THE REAL TENERIFE
AN INSIDER'S GUIDE

BY

ANDREA & JACK MONTGOMERY

ABOUT THE AUTHORS

In 2003 Jack and Andrea Montgomery stepped off the corporate ladder, jettisoned financial security and swapped life in Manchester for the sunshine and fiestas of Tenerife.

Full time travel writers, authors and photographers, their work involves travelling to parts of Tenerife that most visitors and even residents never see, trekking along mountainous goat trails, treading the streets of every town and village, revelling at fiestas until dawn (in the name of research) and spending endless hours poring over books and websites, translating reams of sleep-inducing Spanish text.

The Tenerife Jack and Andrea became familiar with over the the years is one which has a diverse landscape, thriving culture, rich history, colourful traditions, and a tasty gastronomic scene. It's an island whose true personality is often overlooked by even the most reputable travel guides. Having uncovered an island which is a far cry from the popular image of the south's purpose-built resorts, Jack and Andrea are passionate about promoting the island they know so well so that others may discover the 'real' Tenerife's hidden delights.

ABOUT THE REAL TENERIFE

What makes The Real Tenerife different?

The Real Tenerife has been written by professional travel writers who, for more than a decade, have lived and worked on the island, travelling its length and breadth to research, photograph and record every aspect of island life. This is an insider guide in the true sense of the word and it contains information about Tenerife you simply won't find in other guidebooks.

We don't produce reams of hotel and restaurant listings, many of which may be out of date before the virtual ink has dried and all of which are readily accessible through sites like TripAdvisor and Booking.com which most people consult regardless of whether or not they have a guide. Instead, we use these pages to supply information you can't source from anywhere else and which will remain current for years to come. When we recommend a particular restaurant or hotel, it's because we've eaten there and stayed there and have found something worth recommending. When we describe towns, villages, resorts or mountain hamlets, we are describing places we haven't just been shown on a press trip or stumbled upon once, these are places we've visited frequently, at different seasons of the year and over many years.

Part One of the guide takes you into the heart of all things Tenerife - the extraordinary landscape that morphs from arid volcanic to lush sub-tropical; the fascinating history of a frontier island at the crossroads between old and new worlds; the abundant harvest of fish, seafood, tropical fruits, plump grapes and ancient potatoes that produce first-class gastronomy and award-winning wines; and not least, the language, customs, fiestas and costumes of its people. Part Two is a comprehensive guide to every city, town, major village and hamlet on the island, giving an insight into its roots and personality, and highlighting the best of what to see and do.

In the final section you'll find useful insider tips including our favourite things to do on Tenerife and ways to make your holiday money go further.

Is The Real Tenerife a biased account? You bet. It's a compendium of our 14-year experience of living in the Tenerife that exists beyond the holiday brochures and tour operator websites; a showcase of the very best of Tenerife, the Tenerife we know and love; the Tenerife we want you to discover and enjoy.

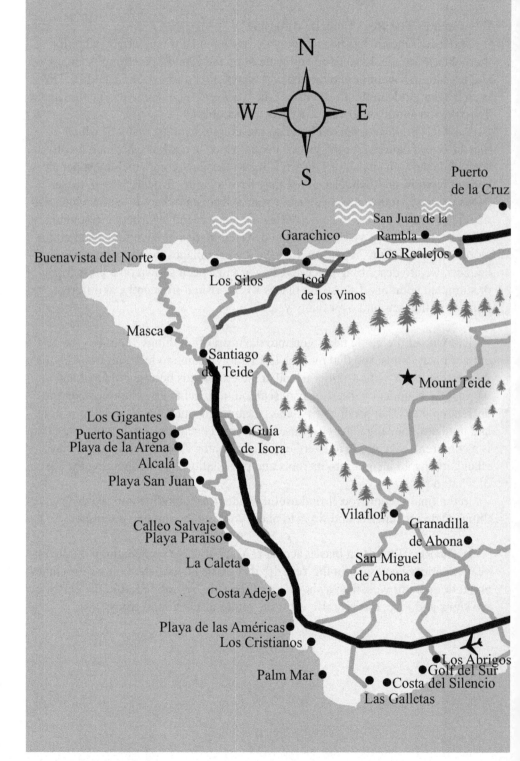

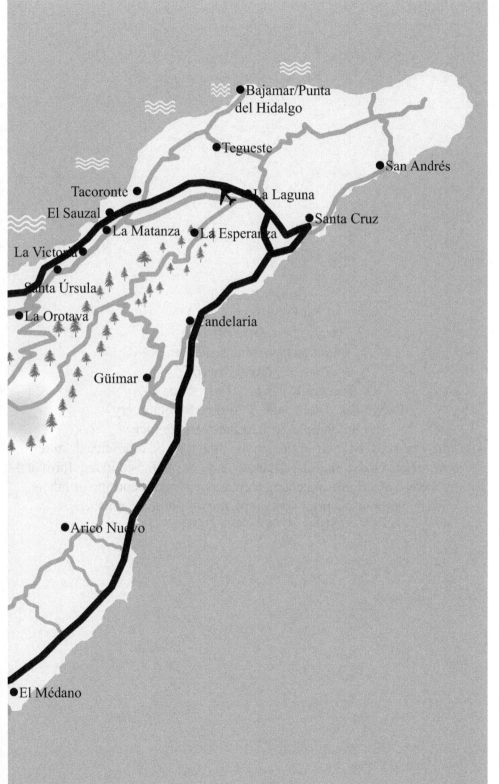

Edition 3, 2020
First Published in 2013
www.therealtenerife.com
Email:jack@realtenerife.com
Twitter: @RealTenerife
Facebook: TheRealTenerife.co
Copyright ©2013 Jack & Andrea Montgomery
All photographs ©2020 Jack Montgomery
ISBN-13: 978-1481926935

TABLE OF CONTENTS

PART 2: GUIDE TO AREAS, TOWNS & RESORTS

An Introduction to Tenerife

Tenerife is an island that attracts over 6 million visitors a year, many of whom believe they know it like the back of their hand and few of whom know it at all.

Sitting 1300km south of mainland Spain and 300 km off the coast of West Africa in the middle of the seven major islands that make up the Canarian Archipelago, Tenerife is the most populous and one time capital of the Canary Islands. It was created by volcanic eruptions between 7 and 12 million years ago and after Hawaii, is the highest volcanic island on the planet, rising to 3718 metres at the magnificent peak of Mount Teide; Spain's highest mountain, the globe's third highest volcano and enduring symbol of the island.

Shaped like an anvil, the island measures just 56 km (35 miles) at its widest point and 86 km (53 miles) in length and is home to a population of 917,841 (2019 – *Instituto Canario de Estadística*), 40% of whom live in the capital city of Santa Cruz or the former capital of La Laguna. A further 30% live in other parts of the north of Tenerife. The four major resort municipalities of Adeje, Arona, Guia de Isora and Santiago del Teide account for the biggest centres of population in the south, comprising 17% of the total population. In some of these areas the non-Canario population outnumbers the Canarian one. In reality, because many incomers still live off the grid, the actual population is probably significantly higher.

(Statistics from ISTAC - *Instituto Canario de Estadística*, www. gobiernodecanarias.org/istac)

Over 40% of Tenerife's surface is protected by special measures. The centre of the island at 2000 metres and above is occupied by the volcanic wonderland of Teide National Park, a UNESCO World Heritage Site. Below that, a crown of dense pine forest known as Corona Forestal National Park circles the peak. In the northern mountains of Anaga, rare laurel forests from the earth's tertiary era still thrive, survivors of the ice age. Throughout the island, steep *barrancos* (ravines) cut into the cliffs are home to many of the 140 exclusive species of indigenous flora and make up some of the 107 areas of special interest.

The ratio of land mass (2034 km²) to height gives Tenerife a range of terrain and micro-climates that take you through arid alpine, tropical, sub-tropical and semi-desert. In winter, you can throw snowballs in the Teide National Park and then sunbathe on the coast within just an hour's journey by car. It can be quite a bizarre sight to see a car arrive at the hot, sunny coast with a partially melted snowman riding the bonnet.

In the far west of the island, you can drive through a tunnel and emerge in an entirely different climatic zone, sometimes moving from dense cloud to unbroken blue skies. Walking Tenerife's myriad paths enables you to clearly see and feel changes in vegetation and air temperature as you cross climate zones from humid to arid and from coast to pine forest.

Tenerife is many worlds inside a single island. Step back from the coastal resorts and you're stepping back in time to a way of life that still holds family values as closely as it holds its Catholic beliefs; where Lent begins with the wild exuberance of carnival; where Easter is the most sacred and solemn of holidays; where Sundays are for mass and for spending with family, and where the Church is a part of everyday life and its plaza the venue for evening socialising and local fiestas.

Away from the resorts too, very few people speak any English at all and there are sparse concessions to tourism, even though it's now the island's number one income generator. Life in rural communities is hard. Narrow terraces still have to be tilled by hand and for many years, younger generations sought easier ways of making money by heading to the coastal tourist towns, leaving many terraces to go fallow, adding dry brush to fuel the not-uncommon forest fires. An unexpected bright side of economic crises has seen a small reversal in that trend with young people being forced to return home where many have turned to the land to help produce food for the family. As a result, some *fincas* (farms) are in better shape than they have been for many years and the island is seeing a boost in local fruit and vegetable production, much of it organic.

For an island that so many people think they know, the vast majority of it bears no resemblance to the mock Las Vegas look, designer label shops and man-made beaches of the coastal resorts. While Costa Adeje invests millions of euros in five star hotels themed on traditional Tenerife villages, in the Anaga Mountains life in the real thing remains much the same as it has done for centuries. Back-breaking farming is a way of life, the flashing neon temperature sign outside the pharmacy is what passes for disco lights and people still live in caves, albeit ones that now have satellite TV.

And it's just as likely that the folks who live in Roque Bermejo and Taganana in the Anaga Mountains know as little about the southern resorts as the millions of visitors who annually flock there know about them.

TENERIFE'S HISTORY IN BRIEF

Pre-Conquest (1BC to 1494)

Tenerife was known as Achinech by the island's original inhabitants the Guanches, who are believed to have settled the Canary Islands somewhere around the 1st or 2nd centuries BC. A primitive people who dressed in animal skins, lived in caves and survived by fishing, livestock-rearing and subsistence farming, with no naturally occurring metals on the island, the lives of the Guanche never evolved beyond wood, bone and stone as their implements and weapons. It was in this Stone Age lifestyle that the Guanche were first discovered and subsequently conquered by Spanish conquistadors in the late 15th century. The origins of the tall, blue-eyed and muscular Guanche is a source of controversy on the islands. It's now generally accepted that they probably originated from the Berber tribes of North Africa but possessing no boat building skills and leaving no evidence of sailing, there's speculation and disagreement as to how they got here; 300km is an awfully long way to swim.

Despite their elemental appearance and abodes, the Guanche had an ordered social structure. Originally ruled by one powerful *mencey* (king), Tinerfe el Grande, the Mencey of Adeje, Tenerife was divided into 9 kingdoms when Tinerfe's nine sons rebelled and refused to share their power. Each kingdom (*menceyates*) was ruled by a king (*mencey*) who oversaw complex political and social systems based on abilities, so hunters for example were afforded a far higher status than fishermen. The Guanche had a sophisticated embalming process for their important dead which began with the body being washed in the sea before the internal organs were removed and then being left to dry in the sun. Finally, the corpse was wrapped in leather or basketry and placed, either on a litter or stone platform or even upright against the wall, in burial caves. The most important of the dead may also have been embalmed with the sap of the drago tree before being wrapped and interred. Many Guanche mummies have been discovered in caves across the island and the best preserved are on show in the Museum of Nature and Archaeology (Museo de la Naturaleza y Arqueología) in Santa Cruz. The Guanche worshipped Achamán as the god of the sky and supreme creator; Chaxiraxi, a mother goddess who would later become the Virgin of Candelaria; Magec the sun god and Gauyota the devil whom they believed lived in Mount Teide (or Echeyde as it was known to them) and which they believed was the place where the earth held up the sky.

The Spanish Conquest

Organised and powerful, the Guanche did not take kindly to 'visitors' to their island, and when Columbus set off to discover what lay beyond the edge of the known world, he refused to dock at Tenerife for fear of the stones and spears of the natives. As Columbus and his crew sailed past in 1492 en route to the unknown, they saw Mount Teide erupting which the ships' crews took to be a bad omen, sailing onward to La Gomera to make their final stop before setting sail on their world-changing voyage. It's generally accepted that the eruption witnessed by Columbus was the last eruption of Mount Teide but contrary to popular opinion, it was unlikely to have been the Lavas Negras eruption and was more probably that of Montaña Boca Cangrejo (Canary Islands, Geology - Kaj Hoernle & Juan-Carlos Carracedo).

For almost a century after Lanzarote and El Hierro had fallen, the Guanche of Tenerife, fiercest of all the islands' natives, successfully protected their island from invasion and their people from becoming commodities in the European slave trade until 1494 when the Spaniard Alonso Fernández de Lugo raised enough money to fund an army of mercenaries and landed on the north east coast where he placed a wooden cross in the ground and said mass around it. Thus the city of Santa Cruz or Holy Cross was founded. Leading his forces south, De Lugo marched on the most powerful of the nine kingdoms, Taoro, known today as La Orotava. Marching through the Acentejo *barranco* (ravine), the conquistadors were attacked from above by the stones and bone-headed spears of the Guanche who decimated their ranks, De Lugo barely escaping with his life. The site became known as La Matanza, the massacre. A year later, at the end of 1495 the Spanish returned with reinforcements and, on higher ground more suited to the Spanish crossbows, defeated the Guanche who were greatly outnumbered and had been weakened by disease brought by the Spanish on their first visit. The site of the final battle became known as La Victoria, the victory. By the beginning of 1496 the island of Tenerife had been claimed on behalf of the Crown of Castille and De Lugo declared himself Adelantado or first governor of the island.

16th to 18th Centuries

Under de Lugo's auspices, much of the north of the island was given to wealthy Genoese, Portuguese and Spanish merchants in return for their financing of the conquest and with the proviso that they plant sugar cane. The cane grew well in Tenerife's climate and throughout the 16th century the island became wealthy on its proceeds. Other than the architectural outputs of the wealth it created, few vestiges of the sugar trade remain today, save for a sugar mill in Los Silos which is now used as a banana storage depot, and the rum factory in Tejina where one of the offshoots of the industry still hangs on in there. At this stage, Tenerife's development was taking place at the same time as the world map was being re-drawn. Columbus had sailed past Tenerife on his voyage of

1492 but with the discovery of the New World came a vast new trading market for which Tenerife was perfectly placed as the crossroads between Europe and the Americas. In a frontier society where silk, spices, gold, fine art and slaves were being exchanged, fortunes were out to be made ... and stolen, and Tenerife became a magnet for merchants, artisans, clerical orders, nobility and pirates. This influx of foreign money and influence is still reflected in the architecture of Santa Cruz, La Laguna and La Orotava where the wealthiest of the settlers made their homes. With its protected inland position, away from pirate attacks, and clear vantage over the Aguere Valley, La Laguna was chosen as the site of the island's first capital and became the political, military and ecclesiastical centre of the island.

When sugar production in the Antilles and Brazil began to undercut Tenerife, the trade started to falter. Even as the last of the sugar cane was being cut down, a new market was opening up in the American colonies where the folks had developed a taste for fine wine. The sweet, white wine produced from the Malvasía grape became the darling of the Colonies and with its rise in popularity, Tenerife's next monoculture was born. Where once the elegant stems of cane bowed in the breeze, now orderly rows of vines thrived on the slopes of Tacoronte, La Orotava, Icod de los Vinos, Garachico and as far as Candelaria on the east coast. Wine production brought a new wave of wealth throughout the 17th and most of the 18th centuries, particularly for the La Orotava Valley where the Malmsey wine was considered the best in the world and the favourite tipple of Europeans. For the little town of Garachico with its deep natural harbour, trade with the New World brought untold riches, making it the island's wealthiest town and even reputedly having one street constructed entirely in marble. But all that changed in 1706 when an eruption from Montaña Negra engulfed a third of the town, including that marble street, and filled the harbour with solidified lava, destroying the town's most valuable asset. With Garachico buried beneath the lava, the trade spotlight turned on the port of Orotava (now Puerto de la Cruz) and then to Santa Cruz where rapid expansion began to attract the attentions of the British. In 1797, led by Admiral Horatio Nelson, English ships attempted to storm the port of Santa Cruz and steal New World gold from the San José which was moored there. The English were resoundingly defeated by the *santacruceros* (natives of Santa Cruz) under the command of General Gutiérrez and Nelson lost his right arm in the battle.

19th and 20th Centuries

In 1821 the Commander General moved his official residence from La Laguna to Santa Cruz, which was awarded the status of capital of the Canary Islands. The second half of the 18th century saw a downturn in the fortunes of Tenerife's wine trade which, strangled by the British stronghold on trading prices, could not compete. The European palate was changing and the new kid on the block, at a fraction of the price, was Portugal's Madeira wine. By the 19th century, Tenerife's wine trade had collapsed and the *tinerfeños* (natives of Tenerife) left in their droves for the New World and the promise of a better life. Families setting sail from Santa Cruz founded the cities of Montevideo in Uruguay and San Antonio (site of the Alamo) in Texas and forged links with the Americas that were to shape the future of the island.

It was a boy from Güímar who was responsible for staving off the complete collapse of the island's fortunes following the demise of the wine industry, by introducing cochineal farming to the island. Cochineal food and cloth dyes came from a small black grub which formed and thrived on prickly pear cactus. Displacing the vines and much of the island's natural pine forest, the black-scarred cactus was considered a blight on the landscape and when the introduction of artificial dyes at the end of the 19th century made its production extinct, there can't have been many who regretted its demise. There's a current resurgence in the demand for cochineal as artificial dyes have been found to contain carcinogens; hopefully it won't mean a return to farming them on Tenerife. Examine the flat surfaces of prickly pear cactus today and you can still find cochineal grubs in their cotton wool nests, clinging to the leaves. It wasn't until the late 19th century when the Frenchman Berthelot brought banana production to the island that Tenerife's fortunes revived and her landscape took on the appearance it still maintains today. Barely had the island got back onto its economic feet when the First World War halted banana exports, causing widespread hardship and sending the *tinerfeños* in their thousands to Cuba and Venezuela.

In 1821 Santa Cruz was awarded the status of Capital of the Canary Islands but it was short-lived. Weakened by the decline of its banana export trade due to World War 1, and seeing its population fleeing to Venezuela and Cuba to escape starvation while Las Palmas de Gran Canaria grew strong due to her steam shipping trade, Santa Cruz capitulated to pressure in 1927 and was forced to share the status of capital with Las Palmas. Santa Cruz became the capital of the Western Canary Islands of Tenerife - La Gomera, La Palma and El Hierro - while Las Palmas became the capital of the Eastern Islands of Gran Canaria, Lanzarote and Fuerteventura.

When, in 1936 a troublesome former Commander-in-Chief of the Spanish army was posted to Santa Cruz to take up his post as military governor of the Canary Islands, the plot to overthrow the Spanish Republican government wasn't ended, it merely relocated. In July of that year, General Francisco Franco left his offices in Santa Cruz for Gran Canaria and onwards to the shores of North Africa from where he began the offensive that would lead to the Spanish Civil War.

The Arrival of Tourism

At the end of the 19th century and the beginning of the 20th, visitors to Tenerife consisted primarily of scientists, explorers and well-to-do Victorians travelling on the advice of their physicians, and after they came ashore at Santa Cruz, it was to La Laguna and the spa towns of La Orotava and Chasna (the old name for Vilaflor) that they were headed. Other than basic coaching inns along the hot and dusty roads and La Laguna's hotels, there were few establishments capable of catering to the needs of visitors until the Hotel Grand Taoro was constructed in Puerto de la Cruz, or Puerto de la Orotava as it was known, in 1890. Quickly established as one of the few 'civilized' (by Victorian England standards) places to stay on the island, the Taoro became a magnet for the great and the good including Queen Victoria, Sir Winston Churchill and Agatha Christie. For those who wished to make the journey from La Orotava to Vilaflor, it was a long and arduous affair which was undertaken along the old *camino real* (formerly literally a royal road, essentially now a merchant trail) known as Camino de Chasna. That route is still passable today and is part of the GR131 walking route that traverses the island. For those with respiratory problems, the fresh mountain air and spring waters of Chasna were a literal tonic, and the village was described by one poetic, early traveller as "...a landscape impregnated with the scent of pine; a haven of peace for the spirit and an environment conducive to good health for the body."

The 1960s brought a tourism explosion to the island. Although the first visitors preferred the green and fertile north of the island, investment in beach building using sand imported from the Sahara led to an influx to the south and in 1978 the southern airport of Reina Sofia was opened, and with it the flood gates to a mass tourism market. Today, the vast majority of Tenerife's tourists flock to the island's coasts and beaches to soak up the winter sunshine, only venturing into Vilaflor on day trips and en route to Teide National Park. But head into the hills and you'll discover a small but growing sector of the tourism market which is rediscovering the Tenerife so loved by the Victorians. Younger Dutch, French, Scandinavian and British visitors are heading to La Orotava, La Laguna and Vilaflor and staying in one of the island's burgeoning boutique rural and spa hotels from which they're striking out to explore hiking trails and enjoy the serenity and traditionalism of an island whose tourism might just be coming full circle.

A Tenerife Timeline

Around 500BC – Tenerife's first settlers mysteriously arrive from the Berber region of North Africa.

1392 – two Guanche shepherds find a statue of the Virgin and child on a beach in Güimar and after firstly attempting to stone her, then to knife her, they finally settle down to worship her and she has remained the object of *tinerfeños'* fervent reverence to this day.

1494 – Santa Cruz founded by Alonso Fernández de Lugo who then leads his troops into an ambush and is soundly thrashed by the spears and stones of primitive warriors; Tenerife 1 – Spain 0.

1495 – de Lugo returns to defeat the Guanche at Aguere and then again at Acentejo; Tenerife 1 – Spain 2.

1496 – Conquest of Tenerife on behalf of the Crown of Castille; final whistle.

1519 – Fernando de Magallanes sails from Tenerife on a journey that leads to the discovery of the Magellan Straits.

1657 – English Admiral Robert Blake attempts to take the port of Santa Cruz and is defeated, setting a trend for the future.

1706 – Port of Garachico destroyed by eruption of Montaña Negra and the English try once again to take Santa Cruz, this time Rear Admiral John Jennings is defeated.

1797 – Rear Admiral Horatio Nelson loses his right arm in the third and final unsuccessful attempt by the English to take Santa Cruz.

1821 – Santa Cruz awarded status of capital city of the Canary Islands.

1927 – Canary Islands split into two provinces and Santa Cruz loses status as capital of Canary Islands.

1935 – André Breton officially declares Tenerife a surrealist island; a fact which comes as no surprise to anyone who's attended carnival.

1936 – General Franco is posted to Santa Cruz from where he begins the Spanish Civil War; presumably the Spanish don't know that old adage 'Keep your friends close and your enemies closer'.

1941 – Los Rodeos airport opens in the north of the island.

1978 – having spent 150 years trying to keep them out, Tenerife opens the Reina Sofia airport in the south, and the British invade.

1983 – Canary Islands become two autonomous regions with Santa Cruz de Tenerife designated capital of the Western Isles and Las Palmas de Gran Canaria capital of the Eastern Isles. Thus begins a rivalry between those two islands which still flourishes today and openly manifests itself whenever the football teams UD Las Palmas play a fixture against CD Tenerife.

ADMIRAL NELSON AND THE BATTLE OF SANTA CRUZ 1797

Whilst bombarding the Spanish port of Cadiz in the summer of 1797, Admiral Horatio Nelson received new orders to sail with his fleet of four battleships, three frigates, and a cutter to an island off the coast of Africa known for being a stop-off point for treasure-laden Spanish galleons making their way back to

Spain from the Americas. His orders were to launch a "sudden and vigorous assault" on the island's port and to capture any ships which subsequently docked there.

The plan Nelson drew up was a sound one – an early morning assault from the sea involving 700 marines and sailors that would catch any lookouts unprepared and half asleep at the end of their watch.

What Nelson failed to appreciate was Tenerife was no sleepy outpost. It was an island which had endured centuries of pirate assaults from the sea. Its ports were well defended and many of its main towns and villages were located inland, a safe distance away from attacks. He'd also been told by a German trader that the port of Santa Cruz was poorly defended.

On the 21 July, under cover of darkness in the hours before dawn Nelson's assault force rowed silently toward Santa Cruz. Strong tides and winds scattered the flotilla of rowing boats and not all were able to make it to land. Meanwhile on Tenerife, lookouts at Igueste spotted the British fleet (the sun comes up early at that part of the island) and lit a bonfire to alert the garrison stationed at the Castillo de San Cristóbal in Santa Cruz. The element of surprise was well and truly lost.

The Commander General of the Canary Islands, General Antonio Gutiérrez, immediately drew up a counter plan. Key buildings in Santa Cruz were evacuated, woman and children were sent to La Laguna, and reinforcements were called for – 1,000 militiamen from Abona, Güímar, La Laguna, La Orotava and Garachico – to help bolster the 600 soldiers and 387 artillerymen from Canarian regiments, 60 Cuban soldiers, and 110 sailors from a French corvette who were preparing to defend the city. Although Nelson ordered a bombardment of Santa Cruz, not enough of his men had made it ashore to launch an effective assault on the city. It was a failure.

But Nelson was determined to capture Santa Cruz. Another attempt was made to land soldiers, this time further east along the coast. However, they were spotted by a peasant woman making her way to the Recova Market to sell her wares. She alerted soldiers at the Castillo de Paso Alto who, assisted by 500 militiamen from Taganana, once again repelled the British assault. By nightfall, the assault force was forced to retreat back to their ships.

Undeterred, Nelson tried a new tack, pretending to sail away before launching a seaborne assault on Santa Cruz, his attack force bombarding defensive installations, but with limited success before, on the morning of 25 July launching yet another assault on the port, this time joining a second wave of attackers himself. One of the groups did manage to take out several cannon, but couldn't successfully storm the Castillo San Cristóbal. Subsequently, a running battle took place on the streets of Santa Cruz as Nelson's men, pursued by Canarian soldiers, took refuge in the Convento de Santo Domingo (now the

Guimerá Theater).

Nelson, meanwhile, struggled to make land; strong waves yet again hampering progress. When his boat eventually did reach terra firma and he jumped ashore, sword raised, grape-shot from the cannon *el Tigre* (on show in the San Cristóbal Castle Interpretation Centre below Plaza De España) shattered his right arm just above the elbow. He was taken back to his flagship, HMS Theseus, where his arm was amputated and opium administered.

On land and at sea, the situation went from bad to worse. The cutter, The Fox, was sunk with 300 sailors aboard and on the streets of Santa Cruz, the assault force was routed. The Battle of Santa Cruz was over, the British requested a parley.

On the morning of 26 July defeated British troops were led to Plaza de la Candelaria where they were given bread, fruit, and wine before being transferred back to their ships whilst wounded British soldiers were treated in Santa Cruz' two hospitals. It was an act of magnanimous chivalry by the Spanish Commander. In response, Nelson sent General Gutiérrez a letter, signed with his left hand, in which he expressed his gratitude for such deferences, as well as a barrel of beer and some cheese. Gutiérrez responded by sending Nelson jugs of Canarian wine. It's not quite how you expect bloody battles to conclude.

Tinerfeños are quite rightly proud of their defeat of England's most famous admiral; you can see the date referenced in street names around the island. There's also a lively re-enactment of the battle held in Santa Cruz each July. And for more information about Nelson's attempt to take Santa Cruz, the Military Museum in the city has an excellent detailed model of the 'battlefield' and an in-depth account of the whole sorry (if you're on Nelson's side) affair.

HISTORY REWRITTEN, THE STRANGE STORY OF THE OTHER BATTLE OF SANTA CRUZ

Nelson wasn't the only British naval commander to experience defeat at Santa Cruz. Admiral Robert Blake also tasted defeat in Santa Cruz in 1657 ... or did he?

According to the Pirate Museum in Lanzarote: 'The name of Robert Blake has been linked to the Canaries since 1657 when he made a frustrated attempt to invade Tenerife.'

But who says Blake's orders had been to invade Tenerife?

On 20 April 1657, during the Anglo-Spanish war, Admiral Robert Blake launched an attack on the Spanish fleet in Santa Cruz harbour. By the middle of the afternoon every single Spanish ship, including the flagship of Spanish Admiral Don Diego de Egues, had been sunk or was on fire. All sixteen ships were destroyed. Not one of Blake's ships were destroyed. Every one of them sailed away from Santa Cruz after the battle was over. As far as casualties are concerned, 48 of Blake's men were killed during the battle as opposed to 300 Spanish soldiers. Whilst some of the treasure that the ships had been carrying had been off-loaded and safely transported to La Laguna, there was still an estimated loss of around ten million pounds.

Nobody disputes this version of events. Where interpretations vary wildly is regarding who actually won the battle.

In Britain, Blake was seen to have won an important victory that helped establish the country as a leading naval power in Europe. The aim of the attack, being the destruction of the Spanish fleet, resulted in an economic loss to Spain that was seen to have dire consequences for their military campaigns, leading to further defeats against the British and the French. Blake was a hero.

Spanish historians saw a very different picture. They claimed that Blake had actually failed to invade Tenerife and hadn't actually recovered the treasure that had already been removed from the ships. There was a lot of rhetoric written by the likes of Viera y Clavijo who described the battle as a clear victory for the local forces. It was a great victory for Spain.

Maybe I'm looking at this in a simplistic way, but the outcome of the Battle of Santa Cruz in 1657 seems glaringly obvious. However, if you can convince your subjects, when you've lost all your fleet and the other guy sails away without having lost even one ship, that you were the victorious party, then I guess you can pretty much feed them any old nonsense. History is fascinating.

GENERAL FRANCO AND TENERIFE

Thanks to the *Ley de Memoria Histórica*, which became part of Spanish law in 2007, you'll no longer see reference to Spain's infamous dictator, General Francisco Franco, on Tenerife's streets. The law was passed to recognise the rights of those who were persecuted, or suffered violence during Franco's reign. An aspect of this law involves removing all references to Franco from public buildings and public areas across Spain. Monuments have been destroyed and street names changed (the reason why Avenida Generalísimo in Puerto de la Cruz is now Avenida de la Familia Bethencourt y Molina).

Although his name has been removed from street signs, it will forever be linked with Tenerife in the history books. It was from the Canary Islands in July 1936 that Franco, then military commander of the Canary Islands, launched a military coup against Spain's leftist-leaning coalition government, an act which ignited Spain's bloody civil war.

Until it was destroyed in 2015 (a victim of the *Ley de Memoria Histórica*) an obelisk at the picnic zone in las Raíces near El Rosario marked the spot where, in June 1936, officers loyal to Franco and Nationalist forces met to iron out the final details of the planned coup.

Tenerife historians record the island was used as somewhat of a training ground for what was to come. In the weeks before the coup, Franco ordered soldiers onto the streets of Puerto de la Cruz, La Orotava, and La Laguna to test the effectiveness of troop deployment. Left-wing political leaders who opposed his actions, like so many others during Franco's reign, simply 'disappeared'. Shortly before the coup took place, there were two assassination attempts on Franco's life; one was by the Iberian Anarchist Federation on the night of 13 July 1936, the other was on 16 July 1936, the fateful day Franco flew from Tenerife to Gran Canaria to launch the military uprising.

Stories about Franco and the Canary Islands are quite scant, and you have to dig quite deep to find detailed information about those dark times – how the island of La Palma opposed the coup for eight days, a period known as *Semana Roja,* until Franco sent the warship Canalejos to the island to help squash opposition; or about conditions in the British-owned banana warehouses which were turned into the concentration camp known as *La prisión de Fyffes*. The 'prison' had the capacity for 600 inmates, yet at times up to 1500 prisoners, mostly political, were confined in what was considered a hellhole. Unsurprisingly, disease was rife and there were regular outbreaks of deadly epidemics which decimated the prison's population.

As in other parts of Spain, any opposition was dealt with severely. Even now there are occasional reports in the Spanish press of suspected mass graves being discovered on the islands.

Oddly, there was one aspect of Tenerife life which Franco basically turned a blind eye to, carnival. In 1937 Franco prohibited acts celebrating carnival across Spain, except for in Cádiz and Santa Cruz de Tenerife where it was such an important aspect of all levels of society that to ban it would be to risk social unrest. Carnival was allowed to continue, albeit under the name of the 'winter festivals.'

Not all monuments to Franco on Tenerife have been destroyed. One controversially still exists - the Monumento al Ángel Caído (Monument to the Fallen Angel) in Santa Cruz. It does appear to glorify Franco, who it's claimed is represented by a figure standing victoriously atop an angel, and it's known locally as 'Franco's Monument.' But, in a bid to save it from destruction, the Santa Cruz council changed its name to the Monument to the Fallen Angel a few years ago.

Top right: Pico Viejo, bottom left: Roques de Garcia, bottom right: Chio road to Mount Teide

TENERIFE'S GEOGRAPHY

Part of the Macronesian Region, the Canary Islands are located to the north of the Tropic of Cancer, and range in age from the 20 million years of Fuerteventura, the oldest of the islands, to 1.2 million years in the case of El Hierro, a mere baby in volcanic terms which is in fact still growing, new land having been formed through volcanic eruptions off the coast of Restinga in 2012. The younger, western islands have deep *barrancos* or ravines, rich vegetation and sheer cliffs while the older eastern islands of Lanzarote and Fuerteventura have smoother, more rounded landforms pocked by volcanic cones. Although they are all volcanic islands and lie within a very short distance of each other (only 230km separates the most easterly from the most westerly islands), each has its own distinct personality. If the only places you visit on every island are the resorts with their homogeneous hotel and restaurant offerings, then you'd be forgiven for thinking they were all the same, but move away from the coast and you'll discover seven very different islands.

Tenerife is the largest island in the Canary Islands and lies some 300km off the coast of West Africa. The north-west of the island is humid, fertile and rich in vegetation, whilst the southern part is hot and arid with a rockier landscape. At the centre of the island lies Mount Teide, the highest mountain in Spain and the third highest volcano on the planet, its steep slopes rising to 3718 metres above sea level, a mere thirteen kilometres from the coastline. The coastal plains are the most densely populated of the three zones and extensive banana plantations are spread in between palm groves, areas of black lava sand and rocky coastline creating dramatic and interesting scenery. Given the presence of Mount Teide and its 'crater', it offers the most diverse scenery of all the Canary Islands which runs the gamut from palm-lined beaches, through terraced hills and dense pine forests to volcanic wonderland, each offering unique landscape features such as ancient, multi-headed drago trees; rock columns wind-eroded into whimsical shapes; a sea of clouds so dense you feel you could simply step onto it; and rivers of shiny, black obsidian flowing through russet and lilac lava fields peppered with rust-red volcanic cones and in early summer, adorned with the ruby, jewelled columns of the extraordinary *tajinaste rojo* flowers. Split into distinct geographic and climatic zones, in winter you can travel from snowboarding in Teide National Park to sunbathing at the coast in a little over an hour. If the day's weather doesn't suit you in one place, simply get in the car and drive to a different weather zone or drive into the mountains to climb above the cloud and emerge into unbroken sunshine and a surreal world that, although now calm and peaceful, still bears the evidence of its violent creation.

Tenerife's Volcanic Nature

The Canary Islands are located on Jurassic ocean crust and are part of a chain of volcanic islands including the Selvagens Islands, formed from the construction of shield volcanoes. Once the constructive, or building phase of the volcanoes has ended, subsequent eruptions and erosions occur in what is known as the destructive phase where the downsizing effects of erosion and wasting outpace the growth created from further eruptions, so over time the size of the volcano reduces. The tectonic plate then shifts away from the magma source and cools, causing subsidence. In Tenerife's case, its highest volcano – Mount Teide – rises 7500 metres from the ocean floor and sits in a crater formed by a mass collapse which indicates that Teide would at one time have been much larger and that it is currently in transition from its constructive to its destructive phase. Experiencing fewer and less violent eruptions than Hawaii (islands which, in volcanology terms are very similar to the Canary Islands), the eruptive history of the Canaries has been moderate over the past 200,000 years, mostly occurring on La Palma, El Hierro and Tenerife, and no casualties have ever been recorded.

There have been four major eruptions on Tenerife over the last 300 years; none have caused human fatalities and with the notable exception of Garachico, there's been very little structural damage as they largely occurred in uninhabited areas high above the island's coastlines.

The site of Tenerife's last volcanic eruption is Mount Chinyero from which, for 10 days in November 1909, molten lava spewed through the forests, destroying everything in its wake as it crept ever closer to the village of Las Manchas in the hills above Santiago del Teide. Fearful of losing their homes, the terrified villagers brought statues of Christ, the Virgin Mary and Santa Ana (their Patron Saint) to a spot below the encroaching lava and prayed for their salvation. It's said the lava flow split at that precise spot and took a course around the village before finally coming to a halt. Tenerife's most famous eruption, and most damaging in structural terms, was the 1706 eruption of Montaña Negro which destroyed 384 neighbourhoods in the little town of Garachico and filled its harbour with solidified lava, robbing it of its status as Tenerife's most important port. Stand on the port today with your back to the sea and look up the cliff in front of you to see the twin frozen streams of lava that caused the devastation.

A volcanologist's dream destination, Teide National Park is a 16 kilometre wide volcanic crater whose surfaces chronicle the eruptive history of Tenerife and whose colours change with the hour of the day, the colour of the sky and the seasons. Many visitors choose to take the cable car to within 200 metres of the peak for a satellite view of the Canary Islands. A walk from the top cable car station to the Pico Viejo (old peak) gives you some of the most stunning views you're likely to see with your feet still on the ground. Walk or drive the Boca Tauce to Chio road and you're passing through the desolate lava fields produced by the last volcanic eruption to take place within the National Park. In 1798 lava flowed from two vents in the flank of Pico Viejo, subsequently known as Las Narices del Teide (Teide's nostrils). A lay-by with viewing platform and information board points to the vents.

CLIMATE

Generally weather forecasts for Tenerife are like 'The Curates Egg'; they're never completely accurate, but neither are they completely inaccurate.

The problem derives from the fact that Tenerife is made up of a series of diverse micro-climates. When there are clear blue skies in one area, it can look as though the end of the world is about to arrive a few kilometres further along the coast. One thing that's certain is that it's very rare for the sun not to be shining somewhere on Tenerife.

As a rule though, there are general patterns that visitors can expect to find in different geographical locations across Tenerife.

South and south west coasts tend to experience the most sunshine and the least rain and subsequently are the warmest parts of the island. The price of this is that they are also dry and barren; good for sun-seeking tourists, but not for farmers. The east coast also benefits from hot, sunny weather but, like many east coasts, can be breezy. The fact that the wind farms are on the south east coast is a bit of a giveaway.

Trade winds from the north east bring a sea of clouds and rain to northern slopes during parts of the year. These clouds settle into folds in the hills between the 600 to 1800 metre mark; spectacular if you happen to be above them but can be dreary if caught underneath or worse, actually in them. Their influence means that temperatures on the northern coasts are a few degrees lower than their southern counterparts and there's more likelihood of rain (except during June – September when there's virtually no rainfall on any coast). The upside is that the northern countryside is lush and sub-tropical and still gets more than its share of sunshine hours.

As soon as you move inland and therefore uphill, temperatures drop noticeably. In the winter, temperatures on Mount Teide's summit are positively nippy by day and can plummet to -10 when the sun goes down. The exception to this rule is during high summer months of June to August when temperatures above 600 metres rise above those at coastal level.

Between November and April, winter snows regularly cloak Mount Teide in a white overcoat, making the mountain even more impressive than usual, especially when viewed from the warmth of the sun-drenched beach. Snow levels can reach the 2000 metre mark and it's not uncommon for roads to the crater to be closed during the heaviest of the snowfalls.

One thing that is constant is the temperature of the sea, it's pretty much the same on all coasts and varies only a few degrees between winter and summer (19 to 23 degrees), so is always pleasant for swimming – unless you're nesh.

But the main thing that most visitors want to hear and that keeps them coming back in their thousands is that you can sunbathe all year round on Tenerife, regardless of where you are on the island, with the good weather having no 'off season'.

Average Maximum Temperatures (Celsius)

	JAN	FEB	MAR	APR	MAY	JUN	JUL	AUG	SEP	OCT	NOV	DEC
Puerto de la Cruz	19.7	19.6	20.8	21.8	22.8	24.8	27.2	28.4	26.9	25.3	22.5	20.7
Santa Cruz	20.5	20.5	21.7	22.7	23.9	26	28.3	29.5	27.9	26.1	23.3	21.7
South Airport	22	22	23	23	24	25	28	28	28	27	25	23

Rainfall (mm)

	JAN	FEB	MAR	APR	MAY	JUN	JUL	AUG	SEP	OCT	NOV	DEC
Puerto de la Cruz	52	43	35	17	7	3	0	1	6	34	61	68
Santa Cruz	44	38	28	13	4	2	0	0	3	29	49	56
South Airport	17	20	15	7	1	0	0	1	4	12	23	30

The tables cover three different areas of Tenerife to illustrate how many people get Tenerife's weather completely wrong. Many weather forecasts consist of temperature readings from the two airports when recording monthly averages. As the one in the south is almost at sea level and the one in the north at 600m, it's quite clearly not a level playing field. Over the years this has resulted in many people misunderstanding and misrepresenting the weather in the north of Tenerife. The location of Tenerife North Airport is a bit of a local joke. It's a great airport, but being located in one of the coolest, wettest and foggiest parts of Tenerife, it isn't representative at all of conditions at the coast. Santa Cruz is also in the north and on the coast, so including it provides a bit more of a balance and hopefully makes for some interesting comparisons.

CALIMA - AFRICA'S SANDY GIFT TO THE CANARY ISLANDS

One of the most unusual and unwelcome of weather phenomena experienced on Tenerife is *calima*, a sand- and dust-filled cloud blown over from North Africa. This cloud doesn't stop in the Canary Islands, it can continue as far as South America and can be so vast it can be seen from space.

Calimas can happen at any time of the year but generally they are most frequent in winter and summer months. Normally *calimas* last around three days, but can whizz through in a day or two as well, usually accompanied by gusting hot winds. The most reliable source for finding out if *calima*, or any type of extreme weather is on the way, is via the Spanish Met Office's weather forecast (AEMET). They can spot an approaching *calima* from around 48 hours in advance and, if it's a serious one, will issue a weather warning for '*polvo en suspensión*', basically tons of dust in the air. Even without Spanish Met Office warnings, it's relatively easy to spot when *calima* is affecting Tenerife. A yellowish haze in the sky blots out the scenery, the wind blows a hooley and layers of dust quickly build up on exterior tables and patios. People who are susceptible might find it feels as though they've a cold as dust particles can irritate the nose and eyes. However, visitors who don't know what to look for aren't always aware of the signs. Someone lying on a sunbed in their hotel complex or looking out to sea might not even be aware there is a *calima*, especially as a feature of *calima* can be temperatures shooting up, something many sunbathers are not going to complain about. The horizon might be hazy, but there's nothing distinct to look at so it's not always as obvious. It might be breezier, but the parts of the island affected most by *calima* tend to be on the breezy side anyway so sunbathers don't always connect it with a weather phenomena. However, look inland and it's not difficult to spot when *calima* has descended. A yellow fog blots out the landscape during the heaviest *calimas*, and creates a nicotine-coloured hazy curtain during light ones.

As *calimas* travel from North Africa westward toward South America, southern and eastern areas of Tenerife are worst affected. Those are the areas where the dust is thickest and the accompanying wind strongest. Northern parts of Tenerife tend to escape the worst of the *calima* thanks to the island's mountainous spine acting as a giant sand barrier, sometimes it's hardly evident there is a *calima* affecting the island in the north as there isn't as much haze and often there's no wind.

Like any extremes of weather which affect Tenerife, *calima* isn't dangerous as long as people are sensible. However, during heavy *calimas* people are advised to stay indoors where possible, especially the old, young and those with respiratory problems. Clearly breathing in a lot of dust and sand isn't good, so walking in the hills during *calima* alerts is a definite no-no.

As well as the danger to people, the dusty wind dries out plants, which in turn increases the risk of forest fires in summer. A wildfire during *calima* is a nightmare. This 'drying out' of the land also has an adverse effect on agriculture. It's said that up to 30% of tomato crops are lost each year because of *calima*.

TENERIFE'S SEA OF CLOUDS

One of the most unforgettable experiences to be enjoyed on Tenerife is when there's a low, grey, cloud blanket blotting out the sun. That's the time when the *mar de nubes* (sea of clouds) is at its most spectacular.

There's a meaty meteorological explanation regarding why Tenerife is an especially good venue for gazing over a fluffy, white duvet of clouds. It involves the cool, humid trade winds which breeze in at a low level from the north east meeting the hot, dry air from the south lording it over the island at above 1500m. The hot, southern air prevents the cooler winds from rising, basically acting as a lid which keeps the cool, trade wind clouds compressed at 800-1000m above sea level.

The presence of trade winds doesn't necessarily mean windy weather on land, often it's more of a pleasing breeze. The term trade winds was coined by mariners who used air currents to navigate and establish trading routes between Europe and the Americas and then the Americas and Asia. They are more prevalent between late spring and mid-summer – which is why the weather phenomena known as *panza de burro* (belly of the donkey), when clouds roll in and don't shift leaving us looking up at the grey 'belly of the donkey', can especially affect some northern parts of Tenerife during that period. As a result, in places such as Puerto de la Cruz, late summer/early autumn and also winter can be a lot sunnier than during the height of summer. The trade winds bringing a cooling sea breeze in summer makes the Canaries a far more desirable/ comfortable destination than other locations in southern Europe. Ironically, when lots of Brits head to mainland Spain's southern coastal resorts in summer, many Spanish mainlanders escape the oppressive heat for 'better weather' in the Canaries.

Although being under the 'donkey's belly' at the coast might be the cause of disappointment for sun-seekers, for anyone interested in memorable experiences the arrival of the 'donkey' should be viewed as an opportunity to witness the sea of clouds. The best time is when dense cloud spreading to the horizon and beyond is stubbornly tucked into the hillside at around the 800/1000m mark and, at the coast, all colour has been drained from the landscape. In the Orotava Valley that's roughly where the last villages in the valley peter out and the pine forest takes over. The first stage involves a bit a dull drive where the views are washed out. This part makes what comes afterwards all the more impressive. Somewhere around 800m you start to see wispy fingers swirling around the trees. This rapidly turns into a pea-souper of a fog as the surroundings start to look more like a cliched horror movie scene. It can be quite unsettling the first time you experience it, especially on narrow, winding country roads. But it's part of the *mar de nubes* experience and, thankfully, it doesn't usually last long as the cloud layer which looks impenetrable from below is only a couple of hundred metres thick at most. You barely get time to register breaks in the mist before it completely dissipates and you find yourself staring into the most intensely blue, cloudless sky. It is a WOW travel moment; the sensation similar to breaking free from the clouds in a plane, but doing so in a car.

Although breaking free from the darkness is quite something in itself, the crowning act is to find a spot where you can stand as close to the edge of the sea of clouds as possible. We've stood in the car park in La Caldera near Aguamansa and watched the cloud bunch up against the low wall right at our feet. Mirador de Mataznos, further along the TF-21, is also a good spot for sea of cloud gazing. In fact, any *mirador* (viewpoint) looking down on the coast (or where the coast should be) above 1000m has potential; although the ones facing into the Orotava Valley are usually best.

Top: Bird of Paradise flower, bottom left: Barbary partridge, bottom right: Tenerife lizard

FLORA & FAUNA

Despite the Canary Islands covering only 1.5% of Spanish territory, the archipelago is home to more than 50% of Spain's endemic species.

Covering the largest surface area of the Canary Islands, and also rising higher above sea level than any of its neighbours, Tenerife boasts the greatest geographical diversity which, in turn, means an incredible range of species of plants, many of which are endemic.

Volcanic origins; abundant micro-climates; the way the land rises dramatically from sea level to high altitude; and the impact of the trade winds, have all combined to create an island with multiple ecosystems. All of which basically means Tenerife is a destination which would suit flower-lovers down to the (rather steep) ground.

Around the more arid parts of the coast, the scene is one of a desert landscape, home to plants suited to dry conditions, strong wind, and little shade – these include the likes of *Euphorbia canariensis* (*cardón*) and *Euphorbia balsamífera* (*tabaiba*) whose sticky resin was used to seal wine barrels.

Between 200 and 600m you find the thermophilic trees; the *Phoenix canariensis* (Canarian Palm) whose sap is used to produce *miel de palma* (palm honey) on La Gomera and whose fronds you can still see being used to sweep streets in Tenerife's capital, Santa Cruz. Also at this level are junipers and, one of the most emblematic plants of the Canary Islands, *Dracaena draco* (the dragon tree).

Then, from 500 to 1000m in northern parts of the island are the atmospheric, and often damp, ancient *laurisilva* forests. Until around 20,000 years ago, laurel forests such as these covered much of northern Africa and the south of Europe but most have long been consigned to the past. The *laurisilva* forests of the Canary Islands and Madeira are among the last of the living remnants of these old rainforests. There are various species of laurel to be found within their dank depths, the most famous probably being *viñátigo* whose wood was a favourite with cabinet-makers.

Acting as a transitional zone between 1000 and 1500m are the Macaronesian heathlands, or *monteverde* (green mountain); a landscape engulfed by the *mar de nubes* at certain times of the year, creating misty, damp forests where, as well as laurels, *brezos* (heather), *faya* (myrtle), and *aceviño* (Canary holly) thrive. As the *mar de nubes* is caused by the trade winds, the Macaronesian heathlands are only found on the northern side of Tenerife, particularly in the Anaga area.

Climbing to almost the highest zones are Tenerife's pine forests, great swathes of which carpet the hills between 800 and 2000m. These forests are dominated by the, thankfully, fire-resistant Canarian pine (*Pinus Canariensis*). These beautiful pines can withstand even the most destructive forest fires, returning to full glory within a couple of years of having been ravaged by flames. In those over 100 yrs old, the heart of these trees, called tea wood, is so dense and hard it was used in the construction of boats and as well as the ornate balconies found in those beautiful colonial buildings in La Laguna and La Orotava.

Beyond the tree line, and over 2000m, lies the high mountain zone – the world above the clouds where the climate is lip-cracking dry, temperatures and weather conditions can be extreme, and the sun rarely stops shining. This consists mainly of Teide National Park. When plants bloom here they can be delightful like the Teide violet (*Viola cheiranthifolia*) or spectacular and out of this world – the *tajinaste rojo* (*Echium wildpretii*).

However, Tenerife's colourful floral face isn't just courtesy of endemic plants. Like the people who have settled on the island over the centuries, there are representatives of many lands - a cornucopia of exotic, foreign flora brought by explorers, botanists and immigrants travelling to and from the Americas, Africa, and Australasia. Historic plazas such as Plaza del Charco in Puerto de la Cruz are shaded by Indian bay trees from Cuba or, in the case of Plaza de la Iglesia in Santa Cruz, brightened up by flamboyant trees (*Delonix regia*) from Madagascar; Jacarandas (*Jacaranda mimosifolia*) from South America and African tulip trees (*Spathodea campanulata*) add elegant colour to charming old streets; and Canarian gardens are riots of vibrant colour thanks to hibiscus (*Hibiscus rosa-sinensis*), flame vine (*Pyrostegia venusta*) and bougainvillea hedges. Most stunningly exotic of them, and found in hotel foyers across the island, is the *Strelitzia reginae* – the wonderful and aptly named bird of paradise flower.

WILDLIFE

In wildlife terms, there's not a lot on Tenerife to excite. There's no big five, there's not even a small five. There are some interesting birds – blue chaffinches, yellow canaries, hoopoes, kestrels, buzzards, fish eagles, *capirotes*, egrets, Barbary partridge, and rare-ish pigeons (Laurel and Bolle's) among others. And there are escaped parrots in some areas (Parque García Sanabria in Santa Cruz is a suitably tropical setting for parrot-spotting). When pigeons are listed as being among the interesting wildlife on offer, it's a sure sign there's not a lot to get worked up about.

Ironically, one of the most fascinating bird-watching experiences we've had on Tenerife was watching scores of owls swooping and hunting from hotel balconies in Costa Adeje. Hotel balconies can be good places for bird watching. We've also spent nights captivated by the cartoon-call of shearwaters.

What creatures actually make up, as one article put it, Tenerife's 'melting pot of fascinating animals'?

There are mouflon, the wild sheep introduced in the 1970s as potential big game to be hunted – a scheme which failed. Since then the mouflon have gone native and become adept at staying hidden. There are official culls twice a year to keep numbers down as they represent a danger to indigenous flora. These aren't so much wild but possibly quite hacked off at being hunted twice a year. In years of walking across Tenerife we've never actually seen one in the wild so, to be fair, I'd be quite thrilled about spotting one of those. Annoyingly, a friend found himself confronted by a family of mouflon on his first foray into Masca ravine.

Then there are rabbits, also incomers and also hunted, which is why they are on every traditional menu on the island. But spotting a rabbit sitting in a field is hardly going to set anyone's pulse racing.

Goats can be pretty good value, especially when they strike poses on the sheer walls of ravines. But goats are livestock rather than wildlife. Although some of the ones which have 'gone native' in Anaga can be pretty wild. Residents often request help to deal with marauding gangs of rogue goats destroying their crops. Talking of livestock, actually seeing some on Tenerife can be akin to spotting a rare animal. They do exist and can be spotted in numbers at agricultural fairs, but cows, sheep and pigs are not creatures you stumble across every day.

Probably best of the pick are the island's lizards; there are lots of them - from big-eyed geckos to coppery skinks. The most striking of all is the endemic *lagarto tizón* (*Gallotia galloti*) whose bright blue spots and vibrant yellow stripes make it as pretty a lizard as you'll see. They're as common as muck and brave as lions. We've had them jump on shoulders and rustle in backpacks in Teide National Park. In Anaga we even had a tug of war competition with one to stop it from making off with the last of my cheese and ham sandwich. What's not common and would constitute spotting relatively big game is to catch sight of the Tenerife lizard's big brother – *Gallotia intermedia* - who can grow to nearly thirty inches in length. It's very, very rare and was only discovered in the Teno region in 1995.

GARDENS OF TENERIFE

Green Tenerife

Mineral rich volcanic soil combined with the perfect botanical climate where it's never too hot, never too cold, and there's adequate winter rainfall, make the north of Tenerife a Nirvana for tree and plant life.

Wander into Valle de Guerra, also known as Tenerife's greenhouse due to its high humidity, and you'll find yourself in a green paradise where the exotic plants that adorn the five star hotel gardens and lobbies of the south are grown in vast plantations. Away from the cultivated terraces, palm groves and neat rows of vines flourish in the north and nature, left untamed, can reclaim a patch of land in less than a season. Willowy cane; neon bougainvillea; prickly pear cacti and seas of lilac convolvulus and orange trumpet vine threaten to take over the island if not checked, while small mountains of surplus peaches, oranges, nectarines and plums are left to rot at the feet of the trees that bore them.

Harnessing that growing power into gardens is not something the Canarios have traditionally been very good at, agricultural and livestock needs taking precedence. As a result, there are not as many gardens on the islands as you might imagine and those that are here have frequently arisen out of some other purpose such as the Botanical Gardens which were created as a holding pen, or else they have the hand of the British somewhere in their creation, like the Sitio Litre and Parque Taoro gardens.

Of those parks and gardens that are open to the public, these are our favourites:

Puerto de la Cruz

Botanical Gardens

Originally known as The Acclimatization Gardens of La Orotava, the gardens were never meant to be gardens at all but were created in 1788 just as a storage or holding pen for exotic plants and trees en route from the Far East and the Americas to the Royal Palace in Aranjuez, Madrid.

Their existence is due to King Carlos III, the Spanish royal Alan Titchmarsh of his day, who commissioned the bringing of ' the most unusual plants existing in the Colonies of the Philippines and America' to the royal gardens. Being only too aware of the differences in climate between their origins and their destination, the King arranged for the plants to be allowed to acclimatize and, having looked around the world for the place that would offer them the best chance of survival, settled on the little town of Puerto with its botanically perfect climate.

It's easy to see, as you wander beneath the giant strelitzias that make you feel like an extra from 'Honey, I Shrunk The Kids' and the strange sausage tree whose fruit looks as if it would fry up nicely alongside some eggs, that everything did indeed survive, and then flourish. Unfortunately the good King underestimated the effect of a Spanish winter on his prize exotics and the first shipment fell victim en masse to the withering frosts of Madrid forcing the plan to be abandoned.

Over time the gardens have experienced years of neglect as funds to maintain them ebbed and flowed with the economy but the plants and trees, oblivious of the bank balance, continued to thrive in their new home, extending tendrils ever further, spreading branches wider and climbing ever higher into the Canarian sky. Today, some of these specimens are over 150 years old, battling for space amongst their 3000 peers including 150 different species of palm trees.

Don't expect neat orderly rows, colourful flower beds or lawns with not a blade of grass out of place, if flowers are your thing you'll prefer Sitio Litre (see below). This is drunk and disorderly tropical foliage where green is the dominant colour and the hand of the gardener is very much subservient to the sheer force of nature.

Calle Retama, La Paz; open 09:00-19:00 summer, 09:00-18:00 winter; entrance €4.50.

Sitio Litre

The 18th century house that sits at the heart of Puerto's oldest gardens was originally the HQ of a Dutch wine importing company but was bought by an English merchant, Archibald Little, in 1774 and rapidly became *the* place for passing dignitaries to stay in when they visited Tenerife. So fragrant and lovely was the garden that Mr Little created, the botanical artist Marianne North found it difficult to prise herself away from it and spent many happy hours producing canvases which now hang in Kew Gardens.

A blend of English garden design with endemic and exotic species, flower and lawn lovers will feel much more at home here amongst the roses, fuchsias, hibiscus and bougainvillea, not to mention the orchids and the Bonsai collection.

Camino Sitio Litre (on the Puerto to La Orotava road, opposite the Cepsa garage); open daily 09:30-17:00; entrance €4.50.

Risco Bello

A wonderfully eccentric garden consisting of five, water rich terraces that step down the cliff side with views across the town to the ocean. Each level is individually styled featuring waterfalls, bridges and ponds in a peaceful environment populated by butterflies, dragonflies, ducks, geese, doves and pigeons as well as the occasional egret.

Moving through the levels down narrow steps; on bridges and stepping stones; over lily ponds; by cascades; and beneath low hanging boughs; the garden's air of decadence makes it feel secret and hidden, somewhere few people know exists. Emerging back onto the dappled lawn with its tea and cakes by the pond and troops of ducklings wending between the reeds, you realise you're not the first, or the last, to enjoy this delightful aquatic corner.

Alongside the former Casino Taoro; open daily 09:30-18:00; entrance €4.

Parque Taoro

Predominantly a park but with impressive gardens that front the former hotel and casino and tumble down the cliffside to the town, the Taoro Hotel was built by the British in 1890, was the first 'great' hotel to be built in Spain and in its heyday attracted such dignitaries as Sir Winston Churchill and Agatha Christie. At that time the hotel was surrounded by acres of English style gardens including tennis and croquet lawns and a circuit for horses and riders to play a popular game known as La Sortija which involved hooking rings suspended on high posts onto a jousting-like pole at full gallop.

Today the gardens are a paradise for joggers who frequent the Camino de La Sortija and the myriad paths through volcanic *malpaís* of cacti and *tabaiba*. To the front of the building an impressive waterfall which every hour, cascades down terraces in a series of pools and rills crossed by bridges and bordered by lush foliage.

The Taoro stands on a volcanic mound above the town of Puerto and is accessible by car and on foot from the Carretera General.

La Orotava

Victoria Gardens
Standing proud above the aristocratic town is the uniformity and regimen of the 18th century, Italianate Victoria Gardens.

Formerly the property of the Eighth Marquis of Quinta Roja, the perfectly manicured beds, close-clipped rose trees and ornate fountains of its seven terraces are presided over by the marble mausoleum of the Marquis himself. On his death, the Marquis, a self confessed Freemason, was refused a Christian burial by the Catholic Church and so this creation was commissioned by the Marquis' mother as the last resting place of her son and a fitting tribute to the Masonic Society, both of whom had been so ignominiously snubbed.

Straying a little from the formal Italian design, the *barranco* that borders the gardens alongside the Taoro Liceo is a glorious riot of trailing ferns, and glancing back up at the gardens from near the plaza provides one of its loveliest aspects.

Calle San Agustín; open Mon-Fri 09:00-18:00, Sat & Sun 10:00-15:00; entrance free.

Botanical gardens
Created in 1788 to accommodate overspill from the La Orotava Botanical Gardens (now the property of Puerto de la Cruz), this lovely, romantic little garden is a delight to wander around with its unkempt inhabitants whose exuberance sends them spreading across paths and through their beds in a profusion of tropical shapes and colours. Much smaller and more compact than its big cousin, the gardens feel more intimate and you get a lot closer to the

Top: Botanical Gardens, Puerto de la Cruz, bottom left, Parque Garcia Sanabria, Santa Cruz, bottom right: Victoria Gardens, La Orotava

exotics. Great for plant photographers. At the heart of the gardens is a quaint little house which is actually clean and pleasant, public toilets.

Calle Tomás Pérez; open Mon-Fri 09:00-14:00, 14:00-19:00, Sat 09:00-14:00, closed Sun; entrance free.

Santa Cruz

Parque García Sanabria

Known as 'the lungs of the city', García Sanabria is a spectacular park filled with tropical plants, an open air art gallery and landscaped gardens. Paths wind through classical Italian gardens, past lily ponds filled with frogs, beneath the branches of banyan trees and through bamboo tunnels to the fountain where the plump knees of Francisco Borges Salas' sculpture, 'Fecundidad', bathe.

Named after the mayor who instigated its creation, Parque García Sanabria has been the city's green space since the early 20th century. First to be initiated was the rose garden set within its wrought iron arches, then the bamboo tunnel and a play area for children. In 1958 the flower clock was donated by the Danish ambassador Peder Larson, and in 1973 sculptures from the city's International Exhibition of Street Art were installed and include such delights as The Cat by Óscar Domínguez.

La Palmetum

Inaugurated in 1995 and opened in 2013, the Palmetum is unique in the world. Over a surface area of 12 hectares, more than 2000 plant species including 472 varieties of palms form a green paradise containing streams, small lakes and cascades. Said to contain the most diverse selection of palms on the planet, you can 'walk the globe' in the gardens, taking in species from Africa, Central America, Australia, Madagascar, Indo China, New Guinea and South America en route. With lots of ocean and mountain viewpoints thrown into the mix so that the scenery is as good looking out as it is looking in, this is a lovely place to escape from the heat of the city.

Avenida de la Constitución; open every day 10:00-18:00; entrance €6 (reductions for children, residents & OAPs).

Icod de Los Vinos

Parque del Drago

We often tell people who want to see the famous *Drago milenario* tree of Icod not to pay the €4 entrance fee to the formal park, but simply to wander up onto Plaza de la Constitución and look over at the tree from there. And that tip still holds good, unless you also have an interest in the endemic plants of the islands in which case, you'll find the entrance fee worth it.

Paths run through various theme gardens encapsulating the variety of endemic flora to be found within the various micro-climates of the Canary Islands, from rain forest to desert and including many medicinal herbs and plants. Naturally, centre stage is the magnificent drago tree itself, reputed to be somewhere in the region of 600-1,000 years old. By paying the fee to go into the park, you get to be much more 'up close and personal' with this ancient of the natural world.

Plaza la Constitución, Icod de los Vinos; open daily 09:30-18:30; entrance €4.

SPRING FLOWERS ON TENERIFE

O were my love yon lilac fair,
Wi' purple blossoms to the spring ...
    Rabbie Burns

There's something about spring which makes it perfect for digging out old poems to quote as you wander over hill and dale, running hands through the tall grasses and swathes of rainbow-coloured blooms. Hedgerows and fields brimming with colourful spring displays might not be a sight everyone associates with Tenerife. When we moved to the island we were regularly told how there were no distinctive changes in seasons. As we drove past bright displays of perky poppies during our first spring on the island, we realised that, for all its popularity, many people still didn't know the island and its patterns very well.

One of the reasons for the 'no variation in seasons' belief was spring flowers don't burst into bloom everywhere. There are specific areas where you get treated to dreamy landscapes which might have the romantic poets reaching for their quills. However, seeing the best displays often requires effort and a bit of a trek.

Valle de Santiago

The Valle de Santiago was the first place on Tenerife where we saw a swathe of wild flowers in bloom. The borders of a field where a mature farmer was bent double planting seeds were bursting with scarlet, yellow and cornflower-blue flowers. They weren't the first wild flowers we saw, those had been corn poppies on the roadside verges on the drive between Icod de los Vinos and Santiago del Teide, but they were the most concentrated. Equally enchanting was a sunburst yellow display in front of the Casa del Patio.

The upper Orotava Valley

The Orotava Valley is a favourite places for walking on Tenerife at any time of the year, but it's at its best in spring when routes around La Caldera come

31

alive with wild flowers and bees. There are many varieties to feast the eyes upon, but one of the most impressive is *echium callithyrsum*, a type of *tajinaste* which, unlike the scarlet variety in Teide National Park, tends to grow in clumps, reaching a height of up to four metres.

Teide National Park

An arid volcanic landscape might initially seem an odd choice as a favourite area for seeing wild flowers, but sometimes less is more. For a start, the towering scarlet *tajinaste* spikes which explode into life in some areas of the park in May are uniquely eye-catching. But they're not the only bright spark in the park - there are violets, laburnums, arnica and one which compliments the strange landscape almost as much as the *tajinaste* - the Teide wallflower.

The Teno Massif

Early spring in the ravines and valleys of Teno Alto can reward with goats skipping across abandoned terraces and hills which are full of flowers - *tajinastes*, Canarian bellflowers, cherry-coloured *tabaibas*, Mediterranean thistles, bladder campion and many more. Steep slopes falling away to a sparkling sea with La Gomera making up the backdrop are carpeted with delicate blue flowers.

Other flowers commonly seen along wooded paths across Tenerife are elegant white and orange asphodels; delicate, papery Canary Island bellflowers tumbling down dry-stone walls; Canary Islands St John's Wort; viper's bugloss; and tall spikes of giant wild fennel.

ALMOND TREES IN BLOOM ON TENERIFE

One of the natural highlights of the winter on Tenerife is to see the countryside perked up by the addition of delicate pink almond blossom. The hills and vales around Santiago del Teide are traditionally the place to go to enjoy the best scenes of almond trees in bloom. At the appropriate time of year, the local council organises guided walks to see the *almendras en flor* (almonds in blossom) and there are even photo competitions for the best 'capture' of the almond trees in bloom.

When the trees are at their most spectacular can vary depending on weather conditions. Normally they're at their best during late January, but if it's been a cool winter (by Tenerife standards), it can be well into February before the display reaches its peak. The downside to Santiago del Teide's blooming almonds is everybody knows about them. At weekends and holidays during almond blossom season, the area can be swamped with locals. Normally quiet hiking routes become clogged with long lines of temporary hikers following the *ruta de almendras en flor*; so many that it's not a particularly enjoyable experience. However, there are other parts of Tenerife where it's possible to enjoy scenes of almond trees in bloom without the crowds.

The countryside around Vilaflor is generally overlooked in the 'almond trees in bloom' stakes, yet it can be just as captivating as Santiago del Teide. Vilaflor, appropriately given its name, is a town where flowers cascade over crumbling walls and scarlet *tajinaste* beside the church can burst into flower long before the specimens in Teide National Park. One approach to the town features an avenue of almond trees, dispersing delicate petals like confetti at a wedding. More almond trees lie in small valleys in the surrounding countryside, hidden away from everyone but farmers pruning their vines and those who explore dusty trails that look as though they lead to nowhere. The almond trees of Vilaflor might not be as famous as those in Santiago del Teide, but that doesn't make then any less magical, if anything it makes them more so.

PEOPLE AND THEIR QUIRKS

In recent times, the islanders have elevated Tenerife's original inhabitants, the Guanche to almost god-like status. Towns, landmarks and hotels have Guanche names, and statues all over Tenerife are dedicated to the proud, primitive people who populated the island pre-conquest. The irony is that the conquistadors decimated the indigenous population so, in truth, islanders are more likely to be descended from the invaders. Yet you'll be hard pressed to find a statue honouring non-Guanche 'heroes' of the conquest.

Some areas remained Guanche strongholds after the conquest; Tacoronte, Santiago Valley, the Orotava Valley and Güímar, where physician and merchant Dr. Eden recorded in 1662 about the Guanche population:

"...the poorest think themselves too good to marry with the best Spaniard."

Interestingly these areas tend to have more than their fair share of beautiful men and women, the tiny town of Santiago del Teide producing at least two Miss and one Mr Spain.

The nationalities of Tenerife's settlers also provide an insight into why the islanders don't primarily consider themselves to be Spanish. The architects, engineers, merchants and farmers who fashioned Tenerife post-conquest were a mix of Spanish, Italians, Portuguese, Flemish, Irish and British; an eclectic bunch which over time combined to produce the '*tinerfeño*'.

The Friendly Island

One of the island's slogans is appropriately *Tenerife Amable* (friendly Tenerife), and *tinerfeños* are generally a good natured, generous and friendly lot. Even in the most remote villages visitors are greeted with a smile and a *buenos dias*. Over the years we have regularly been the beneficiaries of this endemic friendliness, and could reel off any number of examples where a simple question has resulted in an unexpected display of generous hospitality – just asking potato harvesters about their crop in the upper Orotava Valley led to an invite to join them for wine and potatoes during their end of harvest fiesta.

There is none of that wary suspicion that can be encountered in some small communities of Europe. Being at the crossroads of the world for five centuries, the appearance of a stranger isn't exactly something new.

Tinerfeños have a laid back approach to life, 'working to live' rather than the other way around. Nothing is rushed and everything stops for the seemingly endless merry-go-round of fiestas.

Their 'easy come, easy go' outlook can occasionally be frustrating. They queue patiently for hours in the Correos (Post Office) and Concorcio de Tributos (government utility offices) without complaining. When some nationalities, no names mentioned, try to jump the queue *tinerfeños* say nothing. Whilst Brits huff and puff, the *tinerfeños* shrug their shoulders, commenting: "*Tranquilo*, we'll all be served at some point." It's an attitude which makes you feel petty, but it does perpetuate inefficient systems designed to keep Post Office and government workers in a job, rather than having anything to do with customer service.

When *tinerfeños* meet socially, conversations are lively and can sound aggressive, especially those involving dominoes or *brisca* and *chinchón*, Spanish card games played around harbours and plazas, but it's all just good natured banter. Displays of anger are rare.

Driving on Tenerife
A good place for observing the *tinerfeño* character is on the island's roads. If every male on the island lost their left arm tomorrow it wouldn't change their driving habits. The arm hangs limply out the window, never venturing inside for gear changes or to help negotiate corners. It only springs into life to acknowledge friends, or to apologise for cutting you up.

On country roads, some locals drive incredibly slowly, tootling along at 30 km an hour, honking their horns and waving at everyone they pass. If the first two letters of the registration of the car in front is 'TF', sit back and enjoy the scenery, you're not going anywhere in a hurry.

There's a noticeable difference on the island's versions of motorways, the TF roads, especially around the main resort area where there's often an aggression to the driving that doesn't exist in traditional areas, but the culprits there are unlikely to be Canarios. However, there is one island-wide habit that drives us mad – a car will overtake at speed, pull in front, and then slow down so that they then have to be overtaken. A few minutes later, the same car will overtake at speed, pull in front... and slow down. And so it goes on. When this first happened we thought the driver was messing about with us, they weren't; it's just a thing. Drivers seem to be completely unaware they're doing it, but it's annoying as hell.

There used to be regular public service broadcasts on TV to educate drivers about how to tackle 'new fangled' concepts like slip roads and roundabouts. They only had limited success. Most *tinerfeños* still avoid the inner lane of roundabouts altogether. It might go against the grain, but it's safer to stay in the outside lane like everyone else.

Our way is the best way, even when it isn't
Being an island, there can be a tendency to be a little inward looking. Although *tinerfeños* are welcoming towards visitors, they're less open to advice from outsiders, preferring to stick with tried and trusted, but not always successful, methods. This has contributed to a boom and bust economy which

has dogged Tenerife throughout its history. On the one hand, tradition remains strong and there's a wonderful feeling of community everywhere. On the other, development in some areas is painfully slow. In recent years Information Technology has caught up with much of the rest of Europe, but recognition of the power of an online presence hasn't quite matched this. Many businesses still don't have websites, despite the fact that many potential customers lie beyond the island's coastline.

Although tourism has been the mainstay of the economy for fifty years and millions of British descend on the island annually, English isn't as widely spoken outside of the resorts as you might expect, which has resulted in younger Canarios being at a disadvantage when it comes to finding jobs in tourism, where Spanish mainlanders and South Americans tend to fare better.

Tinerfeños have somewhat of an inferiority complex in relation to mainland Spain (the relationship can be a bit like the one between Scotland and England), believing that mainlanders view the Canary Islands as being backward. It's a belief which isn't without foundation. When *godos*, (a slang term for mainland Spanish) descend on the island in the summer, they joke:

"You'll always be behind us ... an hour behind us."

At face value it's an innocent reference to Tenerife time being on GMT whereas Spain is an hour ahead, but the fixed false grin on the *tinerfeño* recipient's face tells you they know what's really being said.

Language

Like so much of its culture, Tenerife's language has its roots firmly in Latin America, not in mainland Spain.

The most immediately obvious differences are firstly, the use of the 's' sound instead of the lisped 'th'; so *'gracias'* is pronounced 'grasias' rather than the Castilian 'grathias' and secondly, the use of *'usted'* and *'ustedes'* to address anyone except children; in Tenerife, the term *'vosotros'* is almost considered an insult. And some words are uniquely Canarian, for example potatoes are *'papas'*, which is rather nice and the bus is known as the *guagua* (pronounced wah-wah) as if everyone were still three years old.

But these pale into insignificance when faced with the spoken word of the majority of Canarios, for it's the almost complete disregard for the letter 's' and the propensity to merge entire sentences into a single sound which confounds even the most practised of Spanish speakers when they arrive here.

One of our first Spanish transactions involved attempting to rent a car, the obscure make of which was an "*Ayaah Eebeea.*" Baffled about what was on offer, we had to seek the assistance of someone who spoke some English. The car was a SEAT Ibiza.

Generally, the 's' sound is dropped from the end of words, so that '*mas*' and '*menos*' become 'mah' and 'menoh', and then they're run together so that the popular sentiment and accurate descriptor of Canarian life; '*mas o menos*' (more or less) becomes 'maomenoh'. This lax use of pronunciation can inevitably lead to confusion, particularly when used in relation to appointments when, for example 2.30 (*dos y media*) and 12.30 (*doce y media*) can sound remarkably similar when said in Canarian.

Particularly confounding can be any conversation which refers to the island of La Palma or the city of Las Palmas, the capital of Gran Canaria, both being pronounced 'La' Palmah'. It can take five minutes to establish precisely where the action is taking place before you get to the plot.

Men are particularly prone to dropping practically all their vowel sounds and running everything together like a blockage on a conveyor belt making comprehension virtually impossible, even amongst themselves. If you listen in to two elderly gents having a conversation, you'll find that a good proportion of it is spent in each clarifying exactly what the other is saying.

For those arriving here having invested time learning the basics of Spanish, it feels a bit like having been taught English and then dropped in Glasgow or Newcastle; you wonder if there are actually two languages called Spanish and you've just learned the wrong one.

You can enrol full or part time at any of the proliferation of language schools on the island or at the University of La Laguna where, for a price, you can move from unconsciously incompetent to consciously incompetent and stay there for quite some time. On the plus side, mumbling over uncertain verb endings will rarely be interpreted as incompetence and can even heighten comprehension. In any case, they'll smile warmly, tell you your Spanish is '*muy bueno*' and continue to talk endlessly to you as if you're taking in every word. Just throw in the occasional '*claro*', '*vale, vale*' and '*si si si*' and you'll be there chatting for hours.

TRADITIONAL COSTUMES

Even though the Canary Islands are an autonomous region of Spain, their culture has evolved from a wide range of influences over the years, and especially from the multiple nationalities which settled on the islands following the conquest. A classic example of this is illustrated by the traditional dress worn in the islands.

Although styles vary from island to island, the traditional costumes worn by men on Lanzarote are completely different from that worn on the Western Canary Islands, the style generally has far more in common with Portuguese traditional dress than it does with most Spanish traditional costumes. Travel to

Top: potato pickers, La Orotava, bottom left: woman at traditional fiesta, bottom right: carnival queen

the Portuguese Azores or Madeira especially and the traditional costumes there are very similar in appearance to those worn in the Canary Islands.

Spend any time in traditional parts of Tenerife and it's difficult to avoid seeing Canarios wearing Tenerife's traditional costume as it is donned by locals at any opportunity. For women, this typically involves ankle boots; a small apron over a long wide skirt which is worn over a petticoat; a blouse under a doublet or embroidered waistcoat; and a head scarf, on top of which is a felt hat (straw in some areas). In the case of men, traditional dress is made up of a linen shirt with wide sleeves and narrow cuffs; a waistcoat (sometimes embroidered); white undershorts which drop just below the knees and which are visible below the knee-length wool breeches which cover the upper part of the leg; a brightly-coloured sash; and a fedora-like black hat.

It's not just different Canary Islands which have contrasting styles. On Tenerife there are variations found in different municipalities. How locals dress for fiestas in Tacoronte is different from their counterparts in Icod de los Vinos. The most eye-catching and vibrant costume is found in La Orotava where the women wear multi-coloured skirts and tight scarlet bodices over white short-sleeved blouses, with a short green cape casually slung across one shoulder. The look is finished off with a petite, straw boater placed jauntily on the side of the head on top of a pale lemon head scarf. The men are equally colourfully decked out, their black, knee-length breeches worn over slightly longer white pantaloons are perked up by embroidery and held up by a scarlet sash. On the torso, a long, sleeveless, embroidered scarlet waistcoat is worn over a white shirt whilst the ubiquitous felt fedora protects heads from the sun's rays.

One of the most emblematic items of traditional clothing is a heavy, woollen cloak worn by farmers which is known as *la manta esperancera* (the Esperanza blanket). The cloak is off-white in colour save for a blue stripe around its bottom edge and is gathered around the neck and worn over the shoulders. It's said to have evolved from a type of cloak the Guanche used to cover themselves but the version which became known as *la manta esperancera* dates back to around the early 19th century when it not only kept farmers warm in the winter when Tenerife's northern hills can get decidedly chilly, but it kept them dry as it was partially waterproof as well. The curious thing about this cloak is that they were made from woollen blankets imported from England. Whereas traditional dress is mainly reserved for fiestas, the Esperanza blanket is still worn as a functional garment. We've met many farmers in Tenerife's northern hills wearing them whilst going about their daily work. Turn up at an agricultural gathering in winter and you'll find plenty of men in fedoras with long wooden staff in hands and Esperanza blankets wrapped tightly around them.

TRADITIONAL AND MODERN SPORTS

On the face of it Tenerife doesn't seem a particularly sport-obsessed island; people are generally too laid back for anything that involves rushing about. And yet there are any number of sporting activities to either participate in or, if getting hot and sweaty in the sunshine doesn't appeal, watch as a spectator. Some of these are quite unique to the Canary Islands.

Arrastre de ganado

Any decent agricultural fair on Tenerife should have an *arrastre de ganado* competition. These are races involving teams of oxen dragging heavy loads on wooden sleds. These teams of oxen can also act like the equivalent of a fairground attraction at agricultural fairs. In the past, the gnarled boards the oxen drag across wheat-carpeted circular arenas were designed for threshing, now children cram onto them to enjoy the ride.

Baseball

Although only founded in 1997, the Tenerife Marlins, whose ground, el Burgado is in Puerto de la Cruz, quickly rose to become the best baseball club in Spain and one of the best in Europe. Between 2010 and 2020 they were crowned champions of Spain six times and won numerous cup competitions. Baseball and Tenerife might seem an unlikely combination, but the team was founded by Néstor Pérez Suárez (known as 'Big Show') a trainer from Cuba where baseball is the national sport. It's particularly popular in the north of Tenerife thanks to the links the island has with Cuba.

Bullfighting

Bullfighting has never taken off on the island, something some locals will tell you proudly as though it gives them the moral high ground over their mainland cousins. Santa Cruz does have a bullring, but it was rarely an arena for bullfights and, until it fell into disrepair, was mainly used for concerts and political rallies. Ironically, although bullfighting is frowned upon, cockfighting is still legal in the Canary Islands, as it is in Andalusia. When we arrived on Tenerife in 2003, cockfights were listed in the programme of events to celebrate the founding of Santa Cruz held each May. In 2017 the Canarian Government began drafting a law prohibiting cockfighting. Three years down the line the fights are still taking place.

Climbing

Some of the most popular areas for climbing lie way off the beaten track, such as in honey-coloured crevasses above Arico in the east of the island.

But others are just tucked away from tourist hots spots. The fantastical rock formations in Teide National Park make for an exciting and visually stunning playground for climbers. Near the start of the Siete Cañadas route in Teide National Park, there's a natural, surreal, burnt orange amphitheatre where if you look closely, you can see carabiners gleaming in the sunshine. Below the Roques de García viewpoint is La Catedral, a huge monolith where you can often spot climbers clinging to its sheer sides. The first time we realised this was after hearing disembodied voices whilst walking the Roques de García circular route. The voices got louder and louder but we still couldn't see their owners ... and then we looked up. Not all climbing areas are in remote places. There are often climbers scaling the Martiánez cliffs overlooking the beach of the same name in Puerto de la Cruz.

Cycling

As people who prefer walking to getting around on two wheels, we can't see the appeal in cycling on an island where the gradient from coast to mountain is so steep. But that's what makes it an ideal training ground for professional cyclists. Finding ingredients that include challenging climbs and adjusting to dramatic changes in altitude, combined with mind-blowing scenery and a climate that mostly guarantees good weather even in the depths of winter has drawn the likes of Chris Froome and Team INEOS (formerly Team Sky) for over a decade. It's common to see international cycling teams take over the Parador de las Cañadas del Teide. We've stayed at the same time as Team Sky on a couple of occasions, nosing at what professional cyclists eat for breakfast. Their presence can make progress through Teide National Park slow for those in cars. Saying that, we once had Chris Froome on our bumper on a downhill stretch where he was able to negotiate the twisting corners far more quickly than we could.

Diving

Although Tenerife may not be as renowned for diving as the dazzling coral reefs of the Red Sea or even neighbouring island El Hierro, the tunnels, caves and strange formations created by its volcanic origins give it an undersea vista worth exploring. In the seas off the coast are rusting wrecks that are home to octopus, moray eels, trumpet fish, and shoals of sardines; weird and wonderful volcanic cascades which look like gigantic steps, a stairway for some mythical aquatic giant perhaps, where dolphins and tuna can sometimes be seen; and sandy, shallow water dives where divers swim amid eagle, manta and stingrays. Dive companies offering experiences for both professional and novice level divers can be found in most coastal resorts.

The Real Tenerife

Football

The island's main football team, CD Tenerife (Club Deportivo Tenerife), play at the Estadio Heliodoro Rodríguez López Stadium in Santa Cruz. The club has had a chequered history, sometimes playing with, and even holding their own against, the big boys of Spanish football in *La Liga*. Two seasons in a row (1991/92 and 1992/93) Real Madrid travelled to Tenerife on the last day of the football season needing to beat the home team to have a chance of winning the league. Both times the *blanquiazules* (blue and whites) beat the mighty Real Madrid in Santa Cruz to deny them the title. However, the last time they played in La Liga was in the 2010/11 season and there's been a revolving door of managers since then as on-the-field dramas tend to now be played out mostly at the bottom of whatever league they happen to be in (Segunda for the last few years). The highlight of any football calendar is the home game against rivals UD Las Palmas from neighbouring Gran Canaria (when they happen to be in the same league) which attracts a level of excitement that would normally be reserved for the arrival of the likes of Barcelona or Real Madrid. We've attended one of these derbies and, whilst it's not on the same aggro level as Rangers vs Celtic or Manchester United vs Liverpool, it's a terse enough affair and we did (accidentally) get caught up in a baton charge by the National Police. Most upsetting of all was watching CD Tenerife fans mutilate Tweety Pie cuddly toys. The nickname for UD Las Palmas players is *pío-pío*, a reference to the sound made by canary birds, and as Tweety Pie is also a yellow bird he makes a good stand-in for a canary. Subsequently Tweety Pie is lynched, decapitated and set on fire whenever the teams meet.

Golf

There are seven full golf courses and two pitch and putt courses scattered across various parts of Tenerife. Buenavista Golf, designed by Seve Ballesteros and located on the coast below the Teno Massif is the most spectacular and remote. Elegant Real Club de Golf in Tacoronte is the second oldest course in Spain and sits at 600m above sea level, nippy in winter months. Abama Golf on the south west coast looking toward La Gomera is the most upmarket of Tenerife's courses, being part of the luxurious Ritz-Carlton Abama Resort. Golf Las Américas is a swish surprise in Tenerife's most bad-mouthed (unfairly) resort, Playa de Las Américas. Amarilla Golf and Golf del Sur are located on the south east coast in what was Tenerife golfing centre, Golf del Sur, which is increasingly known as Costa San Miguel in a bid to make it more attractive to a wider range of holidaymakers. And Golf Costa Adeje on the south west coast fits perfectly with the image of the upmarket hotels located on the western boundaries of Costa Adeje. The two nine-hole pitch and putts are Centro de Gold Los Palos, below Montaña de Guaza on the road to Palm-Mar and Golf

La Rosaleda between Puerto de la Cruz and La Orotava. Golf La Rosaleda has the best location of all in our view, sitting at the foot of the Orotava Valley with Mount Teide dominating the scene. With Tenerife being a year-round sunbathing destination, it's also a year-round golfing destination. But during summer months golfers tend to keep away from Tenerife's courses, even though temperatures in the Canary Islands are nowhere near as oppressive as in the south of the European mainland. We've had more than one director of a Tenerife golf course ponder, bemused, why more British golfers don't use Tenerife as a summer golfing destination.

Hiking

Tenerife is an exceptional hiking destination, its wildly diverse scenery (volcanic landscapes, desert-like badlands, pine woods, ancient *laurisilva* forest; verdant valleys; atmospheric ravines; former merchant trails; historic coastal paths) offering as contrasting a range of walking routes as you'll find just about anywhere. Having created walking holidays in Portugal, France, Germany, Austria, Slovenia, Greece, and mainland Spain we think Tenerife offers some of the best walking you'll find in Europe. Which is why we have a specialist website about it called, somewhat obviously, Walking Tenerife (walkingtenerife. co.uk).

Juego de Palo

Juego de Palo also comes from the Guanche and is a type of martial art which involves fighting with sticks (*palos*), similar in a way to Japanese Kendo but without the protective suits as blows to the body aren't particularly violent.

Lucha Canaria

The most popular sport on the island is *lucha canaria* (Canarian wrestling) which is a bit like sumo wrestling wearing nappies or, as Freddie, a young *tinerfeño* described it to us, "fighting without violence." Nearly every town on Tenerife has a wrestling ring. During the wrestling season, *lucha canaria* is prime time Saturday night viewing on local TV channels. The actual wrestling itself involves fighters have to out-manoeuvre opponents in order to force a part of the body, other than feet, into contact with the ground. This is one of the sports which has it roots in Guanche culture.

Paragliding

Tenerife is one of the best European destinations for throwing yourself off a mountain, with parachute attached obviously. Why? Because you can drive from the coast to dizzying heights of over a 1000m above sea level in a short time. There are a number of launch sites scattered across the island; la Corona on the Tigaiga ridge in the north; Ifonche above the south west coast; la Ladera de Güímar in the south east and from near the observatories at Izaña on the crown of the island at over 2000 metres above sea level. Various companies offer tandem flights so there's no need to go solo. If jumping from high in the heavens seems a tad extreme, some offer tandem flights from sites located a lot closer to sea level.

Salto de Pastor

Although it's mostly practised as a sport now, *salto de pastor* (shepherd's leap) was once a rather nifty way for shepherds and country people to cross small ravines without having to climb in and out of them. Basically, shepherds simply pole-vaulted across the ravine using long, wooden sticks with metal tips, saving themselves a lot of time whilst traversing the island's undulating terrain. Spotting shepherds with long sticks is relatively common in traditional areas, seeing them in use, less so. We've watched shepherds rapidly descend steep slopes using these sticks as we've been cautiously and slowly zigzagging our way down narrow tracks. It's an impressive skill to witness.

Surfing

Although not known as a classic surfing destination, there are still plenty of good surf spots all around Tenerife's coastline, from ones in the centre of Tenerife's purpose-built southern resorts (Playa de las Américas), and off the beaches in traditional resort/towns in the north (Playa de Martiánez in Puerto de la Cruz) to some of the most remote areas of the island, like Almáciga below the Anaga Mountains. Although there's surfing all year, the most powerful waves tend to be between October and March. Every so often a natural phenomenon creates a series of monster swells; super waves which only occur in a few places around the world. One of these places is Punta Brava in Puerto de la Cruz where they're known as *el Bravo* (the brave). It's said Meteorologists can spot them forming about three or four days before they reach land, which gives wave-hunters from across Europe time to descend on Punta Brava. Surfers might relish el Bravo, but the waves do leave the poor buildings on Punta Brava's headland looking battered and shell-shocked.

Windsurfing & Kiteboarding

Breezy El Médano on Tenerife's south east coast is a Nirvana for both windsurfers and kiteboarders, not necessarily a compatible mix. Thankfully, the long beaches at El Médano allow sufficient room for both to exist as harmoniously as could be hoped for given the rivalry. For the neutrals among us, the result is a colourful spectacle of hi-octane extreme sports in a scenic beach setting. As international competitions are regularly held at El Médano it's not uncommon to be able to see the best windsurfers and kiteboarders in the world doing their stuff in the waters just offshore. There are also a handful of windsurf and kiteboard schools in El Médano for anyone who has a hankering to join in.

CULTURE

It has been said in the past that Tenerife has less culture than the average pot of yoghurt and if you were to ask anyone to name someone famous who comes from Tenerife, they'd struggle. Famous writers, poets, musicians, there have been a few, and in the words of Frank Sinatra, "but then again, too few to mention."

Art, Theatre & Dance

Some claim to fame can go to the island's Surrealist connection when, back in 1937, after hosting the second Universal Surrealism Exhibition, André Breton signed a manifesto declaring Tenerife a 'Surrealist Island'. La Laguna-born Óscar Domínguez painted alongside Breton in Paris and his 1937 oil painting 'The Infernal Machine' fetched a record breaking FF2,770,000 in Paris in 2000. The front door to Dominguez' birthplace in La Laguna used to be framed by a large sardine can with the lid rolled open; you get the feeling Dominguez would have approved.

The Teatro Guimerá in Santa Cruz is named after the Tenerife-born playwright Angél Guimerá and was opened in 1851, becoming an obligatory venue for every Spanish theatre company en route to touring the Americas. It's a typical 19th century bourgeois theatre, all gold leaf and frescoes, and today continues to stage theatre and ballet. Several small towns on the island also have theatres which stage surprisingly professional performances; El Sauzal and Arico come particularly to mind.

But the event that really put the yoghurt joke to rest was the opening of Santiago Calatrava's spectacular Auditorio de Tenerife on Santa Cruz' port side in 2003.

Home to the Tenerife Symphony Orchestra, the white tsunami design has become an icon of the city and its 1700 seater auditorium witnesses events ranging from Heineken Jazz Concerts to The Moscow Ballet.

In the south of the island, diminutive Spanish choreographer Carmen Mota stages shows at the Pirámide de Arona, fusing modern and traditional Spanish dancing in her colourful spectaculars. But the Carmen Mota show is one of the few references to mainland Spain you'll find on Tenerife. For although Madrid may rule their heads, *tinerfeños'* hearts belong first to Tenerife and second to

Central and South America.

Tradition

Fiercely protective of their heritage, *tinerfeños* of every age know the words to their traditional songs, the steps to their traditional dances and own a '*mago*' or traditional costume. Far from shunning old, outdated ideas, it's predominantly the young who participate in the fiestas which commemorate, celebrate and preserve their heritage, finding any excuse to don the costume and roam the streets amidst traditional bands of '*parrandas*'. In the bars and clubs it's not UK and US chart sounds that dominate, it's Cuban hip hop, Reggaeton and Latino, an audible link to Tenerife's Latin American pulse which has been 400 years in the making and which beats its way through the food, the music, the language and of course, carnival.

Ties

With an over-reliance on mono-cultures throughout its history, every time the island's main cash crop failed due to economic decline, the lure of the New World beckoned and *tinerfeños* emigrated in their droves to Cuba, Venezuela and Argentina, founding cities like Montevideo in Uruguay and San Antonio in Texas. With them they took their worship of Nuestra Señora; their wooden carved balconies which became known as 'Colonial' style; the Canarian wrestling of *lucha canaria*, and the stick fighting of *juego de palo*. When they returned, they brought cigar & rum production, food, music, and wealth which they invested in building houses and businesses and improving the island's infrastructure. As a result of this cultural exchange, there's barely a Tenerife family that doesn't have a cousin, a brother or a son who lives in South America and as *Los Reyes Magos* (Feast of the Epiphany, or The Kings, at which youngsters get their presents) approaches, queues the length of a football pitch form at the *correos* as parcel after parcel waits to be weighed and stamped en route to the Americas.

The unique mix of *tinerfeñan* and South American has produced a smiley, friendly people for whom life still moves at a slower pace than for much of the rest of the developed world and for whom time spent with family and friends in their island's benign climate is still far more valuable than money or material possessions. Long may it remain so.

FIESTA CALENDAR

January 5th: Epiphany - island wide
The children's fiesta. On the night before the Epiphany, *Los Reyes* (The Three

Kings) arrive in towns all over the island (on camels in La Orotava, Garachico and Los Cristianos) bestowing gifts and throwing sweets to the crowds with such enthusiasm it could have your eye out.

January 17th: San Abad - Buenavista del Norte, La Matanza
Over 1500 oxen, goats, horses, donkeys and the occasional iguana on a lead have a day out in town for their annual blessing.

February/March (dates vary depending on when Easter falls): Carnival - Santa Cruz and Puerto de la Cruz
The biggest fiesta of the year and the time to slip on the fishnets and sexy little black number, if your wife will let you, and join the week-long party.

April: Semana Santa (Easter) - La Laguna and Adeje
Solemn, silent and evocative processions involving cloaked, barefoot and chained brotherhoods. La Laguna on Good Friday.

The Passion of Christ - most of the townspeople take on roles in an emotive and biblical-sized re-enactment of the crucifixion. Adeje on Good Friday.

April 25th (Sunday closest to): San Marcos - Icod de los Vinos and Tegueste
A cross between a harvest festival and a county fair, galleons on wheels lead Tegueste's colourful and unusual *romería*.

May 3rd: Fiestas of the Cross - Santa Cruz, Puerto de la Cruz and Los Realejos
Crosses are ornately decorated on the streets and in houses, but let's be honest, it's the three hour long firework display in Los Realejos we really want to see.

June (dates vary according to when Easter falls): Corpus Christi - La Orotava, Santa Cruz, La Laguna and Tacoronte
Flower power in La Orotava when the old cobbled streets are carpeted with beautifully ornate floral images ... only to be trampled on by the clergy. Carpets are also created in Santa Cruz, La Laguna and Tacoronte.

June (Sunday following Corpus Christi): Romería - La Orotava
One of the largest on the island with beauty queens on camels, over 70 carts pulled by oxen, traditional singers and dancers and as much wine and food as you can catch, literally.

June 23rd & 24th: San Juan - Puerto de la Cruz, La Caleta de Interián, San Juan de la Rambla, Garachico and various beaches

On the night of the 23rd there's a huge party with bonfire, fireworks and live entertainment on Playa Jardín – bring your own candles, flowers and food and be prepared for a midnight dip. The following morning the town's harbour is filled with goats in honour of an ancient Guanche ritual. In La Caleta de Interián (beyond Garachico) they light the beach with hundreds of burning torches; in Garachico people camp on the beach for the bonfire and fireworks and in San Juan de la Rambla they roll fireballs down the hillside. Smaller beach parties take place across the island including in Costa Adeje and Los Cristianos.

July 16th (Sunday closest to): Virgin del Carmen - fishing communities all over Tenerife, particularly Puerto de la Cruz

Mariners carry their patron saint through the streets before taking her on a sea trip (Santa Cruz, Puerto de la Cruz, Las Galletas). Alcalá swims against the tide, holding theirs on 15th August.

July 25th: Anniversary of Nelson's defeat - Santa Cruz

The capital celebrates the defeat of Nelson in 1797 by staging a re-enactment of the heroic defence of the city. Brits can participate as long as they don't mind losing.

August 14th & 15th: Nuestra Señora de Candelaria - Candelaria

Pilgrims travel (many on foot) from all over the island to celebrate their Patron Saint's day and watch a couple of 'cavemen' do a Laurel & Hardy routine while they re-enact the finding of the Virgin, aided and abetted by animal skin-wearing locals and a herd of goats (the goats are the best actors – by a margin).

August 16th: San Roque - Garachico

Free food and drink dished out by lads and lassies dressed in colourful traditional costumes from oxen-drawn carts. Local *parrandas* (musicians) join the general 'eat, drink and be merry' throng.

August 18th: Fiestas del Santísimo Cristo - La Laguna

One of Tenerife's most beloved icons, a Gothic carving of the crucifixion, is paraded through the town.

August 24th: Hearts of Tejina - Tejina

The townsfolk of La Tejina construct giant hearts from flowers and fruit and hurl insults at each other.

Top: Carnival queen, bottom left:
alfombrista, La Orotava,
bottom right: romería

September 7th: Fiestas Del Socorro - Güímar
The people of Güímar carry their Patron Saint's image across the *malpaís* (badlands) to a sanctuary by the sea.

October 12th: Día de la Hispanidad - Island wide
Anniversary of Columbus' discovery of the New World and a public holiday in Spanish-speaking countries.

November 29th: San Andrés - Puerto de la Cruz and Icod de los Vinos
An excuse for quaffing the new wines in Puerto de La Cruz and then careening down an almost vertical hill on a metal tray in Icod de los Vinos (see details in Part 2, Icod de los Vinos).

December (1st week): Fiesta del Cuento - Los Silos
Los Silos becomes even more enchanting during the International Storytelling Festival.

CARNIVAL ON TENERIFE

History of Tenerife's carnival - The feast before the famine
Carnival originated in Italy as early as 1268. The name originates from the Latin *carne valle* meaning 'goodbye to meat' alluding to the need to use up meat and animal products, such as eggs and milk, before devout Catholics give them up for Lent; hence Pancake Day in Britain; the only practice to survive the Reformation. Carnival quickly spread throughout the Catholic countries of Europe and arrived in the Canary Islands with the Spanish conquistadores in the fifteenth century.

Thought by the church to be blasphemous and by the authorities to be subversive, attendance at *carnaval* (the Spanish spelling) was frowned upon and so the practice of wearing costumes and masks developed to hide an individual's identity and allow them to carouse without fear of recrimination.

Franco banned Carnival in Spain in 1937 on the grounds that it provided the ideal climate for crime to flourish undetected. With the Second World War and Franco's ban in place, Carnival kept a low profile until 1945 when it re-emerged clandestinely in Tenerife, people wearing cloth hoods with holes cut for eyes and mouth and confining their revelry to their homes. Being a former Governor of the Canary Islands and knowing how important the celebrations were to islanders, Franco chose to turn a blind eye to what became known as the Winter Fiestas to get round the country-wide ban. Franco never repealed his ban on carnivals; it stayed in place until his death in 1975. The following year, for the first time in nearly 40 years, festivities could be once again openly paraded under the true title of 'carnaval'.

Tenerife carnival - something old

Over the years, much about Tenerife's carnival has changed; the traditional masks have virtually disappeared and costumes have become more elaborate, covering a wider spectrum of disguises and in some cases, not covering very much at all ... even in February after-dark temperatures.

However, the election of Carnival Queens still heralds the start of the main festivities and the opening parade sees them, their Maids of Honour and entourages, being driven through the main streets of Tenerife's bigger towns, accompanied by the traditional 'murgas' in clown costume and assorted groups and individuals in fancy dress.

The Burial of the Sardine (*entierro de la sardina*) used to denote the demise of carnival but nowadays in the likes of Santa Cruz and Puerto de la Cruz marks the half way point on Ash Wednesday, where hordes of weeping 'widows' follow a funeral cortège for a giant papier mâché sardine down to the harbour where the 'corpse' is set alight amidst an extravaganza of fireworks and a cacophony of banshee wailing.

The Gran Cosa Apoteosis (closing parade) used to involve the throwing of *huevos tacos* which were eggshell and cloth balls held together by paste and thrown onto the passing parade from windows and balconies. In 1906 they were banned on health and safety grounds as some people were apparently being over zealous in their use, to be replaced by the confetti and streamers that we see today; the expression ' you'll have somebody's eye out' must surely have come into the discussions. But carnival hasn't just lost some of its old traditions; it's also re-discovered some others and invented entirely new ones.

Tenerife carnival - something new

Now one of the highlights of carnival in Puerto de la Cruz, and attracting thousands of spectators and more and more participants, registration for the Mascarita Ponte Tacón (High Heels Drag Marathon) takes place in Plaza del Charco where contestants have their heels measured for regulation minimum height by the event's compère; a Lily Savage lookalike in bouffant wig, false eyelashes that cause a draft when she blinks and heels that would induce vertigo in a lesser mortal.

Outrageously shocking costumes are de rigueur and lashings of free beer is on tap for participants at the side of the main stage (not for these insouciant athletes the isotonic properties of a high energy drink) before racers negotiate an obstacle course, and cobbled streets, on their high heels. It's a hoot and not for anyone who's easily shocked.

Getting the best from carnival

Tenerife's carnival parades are fantastic extravaganzas to witness, but they involve stamina and a lot of standing around. You'll need to be in position about an hour before the 'official' start to get a prime spot. Although the parades are great spectacles, the true heart of carnival in Tenerife lies in its street parties. Instead of being a spectator, become a 'carnival-goer.' All that's required is to use a bit of imagination and dress up a little. If you're a man visiting with your female partner, then borrowing her clothes is perfectly acceptable (maybe not to her). Cross-dressing is pretty much obligatory, but anything will do. Trust us, it does make a difference. Wearing fancy dress you'll see a very different carnival in Tenerife; one that's unforgettable.

Don't arrive too early. Carnival in the street doesn't hit its stride until around midnight. By then those not in fancy dress will feel the odd ones out. From then enjoy the party; it's a great atmosphere and one which many visitors never experience.

Misconceptions about carnival on Tenerife:

Carnival on Tenerife takes place each February

As carnival is linked to Lent, and Lent is a moveable feast, the dates of carnival change each year. This means the main events can take place in February or March. The traditional carnivals on Tenerife observe these dates, well, religiously. The good thing about this is that you know years in advance when the traditional carnivals on Tenerife will be taking place. However, non-traditional carnivals on the island aren't linked to Lent.

How long carnival in Santa Cruz lasts

Some travel publications state that carnival lasts a week, some that it lasts two weeks, and others that it lasts for weeks and weeks. The last isn't technically wrong as the period from the first official carnival date to the last can span three months. But it's not all party, party. The run-up involves various competitions – Carnival Queens, dance troupes (*comparsas*) and *murgas* (satirical singing groups) competitions etc. But the part of carnival which involves parades and street parties kicks off after the election of the Carnival Queen and is known as *carnaval en la calle* (carnival in the street). In Santa Cruz this lasts for ten days.

Carnival celebrations begin in Santa Cruz before continuing across Tenerife

Carnival celebrations take place at exactly the same time in many traditional towns on Tenerife, because the dates are linked to Lent. But there are non-traditional carnivals, especially in southern areas which have developed mainly thanks to tourism. Once the big (and smaller) northern carnivals are over, these non-traditional ones can begin. The downside to these carnivals is, because they're not linked to Lent, it's more difficult to plan exactly when they'll be taking place. The upside is that locals in those areas can enjoy a traditional carnival like the one in Santa Cruz, and then their own as well.

In reality, there are loads of carnivals across Tenerife. How long each lasts can vary from town to town.

THE CORPUS CHRISTI FLOWER CARPETS OF LA OROTAVA

In June 2020, for the first time in 101 years and only the third time in its 116 year history, the cobbled streets of the old quarter of La Orotava remained free of flowers and the large space in front of the Town Hall remained void of Teide's soil. As a prayer to the pandemic which prevented the town from celebrating its most important day, and as a tribute to the memory of all its victims, a 20 square metre tapestry was constructed in the aisle of the Church of Nuestra Señora de la Concepción over which the Corpus Christi procession was able to walk. Despite the beauty and poignancy of the piece, it was all a far cry from the bustling activity and perfumed streets that annually attract visitors in their thousands.

The feast of Corpus Christi has been celebrated in Tenerife since the end of the fifteenth century when, following the Sevillian model, local guilds paraded through the streets of La Laguna's old quarter carrying their traditional trade banners. Over the centuries, celebrations became embellished until in 1847, Leonor de Castillo Monteverde whose mansion stands on Calle del Colegio, one of the streets along which the Corpus Christi procession passes, decided to do something special. Using flowers and petals, Leonor created a small carpet of flowers on the street outside her house in homage to the procession whose feet then destroyed the transient art. This act of homage was so well-regarded by all who witnessed it that the following year, several of Leonor's neighbours decided to follow suit, creating their own flower carpets outside their homes. Thus began a tradition which quickly led to four entire streets and three plazas being decorated in flowers, petals and grass seeds, some thirty individual carpets in all.

It was to be another 72 years before the intricate tapestry of the Town Hall joined the Corpus Christi celebrations. Adorning the large space outside the Town Hall was originally conceived, not in relation to Corpus Christi, but as part of the celebrations to mark the completion of the Plaza de Alfonso XIII, designed by renowned architect Mariano Estanga in 1912. The following year the Corpus Christi procession passed through the Town Hall plaza for the first time but it took another six years before the space was decorated in honour of the occasion. Although the original designs were constructed of flowers, seeds and grasses, over the years as the *alfombristas* (master carpet-makers) added such intricacies of design as perspective, nuances of shade and trompe-l'oeil, the medium morphed from petal to volcanic sand, all of which comes from Teide National Park.

What began as a single day's work placing petals and seeds in a carpet pattern now takes many months at the end of which, an intricate tapestry woven with religious and contemporary themes is designed, outlined and created – a magnificent, transient work of art, born to dazzle for just one day.

The Fiesta of Corpus Christi takes place on the Thursday following Corpus Christi but one of the real joys of this event comes from visiting a day or two ahead of the day to watch from the steps of the Town Hall as the *alfombristas* create their masterpiece.

THE MAGICAL NIGHT OF SAN JUAN

The *Noche de San Juan* (June 23rd) is the longest day and shortest night in nature's annual cycle. Midsummer's Eve is the time to cast out the old and welcome in the new; a time of re-birth and a time of heightened magic.

Celebrating San Juan is a big thing on Tenerife, especially in areas where traditions are strongest and reach back centuries. Its origins lie with the island's aboriginal people the Guanche who, like many primitive civilisations, believed that the sun cast powerful magic when it was at its midsummer peak. Another name for the San Juan celebrations is the Fiestas of the Sun.

Festivities begin on the eve of San Juan; a night of fire festivals and love magic when the twin elements of fire and water have potent qualities and, legend has it, whatever is dreamed will come to pass. In towns on Tenerife's northern slopes, figures festooned with flowers, and bonfires are set alight; the Guanche believed flames from fires added strength to the sun. In some towns young men practice the custom of leaping over bonfires to demonstrate their prowess.

All across Tenerife from traditional towns to resort areas, people take to the beaches, or light fires in the hills, to celebrate. What form that celebration takes varies from location to location. In less traditional areas it can be more of a casual beach party. In other places there are more obvious links with age-old customs.

The best celebrations take place in Puerto de la Cruz where families armed to the gunwales with supplies of food and flagons of country wine fill Playa Jardín. Whilst elaborate feasts are prepared, children excavate holes in the sand, some with depressions of volcanic crater proportions, which are then decorated with displays of shocking pink bougainvillea and luminescent yellow hibiscus from the beach's gardens; the flowers are important symbols representing love and partnership. Following a night of live music, there's a firework display and a mass bathing at midnight. The Guanche believed the sea at midsummer was bubbling with magic; bathing in it as Midsummer's Day dawned ensured good fortune for the coming year as well as rejuvenating skin, banishing harmful spirits and guarding against illness. The magic water is also supposed to be a strong source of fertility. It would be interesting to know if there was a baby boom on the islands every March. It's also claimed that anyone who stays awake to see daybreak will hear a chorus of mermaids before the mythical island of San Borondón appears briefly on the horizon.

All along the north coast, are more intimate San Juan celebrations; from small fires laid out along the curving beach at La Caleta de Interián and the coastal road being blocked by cinders from an over-sized fire on the beach at Garachico to torch-lit processions in the old streets of San Juan de la Rambla.

El baño de las cabras

One of the most bizarre traditions to be found on Tenerife takes place at the harbour in Puerto de la Cruz on the morning of 24 June, *el baño de las cabras* - the bathing of the goats.

From first light, goatherds from the Orotava Valley drive their herds through Puerto's streets, filling the harbour's pebble beach with anxious-looking goats. The air is soon filled with tortuous cries as each indignant creature is dragged into the water and dunked. This is no display put on for tourists,

Local goatherds believe this ritual will benefit their animals. Whether they actually consider the water enchanted, who knows, but veteran goatherds claim the bathing results in increased fertility amongst female goats, improving their chances of falling pregnant and ensuring the continued growth of the herd.

When the last of the goats are dunked, it's the turn of other animals. Dogs are drenched and *caballeros* ride their steeds into the sea in a display of equine formation bathing.

ROMERÍAS

The *romería* is the most emblematic fiesta of Tenerife and can be found liberally dispersed across the island between May and September. Literally meaning a pilgrimage or excursion, at its simplest description the *romería* is a procession but in reality, it's a celebration which combines both pagan and religious roots; a fusion of village fête, harvest festival and county fair with a sprinkling of religious worship. Originally a fiesta of the upper classes, it celebrated rural life on Tenerife and usually featured the pursuits and fruits of those who toiled the land by way of a procession of the farm workers who shared the spoils of their labours with onlookers. Quickly gaining in numbers and popularity, the *romería* evolved into the main event in a village or town's

Top: Corpus Christi sand tapestry, bottom left: bathing of the goats, bottom right: chestnut braziers

annual fiesta calendar, often coinciding with the Patron Saint's Day, and became a 'fiesta of the people'.

Keeping the Faith

The *romería* is seen by local farmers, livestock-rearers and suppliers as an opportunity to offer the fruits of the harvest to the saintly guardian of the town and its people. For some, the day commemorates deeply held beliefs which date back centuries.

For 400 years the townspeople of Garachico have given thanks to a diminutive Saint from Montpellier in France for answering their prayers when in 1601 bubonic plague arrived on two cargo ships from the Spanish mainland. The pestilence quickly spread to neighbouring municipalities and for five years it ravaged the area, killing thousands and bringing trade to its knees. It wasn't until a group of pilgrims arrived at the little Ermita of San Roque and carried the image of the Saint to the Church of Santa Ana where a mass was held that the disease finally abated and the port and town could begin to recover. In thanks the people of Garachico and its surrounding municipalities made offerings of animals, food and wine; a practice which has continued to the present day in its Romería de San Roque.

In 1745 the town of Arafo suffered calamity when a landslide buried the natural spring of Añatigo, the source of its water supply. For five years the townspeople laboured in vain to dig out the spring. Then one night in 1751 they carried the statue of San Agustín in a procession down to the site of the landslide and held a mass. A storm brewed up and, leaving the saint at the scene, the people fled home to take shelter. The next day they returned to find the statue unharmed and the source of the spring freed as a result of the torrential rains. Today, the Romería de San Agustín celebrates the 'miracle' of Añatigo.

Country Pursuits

Every *romería* has certain characteristics that define it. The main event takes the form of a procession of decorated carts pulled by oxen and accompanied by assorted livestock and the town *parrandas*, or folk musicians, who provide the music to which everyone sings along.

In the small town of Tegueste the carts are decorated to look like small galleons with white billowing sails; a tradition which commemorates a 16th century offering to San Marcos to keep a virulent plague at bay. The land-locked municipality chose to make as an offering something they would not normally have; boats. Clearly impressed, San Marcos obliged and kept the town free of disease. Now, every year the 'galleons' of San Marcos raise their sails and provide one of the most colourful *romerías* on the island. In Los Realejos the carts are festooned with flowers, branches, farm implements and the head of a goat sacrificed for the fiesta. The streets of the town are so steep that the carts are mounted onto the back of lorries rather than pulled by oxen; a rare triumph of health and safety over tradition. In La Orotava, one of the largest *romerías* on the island, the procession is traditionally led by camels. As well as the *parrandas*, there are groups of traditional dancers to accompany the carts through the grand, historic streets and there are so many carts that it takes more then three hours for the full procession to pass.

Rural games and traditions feature heavily in *romerías,* with exhibitions of *lucha canaria* (wrestling), *juego de palo* (stick fighting), wheat thrashing and goat milking amongst them and there are sometimes fairs featuring pottery, embroidery, weaving and pudding making.

There are always offerings of food and wine liberally dispensed to participants and onlookers alike. As each cart rolls past, its occupants throw food into the crowds which eager spectator hands grab and snatch with practised aplomb. Over our years attending Tenerife's *romerías*, we have caught bags of popcorn, little rolls spread with chorizo paste, hard boiled eggs, fruit, pork chops and chunks of steak wedged into a doorstop slice of crusty bread. To accompany the food, huge vats of wine are syphoned off into jugs and sloshed into the frenzy of cups and glasses which are thrust at every cart by the crowds. Seasoned *romería*-attenders have their own glasses that hang around their necks, ready to be lunged towards anyone holding a jug of wine as the carts trundle by.

A photographically colourful affair, the wearing of traditional costumes by participants during the *romería* is absolutely de rigeur. More than anything else, the wearing of costumes unites participants in the recognition of their heritage; farmers and livestock-rearers whose knowledge of the stars, of nature and the healing power of plants and herbs earned them the nickname *magos* or magicians. The *romería* is a way of keeping those skills and traditions alive; a piece of *tinerfeño* magic for everyone to share.

The best way to enjoy the *romería* is to wear some comfortable shoes to help alleviate the syndrome known as '*romería* feet' from all that standing around. If you see one, buy yourself a small glass that hangs in a leather pouch around your neck from one of the '*vaso*' vendors in the street and liberally partake of all the offerings given to you. Don't be shy to hold up your glass for refills or to ask for food, it's not considered rude, it's expected.

Tenerife's Main *Romerías* (in calendar order):
San Marcos, Tegueste – Sunday closest to 25th April
San Isidro, Los Realejos – last Sunday in May
Las Mercedes, La Laguna - last Sunday in May

San Isidro, La Orotava – Sunday after Corpus Christi
San Antonio de Padua, Granadilla – in first two weeks of June
San Benito, La Laguna – second Sunday in July
Nuestra Señora de la Esperanza, El Rosario – first Sunday in August
San Roque, Garachico – 16th August
San Agustín, Arafo – last Saturday in August
Nuestra Señora del Socorro, Güímar – 7th September

THE FIESTA OF THE CROSSES AND FUEGOS DE MAYO

To visitors it might be the light show of the year in the Tenerife sky, but the *Fuegos de Mayo* firework display which lights up the sky above the Orotava Valley on the night of the 3rd of May has its roots in a class war.

The 3rd of May is a big day in the Spanish Calender, it's the day of the Fiesta de las Cruces (Festival of the Crosses, also known as the Cruz de Mayo) when crosses all over Spain and South America are decorated to commemorate, so the story goes, a search for the cross on which Jesus died.

Coincidentally, or conveniently, both Santa Cruz de Tenerife and Santa Cruz de la Palma were founded on 3 May (different years), so there's a good reason for throwing a big bash in the Canary Islands.

In Santa Cruz, Los Realejos and Puerto de la Cruz especially, the local people go to town when it comes to dressing up crosses for the big day. It's worth visiting any to wander around the streets seeking out well-dressed crosses. The most obvious example in Puerto de la Cruz is the cross on the side of Casa Aduana, the old customs house beside the harbour.

In Los Realejos upwards of 300 crosses are decorated. The best way to see them is to simply stroll the streets popping into houses (it's the done thing), *ermitas* and churches to have a look at the variety of designs. They look their best when lit up after dark, but that's when the streets are at their busiest, full of people in town to enjoy the main event, the *Fuegos del Mayo*.

Los Realejos, *Fuegos del Mayo* is the biggest firework display of the year in the Canary Islands. Locally it's claimed to be one of the biggest in Europe, but we're always a bit wary of such grand claims. Whatever the truth, it is an impressive event and the most spectacular firework display we've enjoyed anywhere.

It initially started in 1770 as a bit of rivalry between two streets, Calle del Medio (home to farm labourers and manual workers) and Calle del Sol (where the professional classes lived) and involved a contest to see who could decorate their neighbourhoods with the most elaborate floral displays. After the Hermanos Toste opened a fireworks factory in the town in 1788 the floral displays were added to with something which had a bit more fizz, and the battle of the fireworks erupted in spectacular fashion. Since then the event grows louder every year as both streets, with the help of two firework factories, strive to design bigger and better displays in a bid to outdo each other in this most exuberant and colourful of class wars. The story goes that one of the streets once introduced a cannon to try to outdo their neighbours.

The first time we went to the *Fuegos de Mayo* we didn't really know what to expect. Information about what happened at fiestas was usually quite shallow – more basic rehashes of press releases rather than articles by people who'd actually experienced events first hand. So we found out the hard way by standing for hours shivering (stupidly a friend and I wore short sleeve shirts – because it was May in the Canary Islands we expected a sultry night not realising how cool it could be after dark in the hills at that time of year).

The firework display doesn't start until quite a bit after a procession leaves the Iglesia de Santiago Apostle at 10pm. By that time we were numb having arrived in the town around 8pm. A single firework at various stages along the route signals the procession's progress ... which can seem to take an interminably long time.

However, once the first 'proper' firework lights up the sky, the magic begins and numb cheeks are forgotten as the fiesta in the heavens begins and wave after wave of multi-coloured spheres explode sending twinkling, man-made shooting stars arcing back towards the earth.

What makes it stand out from any other 'spectacular' firework display is that, thanks to the involvement of the fireworks factories, there are often imaginative and innovative fireworks you simply don't see anywhere else. We've witnessed some beauties over the years which have left us standing open-mouthed as one street unleashes a beautiful barrage and then the other street counters with an equally bewitching response.

The official blurb tells you the display lasts three hours, which it usually does ... more or less. But that's from start to finish, not how long the actual fireworks display lasts. There are quite long gaps between each pyrotechnic skirmish. That doesn't make the *Fuegos de Mayo* any less of a WOW experience, but don't go along expecting three hours of non-stop explosions. And remember to take a jacket.

The Belén, a Christmas Tradition

Seeing a *belén* unlocks the inner child, there's something magical about these beautiful nativity scenes. They fascinate, especially the most elaborate ones where all village life is depicted. We can stand for ages marvelling at the detail and wit to be found as our eyes wander the little streets, pausing to peek in windows like a giant voyeur. There is an air about them which stokes nostalgic memories of past times, when Christmas was all about innocent wonderment, about family and compassion rather than frantic consumerism.

Belénes are nativity scenes that can range from the classic basic – a few shepherds, Mary and Joseph, the baby Jesus, a donkey, an ox ... you know, the main team – to whole towns with working parts that are populated by beautifully detailed mini people. The tradition of creating *belénes* at Christmas goes back to Italy and is said to have been started by St Francis of Assisi in 1233. It wasn't until the 18th century that it caught on in Spain. Traditionally *belénes* should appear from the 7th December.

There are hundreds of *belénes* across Tenerife, with some of the bigger towns having *belén* exhibitions and even *belén* routes. In Santa Cruz there are good ones in the Town Hall and in the Meridiano shopping centre; in Laguna you can stumble across them in the city's religious buildings and historic courtyards; in La Orotava they're found in churches and even in the back room of an ironmonger's shop. In Puerto de la Cruz there's an exhibition in Casa Ventoso which is overlooked by many visitors because it's tucked away in a courtyard in a colonial building away from the busiest streets. Although most *belénes* depict a Biblical scene, some stray from the path. There are those which feature exquisitely detailed, flamboyant Italian characters as well as a few which depict life in Canarian towns. A few years ago in Garachico we saw one which was based around a Guanche village. Some, like the *belén* in front of the Town Hall in La Orotava are life-sized affairs. The most magical of the *belénes* also change appearance as day quickly turns to night, little houses light up and camp-fires give off a cosy glow. It's always worth taking time to look at the scenes very closely. There is much to discover in the most detailed of them. Peek inside windows and you'll see all sorts of shenanigans, from *abuelas* baking bread whilst *abuelos* laze in bed, to mothers breast-feeding their babies. Cheekiest of all is *el caganer,* the guy who's been caught short outside. To be fair to him, he's not always caught short outside. Sometimes he is actually using a bona fide toilet and is simply the victim of a faulty door which swings open at an inconvenient moment. Why he's there is a bit of a mystery and the subject of much debate. It looks as though his roots lie with the Catalans and he's thought to have first appeared in the late 17th century. It's claimed that he's a figure of good luck, his 'deposits' fertilise the soil which in turn results in a good yield. Subsequently his presence promises good luck and happiness. Leave him out and you're asking for trouble. But he's also seen as a mischievous wink at the Catholic Church; a nod that seems to say 'don't take yourself so seriously.'

FOOD AND DRINK - OVERVIEW

Canarian eating habits are much the same as in the rest of Spain, the main meal being taken in the afternoon, followed by a *siesta* period. Apart from those in purpose-built tourist resorts and in modern shopping centres, most shops shut between 13.30 and 16.30 and even the capital, Santa Cruz, can be eerily quiet during these hours.

Although five hundred years of Spanish, Italian, British, Dutch and Portuguese influence has left its mark on Canarian gastronomy in general, you have to know what influences to look for to be able to spot them. For example, the famous Canarian *mojos* are spicy sauces, but spicy food is not something you'll find much evidence of in either Canarian or Spanish cuisine. The clue to where the influence for these more-ish sauces comes from lies in the name. The Spanish word for sauce is *salsa*, whereas the Portuguese, who *do* like spicy food, call sauces *molhos*. Despite its proximity to Africa, you'll struggle to find much African influence in the food. Thanks to the influx of emigrants returning from South America in the 1970s, it's easier to find South American influences than African. A classic example is the Venezuelan *arepa*. This tasty and cheap, filled cornbread pancake is sold in cafes and *areperias* in all traditional parts of Tenerife, but not so easy to find in resort areas. Overall though, traditional Canarian cuisine consists of simply cooked, good quality ingredients. Subsequently traditional menus have changed little in centuries. Accounts written by travellers in the 18th and 19th centuries describe meals which aren't very different from that which the modern day visitor will be offered.

"The staple dish was *puchero* ... which antiquated travellers still call '*olla podrida*' (pot pourri)" – Richard Burton, 19th century, 'To the Gold Coast for Gold'.

On the coast, grilled or fried fish is the norm and what a choice; sea bass, bream, sole, hake, monkfish, swordfish and even shark. However, if you're going to eat only one fish on Tenerife it should be *vieja* (parrot fish) whose sublime smoky flavours have earned it the distinction of being the islanders' favourite fish. Another popular and wallet-friendly choice is *cherne* (wreckfish/stonebass), a meaty fish similar to cod in texture and ideal for anyone who gets bored picking bones out of their teeth.

Inland is more traditional country fare; huge slabs of meat cooked on wood burning grills, *conejo en salmorejo* (rabbit in sauce), and hearty stews like Burton's *puchero* (an 'everything but the kitchen sink' mix which usually includes chickpeas, pumpkin, potatoes, carrots, beans, corn and whatever leftover meat is to hand) warm the cockles against the sometimes brisk mountain air.

Meals are usually served with '*papas arrugadas*' (delicious small potatoes boiled in seriously salty water until they wrinkle) and two sauces - *mojo verde* and *mojo rojo*; one made from coriander, the other from chillies. An ingredient which predates the Spanish conquest is *gofio* (a flour made from toasted cereals) which was a staple of the islands' original inhabitants, the Guanche. It's still used extensively today to thicken and flavour stews, or is mixed with cheese or nuts and cut it into small cakes (*asado*). *Gofio* is also a forerunner of power drinks; Jesús, a *gofio* mill worker in La Orotava, swears by it, saying a glass of *gofio* and milk in the morning gives him bags of energy and staves off hunger until lunchtime.

In the last decade or so, Canarian gastronomy has experienced somewhat of a renaissance in, particularly on Tenerife which is arguably the capital of Canarian gastronomy. Tenerife simply offers the greatest wealth of dining options. If proof is needed, at the time of writing Tenerife boasts five Michelin Star restaurants. Only Gran Canaria, with two Michelin star restaurants, can come close to that tally.

The catalyst for this renaissance is the island's southern resorts. Ironically, areas which are often dismissed as being 'all day British breakfast' territory have been responsible for Tenerife's gastronomy being elevated to tastebud-delighting levels. Not the general resort restaurants, which invariably disappoint with mediocre offerings being dished up at far higher prices than *tinerfeños* pay for superior meals in traditional areas. No, the source of this culinary renaissance is to be found in the kitchens of the luxury hotels that started appearing in numbers in the south west of Tenerife at the start of the 21st century. Five star hotels *have* to offer five star gastronomic experiences, and subsequently top chefs were attracted to Tenerife. Now you have restaurants reflecting the creations of some of the most renowned Spanish chefs, such as Catalan superchef Martín Berasategui's two Michelin star M.B. in the Ritz-Carlton Abama near Playa San Juan. This has had a hugely positive trickle-down effect as young, local chefs have taken the experience they've picked up in these creative kitchens, and in ones further afield, and are now applying them in their own restaurants, breathing exciting new life into classic Canarian dishes in the process.

What all of this amounts to is that Tenerife has become a superb culinary playground for foodies. If good traditional local food is your thing, it exists in hundreds of restaurants. But if more sophisticated, creative gastronomy rings your bell more, there are numerous, excellent contemporary Canarian restaurants to be discovered all around the island, as well as in the dining rooms of the top hotels.

DISCOVERING CANARIAN CUISINE

Eating out is an important part of Canarian culture, subsequently there are good Canarian restaurants to be found all over Tenerife. With a population that hovers around the one million mark that means there are a lot of restaurants which exist first and foremost for the local population. Drive along Tenerife's older roads and you find yourself falling over traditional restaurants. There are more to be discovered in the north than in the south for one simple reason - the majority of Canarios live in the north. There are whole stretches between Los Realejos and the capital, Santa Cruz, which are renowned for their gastronomy. Whenever we eat in these areas there are rarely any other English speakers around; even though restaurants might be packed to capacity.

It's important to know the specialities of any location's cuisine to know when seeking authentic local food, especially in a popular holiday destination like Tenerife where a significant number of 'authentic' restaurants in resorts might not actually be Canarian. In some ways, the most basic Canarian cuisine isn't very different from many other destinations around Europe, tending to consist of simply-grilled meat, fish or seafood served with potatoes or French fries. However, there are plenty of dishes which have 'made in the Canaries' stamped all over them.

Starters

Some common starters will be familiar to people who have eaten in restaurants on the Spanish mainland – *pimientos de Padrón, jamón iberico, croquetas, papas bravas, boquerones, ensaladilla rusa, gambas al ajillo* etc. Others are distinctly Canarian. These include *rancho canario* (a soup of meat, veg and noodles), *potaje de berros* (watercress soup), *queso asado con mojos* (grilled cheese drizzled with sauces and honey), *almogrote* (a pungent cheese pate from La Gomera), *escaldón de gofio* (a thick paste consisting of toasted flour mixed with stock), *ropa vieja* (literally translated on some menus as 'old clothes', a mish-mash of a dish made with chickpeas, chicken, beef or pork, potatoes, tomatoes, onion, garlic, stock, wine, thyme, bay leaves, paprika, parsley and wine), *carne fiesta* (chunks of marinated pork), *garbanzos compuestos* (another chickpea and meat stew), and *papas arrugadas* (wrinkled potatoes).

Egg dishes also feature regularly and could either be starters or mains as some can be hearty affairs. Everyone knows *tortilla española* but also look out for *revueltos* (scrambled eggs with other ingredients), *huevos estrellados* (egg and chips, which comes in a few guises) and *arroz a la cubana* (an odd mix of fried bananas, egg, tomato sauce, rice, and a sausage).

Meat

Anyone who heads straight to the meat part of the menu and orders steak, chops etc. probably isn't going to notice much difference in what arrives on

Top: Tenerife potatoes, bottom left: cheese & country wine, bottom right: lapas

their plate than if they'd ordered similar in any other European destination. The dishes which reveal a menu is truly authentic Canarian include *cabrito* (goat), *conejo* (rabbit), *cochino negro* (black pig), *costillas con papas y millo* (a messy concoction of corn on the cob, pork ribs and potatoes), and *puchero* (another meat and vegetable concoction featuring numerous ingredients). It's not always possible to just choose *puchero* from a menu. Some restaurants only prepare and serve it on certain days, whereas in others, diners have to order it in advance.

Fish and seafood

For lovers of fruits of the sea, Tenerife is a treasure chest filled with all sorts of goodies. Every town by the coast has access to fresh fish which means no matter where you stay on Tenerife, you should have a choice of restaurants in which to get to eat the cast of characters that populate the surrounding waters. Places that have a fishing community are best (Bajamar, Los Abrigos, Las Galletas, Puerto de la Cruz, San Andrés, Los Cristianos, Playa San Juan etc.) but you won't struggle to find seafood restaurants in purpose-built resorts like Costa Adeje and Playa de las Américas.

The fish selection on Canarian menus often includes *vieja* (parrotfish), *cherne* (stone bass/wreckfish), *bacalao encebollada* (salt cod with onions and peppers), *atún en adobo* (tuna marinaded in herbs, spices, oil and vinegar), and various types of bream with numerous different Canarian names (*sama, sargo, parga, chopa, bocinegro)*. A less common speciality to look out for is *moreno frito* (fried moray eel). The fish dish most connected with Tenerife is *chicharros*, which are small fried horse mackerel. It was so popular that the residents of Santa Cruz were called *chicharreros* because they ate so much of it.

As far as seafood goes, *lapas* (limpets drizzled with a garlic, parsley and olive oil) are very popular in the Canary Islands as is *choco* (cuttlefish), *pulpo* (octopus), and squid in various formats (*calamari, chopitos, chipirones*). Wander harbour areas in traditional towns and you're likely to see blackboards with 'Hay Camarones' scrawled on them. *Camarones* are bright pink shrimp flavoured by salt, bay leaves and olive oil.

Desserts

In our view, desserts aren't the strong point of traditional Canarian cuisine. Too many restaurants are guilty of dishing up unappetising, wobbly, pre-prepared desserts served in those old-fashioned, glass dessert dishes. Canarian puddings to look out for include *bienmesabe* (almonds, water, sugar, egg yolk, cinnamon, lemon peel); *frangollo* (milk, egg yolks, flour, raisins, sugar, cinnamon, almonds, palm honey, butter, lemon peel); *prince Albert* (chocolate mousse with hazelnuts, almonds, and eggs); *gofio mousse* (a mousse made with toasted flour); *leche asada* (roasted milk, which is far nicer than it sounds); and *quesadilla* (a type of dry cheesecake from El Hierro).

And to finish

Good Canarian restaurants should end the meal with a *chupito*, a small shot of something alcoholic, usually *ron miel* (honey rum).

TAPAS ON TENERIFE

Most of us know that in mainland Spain a *tapa* is traditionally a small snack, used to stave of hunger between meals. How it came about remains disputed, but the most plausible explanation involves a *tapa* (lid) of ham or cheese placed on a glass of wine. The reason for that is also the cause of much debate. It was either to keep flies out of the drink (but not off the food), or strong *jamón serrano* and sweaty cheese lids helped disguise the taste of poor wine. Whatever the truth, eating tapas has become massively popular and tapas now encapsulates a range of dishes which have evolved way, way beyond their humble origins. Like both drinking sangria and watching flamenco dancers, eating tapas in a Spanish destination is a holiday crowd-pleaser and subsequently you'll find restaurants in Tenerife's purpose-built resorts with tapas menus. But although the food might be decent, the experience won't have much in common with picking at *pintxos* in a bar in Barrio Gotico in Barcelona. Which is probably why we regularly read comments about there not being authentic tapas on Tenerife.

Pop into most 'local' bars in any traditional town and you'll generally find a glass cabinet with a few trays of tapas underneath. What's under the glass usually tends to be the same limited selection of tapas. You'll probably also find a blaring television screening bad soaps or the same news item over and over, a couple of grizzled geezers propping up the bar and, if you're lucky, a stand selling cassettes of Latino music. These places might not fit the average holidaymaker's idea of going to a bar for tapas, and the tapas may not be the best you'll ever try, but they're 100% authentic. Petrol stations are especially good places for tapas. Most have a cafe attached which is invariably packed with locals. Santa Cruz bus station does good, basic tapas. The bar there is more likely to be populated by bus drivers as it is travellers passing through. It's authentic but, again, maybe not what tapas-seeking visitors are looking for.

At Tenerife's agricultural markets you usually find stalls selling wine and a small selection of tapas. One side of the Mercado de Señora de Africa in Santa Cruz is lined with little kiosks such as this. Sharing counter space at one with a *chicharrero* is a seriously authentic way of trying a *tapa*. A bit less intimidating is to pop to the underground fish market where there's contemporary as well as traditional tapas, and a bit more elbow room in which to eat them.

If a fiesta doesn't have pop up stalls serving *pinchos morunos* (skewers of marinated pork) it's not a proper fiesta. There are always food stalls at fiestas serving traditional snacks, which is basically what tapas are. At some, like Noche en Blanco and Noche de San Andrés, you get a greater selection of tapas than at others.

The problem with most of these suggestions so far is they require visitors to venture into what might be completely unfamiliar territory; places where non-locals are few and far between and the local accent is thick and difficult to understand even when you know some Spanish. It took us time to build up confidence to dive into a thick throng of locals surrounding fiesta kiosks in off the beaten track places. But the more we did it, the easier it became ... and we always ended up with a memorable experience.

In the likes of La Orotava, La Laguna, Santa Cruz and Puerto de la Cruz there are plenty of very good tapas restaurants with the sort of ingredients a lot of people want when they go seeking a tapas experience. There are tapas restaurants in pretty squares, on historic streets and located inside colonial buildings; some are traditional (think rows of hanging hams) whereas others are ultra contemporary with more imaginative menus to match. There are even chain tapas restaurants such as Lizarran, where you choose your *pinchos* (small, open-topped sandwiches with various toppings) held together with cocktail sticks and then present the *pincho*-less sticks to the cashier when you want to pay the bill.

The best way to try lots of interesting tapas is to follow an official *ruta de tapas* (tapas route). These are held throughout the year and all across the island and are a super way of trying unusual tapas (a drink and a *tapa* cost around €2.50) as well as discovering good new restaurants and bars.

What is generally thought of as tapas comes in a variety of sizes and occasionally with different names on Tenerife. You can wander into a Canarian bar and point at a selection of dishes in a glass cabinet on the counter. Sometimes you might find your *cerveza* arrives with a little complimentary 'snack,' but not usually of the type of *tapa* that was once common in mainland Spain. Most common are restaurants whose menus have a tapas section. But it's also worth checking if menus include *raciónes*. *Raciónes* are like big tapas portions. Anywhere with *raciónes* usually offers ½ *raciónes* which are closer to tapas size. Another word to look out for on Tenerife menus is *picoteo* – food to pick at, to share. In other words, tapas.

Although there's been an increase in speciality restaurants serving more imaginative and diverse tapas, most of the time Tenerife tapas menus tend to have a similar look to them. *Tortilla española* and *papas arrugadas* (the island's speciality wrinkled potato) are everywhere, so not exclusive to tapas menus. These dishes, on the other hand, are to be found mainly in establishments with tapas menus.

Churros de Pescado

These are a must try – small goujons of white fish encased in batter (a crispy, herby one if the restaurant is good). Fabulous on their own, they're even better when dipped in the little bowl of *alioli* (garlic mayonnaise) that often accompanies them.

Queso

We're using an umbrella term as there's a variety of cheesy choices on good tapas menus. If drinking a glass of red wine, a *tabla de quesos* (cheese board) is the perfect partner. Go for Canarian cheeses as the islands produce some real belters. Alternatively, the cheese used for *queso asado* and *queso a la plancha* (fried/grilled cheese) doesn't pack a powerful punch but it's livened up no end by being drizzled with *mojo rojo, mojo verde* and honey.

Jamón

If you have cheese and wine, you really should have a *tabla de jamón serrano* and/or *ibérico* (thinly sliced cured hams) as well to complete a seriously tasty trio. There's been an increase of speciality *jamón* bars and delicatessens in Tenerife in the last few years so not too difficult to indulge in some authentic *jamón* and wine tasting.

Boquerones

Menus translate *boquerones* as anchovies, but they taste nothing like the salty version found on pizzas. These are simply tiny, filleted fish which have been marinated in garlic, olive oil, white wine vinegar and herbs. Perfect for picking at.

Croquetas

Croquetas are nearly as common place as *tortilla*. Although they are supposed to have fish, ham, chicken fillings, many taste more like flavoured potato than anything else. It's worth seeking out *croquetas caseras* and also places that are a bit more adventurous with their *croquetas*. We've had wonderful spinach, blue cheese, chicken curry, banana and even beetroot *croquetas* in various bars around Tenerife.

Small squid

Another tapas that comes in various forms. Many people automatically opt for *calamari* but *chipirones* (small squid) are more tender and have more flavour whilst *chopitos* are tiny, fried squid in batter.

Ensaladilla Rusa

We've no idea why a salad said to have been created in Russia is so popular in Spain, but you can get this savoury mix of tuna, mayo, peas, potato, boiled egg and carrot (that's the basic version) everywhere. It looks a bit of a mess on the plate, but we're often drawn to *ensaladilla rusa* as it's so tasty.

Pimientos de Padrón

Simple, but special, green peppers fried in olive oil and sprinkled generously with rock salt. By now everyone knows that one in ten should be as hot as the inside of a furnace, but here in Tenerife they rarely are. Every so often though one will catch you with your guard down and when it does ... yowza. More-ish whether spicy or not.

Pulpo

Octopus is another very common tapas on Tenerife and usually shows up as a zingy salad in Canarian bars. We prefer *pulpo a la gallego* where it comes on a bed of potatoes and is sprinkled with paprika. Best of all is when the potatoes are mashed. Octopus and mash is a heavenly combination.

Meat and Potatoes

Finally, this one can be more like a small meal than a tapas, but a variation of it regularly features on tapas menus. *Carne con papas* is as it sounds – meat with potatoes. More flavoursome is *carne fiesta* which is spiced pork and far tastier. Either way, you normally get potatoes or chips, so a bit too filling for tapas.

GUACHINCHES - TENERIFE'S MOST AUTHENTIC DINING EXPERIENCE

Guachinche – it's a delicious sounding word, pronounced *gwah-cheen-chay* with the G so soft it's like a whisper on the wind you aren't quite sure you actually heard. The word *guachinche* sounds as though it should have Guanche origins, but apparently it doesn't. It's actually a bastardisation of English and dates from a time when British merchants travelled the road between Santa Cruz and La Orotava. Small stalls by the side of the road were set up by wine growers for the merchants to try their harvest in the hopes they would then buy it and export it. As the growers were pouring samples, the merchants would say "I'm watching you!" so they could be sure the wine being tasted was only from that owner's vineyard and not being supplemented from other sources. Over time, 'wat-ching-you' became *'gwah-cheen-chay.'*

As merchants sipped their wine, stallholders prepared a small selection of tapas to accompany it, and from this practice these rustic eating stalls developed.

Now *guachinches* are rough 'n' ready makeshift restaurants that can be found set up in garages, gardens, interior courtyards, or even in the middle of banana plantations. To tag a trendy name to them, you could describe them as pop-ups. What they most definitely are *not* are restaurants. In recent years, as more and more visitors have heard about them, quite a few conventional restaurants try to cash in on the act by calling themselves 'guachinche.' when they're not. Whilst *guachinches* come in all shapes and sizes, if the one you're in looks like a restaurant and has menus, the chances are it is a restaurant, not a *guachinche*. They don't have the same licences as a restaurant, nor pay the same taxes. As a result, they are bound by laws which are completely unique to them. For a start, the owners of *guachinches* can only sell wine they've produced themselves. As well as wine, the only other 'beverage' they can offer is water. *Guachinches* can only open for between four and six months a year, and must close as soon as the wine stocks run out. In terms of food, there should be a maximum of three dishes on offer, plus any pickles, nuts, or fruit produced by the owner. The food should mainly be made with home grown ingredients or with produce from the immediate area; so we're talking fare which is as basic as its surroundings. We've eaten in a lot of *guachinches*, and not one has stuck rigidly to those rules, that's part of what makes eating in one fun. They have a below-the-radar ambiance, like drinking at an illicit still in the forest.

At fiestas and during wine harvest, *guachinches* spring up all over the place. Over the rest of the year they can be found in large numbers along Tenerife's northern slopes. The best hunting ground for them is between Tacoronte and Los Realejos. Whilst *guachinches* are historically unique to the north of Tenerife, some can be found in other parts. Gran Canaria has a variation of them called *bochinches*, but those are a relatively new creation. There are some around Güímar, Arico, and Arafo, but the further south you go the fewer there are. They've become so well known that there is even an app highlighting where to find them; however, the best way to experience a *guachinche* is to do so in a spontaneous manner. Follow the old roads heading west above the north coast and look out for signs on posts or scrawled on cardboard and nailed to trees, then simply follow the signs for a memorable and authentic Tenerife dining experience.

TENERIFE'S GOURMET POTATOES

Almost without exception, visitors to Tenerife fall gastronomically head over heels for the speciality dish of *papas arrugadas con mojo* (wrinkled potatoes with sauces). But if you've ever tried to re-create those delicious babies at home and have ended up with soggy, over-salted spuds on which you pour your souvenir *mojos* in a failed attempt to make them edible, you'll know just how important the particular brand of potato is to this humble dish.

Potato roots
The potato was born in South America on the high terraces of the Andes alongside Lake Titicaca over 7000 years ago. It wasn't until 1536 that the joys of potatoes were discovered by Spanish conquistadors who decided to bring some back to Europe to see if they would grow. Crops quickly adapted to the different environment, soil and weather conditions of Europe and new varieties were cultivated that shortened the growth cycle from five to three months. But here on Tenerife, the conditions in the upper terraces of Icod de Los Vinos where the

first crops were planted, bear a remarkable similarity to the conditions of origin in the Andes and, planted as a winter crop, hours of daylight remained equally close. As a result, some of the potatoes still being farmed on Tenerife can trace their tubers back to those original Peruvian Andes and are considered actual relics by those in the potato know. The first written accounts of potato cultivation on Tenerife date back to 1622 but it's believed the crop has been cultivated here since the 1570s.

Generation after generation of Tenerife farmers have cultivated various antique varieties of potatoes, exchanging seeds between north and south which helped to eliminate pests and to 'clean' the seeds year on year. When new varieties of the so-called 'short cycle' potatoes arrived from Europe, the poor farmers of Tenerife's central lowlands couldn't afford to experiment lest their crops failed and hunger ensued so they continued to farm their original varieties and have done so to this day.

Prized specimens

There are currently 46 varieties of potatoes cultivated in the Canary Islands and 25 of those (18 of them in Tenerife) can be traced back to those original Andes potatoes. These are varieties that never made it to the terraces of England, Ireland, France or Spain, nor to the United States and are today unique in Europe. In recent history a resurgence of interest in gastronomy using local produce has led to the recognition of these potatoes as rare and exquisite gourmet items and the humble potato received its own Denomination of Origin from Brussels at the end of October 2012 - *La papa antigua de Canarias*.

You'll find the greatest variety of potatoes on sale in Tenerife at farmer's markets in Tacoronte, La Orotava, La Laguna, El Rosario, Cruz del Carmen (Anagas), Puerto de la Cruz, San Miguel and Nuestra Señora de Africa in Santa Cruz. Look out also for special displays of winter variety harvests in major supermarkets through December and January.

Top of the crops for potato aficionados are *Bonita Negra, Negra Yema de Huevo, Torrenta, Azucena Blanca, Azucena Negra* and *Bonita Blanca*. They don't come cheap, but then how much would you expect to pay for a 500 year old, authentic Andean antique that also happens to taste sensational?

GET YOUR TENERIFE MOJO WORKING

A staple of the Canarian kitchen, every cook will have their own recipe for *mojo*, often using their own, home grown herbs and improvising on ingredients depending on what's available. You'll find subtle differences in taste and strength, both within Tenerife and across the Canary Islands as a whole. On La Gomera for instance, the *mojo* is generally much spicier than it is on Tenerife.

But *mojo* isn't simply the red and green sauces that you get with your Tenerife potatoes, in fact, *mojos* come in many different colours and flavours, even the ones you think you know so well.

Closer inspection of the ubiquitous *mojo rojo* and *mojo verde* that appear on every restaurant table from Los Cristianos to Santa Cruz, reveals that there are more varieties than meet the eye. *Mojo verde* (the green one) can be *cilantro* (coriander), *perejil* (parsley), or *pimiento verde* (green pepper) while *mojo rojo* (the red one) can be *pimiento rojo* (red pepper), *pimentón* (paprika) or *pimienta roja* (cayenne pepper). Although there are no real rules as to how you eat your *mojo*, in fact the red one is best eaten with meat while the green one goes with fish, the *mojo* equivalent of red and white wine. Both red and green will also contain more than a touch of garlic so if you don't want to end up singing 'Got My Mojo Working' on your lonesome, it's best to ensure your loved one gets their *mojo* on too.

Red and green aside, there are also lots of specialist *mojos* which you may find adorning your dinner table depending on the restaurant. Finding increasing popularity on the bread board is La Gomera's speciality of *almogrote* which is made from mature (for 'mature' read pungent) cheese mixed with *mojo* and can on occasion be something of an acquired taste. But toned down, it makes a delicious dip and we have recently found it cropping up on Tenerife tables as far apart as Vilaflor and El Tanque. A dangerously addictive *mojo* often accompanying bread rolls is *alioli*, or garlic mayonnaise, another one for sharing if you don't want to scare off everyone within a 20 metres radius every time you open your mouth. Other traditional, specialist *mojos* that you'll find across the Canary Islands are *mojo de almendras* (almonds) and *mojo de huevos* (eggs), both from La Palma; *mojo de queso* (cheese - not to be confused with *almogrote*) from Gran Canaria; and *mojo de aguacate* (avocado) which is usually served with *arepas*.

This list is not definitive, there are plenty more out there.

ANDY'S TRIBUTE TO TENERIFE'S BANANAS

Anyone who's ventured beyond the beach on Tenerife can't fail to have noticed the ubiquitous banana plants that grow all over the island, their tattered and torn leaves happily wafting in the breeze, or else contained within their ugly polyethylene greenhouses.

Now the island's number one agricultural export, the banana was first thought to have been commercially introduced to Tenerife in 1855 by Sabine Berthelot who brought the 'Chinese' banana to the island. In 1880 the firm of Wolfson and Fyffe made their first commercial delivery of bananas to London and for almost fifteen years, the trade thrived. But then, just as the exports were reaching

their zenith, World War 1 brought trade to a halt and changed the course of the Tenerife banana's history. With Fyffes switching their UK banana import business to the Windward Islands, Tenerife's bananas are now mainly exported to the Spanish mainland. Today, it's the Dwarf Cavendish variety of banana which is predominantly grown on Tenerife and across the Canary Islands. The plants are grown from rootstocks or rhizomes which throw shoots up from the ground to produce new plants. At any one time you can see three banana plants growing together – the 'adult' plant which will produce the current crop, the new plant for the following crop and a baby shoot for the crop after that. It takes 11 to 15 months for the plant to reach full maturity and it takes 4 to 7 months from the flower appearing for the bananas to reach harvest-ready ripeness.

One summer, whilst on assignment for an in-flight magazine, I was driving along the south west coast from Los Gigantes to Playa San Juan and was just approaching Alcalá when I spotted some banana workers in one of the plantations that line that entire stretch of road. As my assignment was about the burgeoning gastronomic scene on the island and its excellent home-grown produce, it seemed like the perfect opportunity for a spot of ad hoc banana photography.

There were about ten banana workers in total, including the guy who loaded the truck, and every one of them was filthy and sweating profusely. When I first arrived they had just cleared one plantation and were moving to the next so they invited me to watch and photograph as long as I didn't get in the way. The truck was parked in the middle of the plantation and the workers dispersed in pairs, disappearing into the dense forest of banana plants. Each pair approached a ready-for-harvesting plant and while one guy carefully placed the whole stem onto his shoulder, the second guy cut the stem cleanly from the stalk using a half moon blade attached to a long pole. Each stem was then carried out to the truck and stacked upright, every alternate one wrapped in a sack to prevent the fruit from bruising. When the lower level was full, a board was placed on top and a second layer of bananas was stacked.

It must have been 32° C in that plantation with the sun beating relentlessly on heads. Each inflorescence (the whole stem containing all the hands of bananas) weighs between 40 and 50 kilos (6 to 8 stones) and has to be carried on shoulders through the plantation, up the ramp to the truck and gently lowered into position. While I photographed and asked questions, the guys never once stopped working. When one man of slight stature who must have been in his sixties paused for a moment for me to photograph the particularly large inflorescence he was carrying, his co-workers good-humouredly called for him to carry on working instead of posing and trying to impress me with the size of his stem.

In less than 12 minutes these guys had filled the truck to capacity, which must have been something in the region of 40 stems in total. While the truck moved

Top: banana workers, bottom left: mojo, bottom right Arico cheese

off, they walked on to the next plantation where the next truck was waiting to be filled. Before I left, they gifted me a part of an inflorescence that had ripened beyond harvesting. Although it only contained a fraction of the number of hands of bananas on a full stem, it was really heavy and it reinforced just how hard these men worked. For the next two days while I was on the road the car smelled delicious and I had a ready store of sweet bananas in the boot.

So to the banana workers of Tenerife I say: *"Gracias. Thank you for the hard work you put in to bring me my weekly supply of bananas and every time I see a banana plant I remember you and your big stems and I smile."*

GOFIO - THE BREAKFAST OF CHAMPIONS

It may require a leap of imagination of JK Rowling proportions to link the little heaped pyramid of *gofio* which accompanies soups and stews in many Canarian restaurants with the birth of civilisation; however, the cultivation of grain, and therefore products like *gofio*, led to ancient man setting down roots and establishing permanent communities.

Cheap, nutritious and easy to produce, grain products have been an essential part of our diet for almost ten thousand years, with most cultures developing their own methods for transforming grain into food products. On Tenerife and the other Canary Islands there's a rather unique example of this, *gofio*; a toasted flour introduced by the island's original inhabitants, the Guanche. The word *gofio* is somewhat of an umbrella term given that it can be derived from wheat, maize, barley, millet, chickpeas or even a mix of these. Harvested grain is toasted before being milled to a fine yellow powder; a process which lends it a distinctive taste and smell. Initially laborious, the Guanche ground grain by hand until, following the conquest, the process was simplified by the introduction of water mills; some of which, like La Maquina in La Orotava, are still churning out *gofio* today. It's easy to know when you're in a town where there's a *gofio* mill; the slightly nutty, slightly sweet aroma emanating from their ovens will guide your nose straight to their doors.

There are a number of reasons why the consumption of *gofio* has remained popular with islanders since Guanche times. Throughout its history, Tenerife has suffered periods of extreme hardship; *gofio* proved a reliable source of nutrients such as protein, fibre, magnesium, iron, calcium and sodium when other food was in short supply. When outbreaks of rickets were rife throughout Spain following the Spanish Civil War it's said the Canary Islands were rickets-free because of the nutritional qualities found in *gofio*. It's also said to be good for helping lower cholesterol, regulate blood sugar levels and can be suitable for diabetes sufferers. *Gofio* is particularly popular in agricultural communities where its nutrients give farmers strength and energy to get through a hard day toiling in the terraces. For similar reasons, practitioners of the Canarian sport of *lucha Canario* (wrestling) swear by it, believing that including *gofio* in their diet is essential in their bid to become champions of their sport.

So how is it prepared and eaten? The answer is pretty much any way you want. Many *tinerfeños* call it the original power drink, claiming that a breakfast of a couple of teaspoons of *gofio* mixed with warm milk will set you up for the day and banish hunger pangs for hours - it's even possible to buy *gofio* energy bars; children love it mixed with condensed milk, honey and mashed bananas (maize *gofio* has a flavour reminiscent of crushed ice cream wafers); it's ideal for thickening and adding flavour to soups and stews like the traditional Canarian dishes of *puchero* and *escaldón*; more recently chefs have been experimenting with it in desserts, ice creams and even chocolate. Its sweet, savoury flavours make it suitable for using with breakfast, lunch and dinner.

SAY CHEESE

The Canary Islands have been producing excellent goats' cheese for centuries and have been winning accolades for it on the world stage for decades. At the 2019 World Cheese Awards, no less than 29 Canary Islands cheeses were in the medals – not bad for a little archipelago in the Atlantic.

Made from goat, cow and sheep's milk, sometimes only one of those and sometimes a blend, the rich pastures on which the herds graze give Canary cheeses their award-winning flavour. Although every island produces its own cheeses, Fuerteventura is in fact the front runner in the islands with their Majorero and Maxorata brands sweeping awards year after year.

The Canaries produce a staggering amount of goats' cheese every year and unsurprisingly, given how good the stuff is, they also consume more of it than anywhere else in Spain. On Tenerife, the penchant is for *queso fresco*, the soft, white, fresh cheese that can be eaten straight from the day it's made. It's available in natural or smoked form and with or without salt. Unless it's lightly grilled and drizzled in honey and *mojos*, we find it a bit too bland and prefer our cheese to have more attitude, like the *semicurado* which has been matured for more than 35 days and has a harder texture and stronger flavour. You'll find *semicurado* often sold with a coating of *gofio* or paprika to give them a distinctive taste. Plenty of bite and full flavour with a memorable after taste, this is our favourite. Finally we come to the Anthony Joshuas of the goats' cheese world, the *curados*. These babies have been matured for more than 105 days and can take the fur off your tongue soon as look at you. Pungent and packed with cheesy flavour they can tread a fine line between delicious and dangerous. They can be natural, smoked or coated in paprika or *gofio*.

It's not difficult to pick up good local cheeses; there are *queserías* (cheese producers) all over the island in Arico, Santa Ursula, Tacoronte, Guia de Isora, El Sauzal, Santa Cruz, La Laguna and Güímar. Easier still, just check out the cheese aisle of the nearest supermarket.

A TASTE OF HONEY

2000 years ago in the first known text which referenced the Canary Islands, Roman scholar Pliny the Elder wrote about there being an abundance of honey on the islands. Nobody is completely sure where he was being literal or figurative, but what is certain is there is a lot of honey on Tenerife.

It's thought the Guanche ate honey from wild hives; however, beekeeping and honey production as we know it arrived with the conquistadors. Tenerife's perfect climate made it a Garden of Eden and colonists soon exploited the diverse range of plants and the island's black bee population to make as sweet a range of honeys as you're likely to find anywhere. *tajinaste* and broom at high altitude produced honeys with delicate flavours; pine and laurel forests in the hills created honeys flavoured by chestnut, heather and wild herbs; whilst at coastal areas orange blossom, avocado and even bananas created jaunty, fruity honeys. For centuries, the island's beekeepers have moved mobile hives made from palm trees (*corchos*) to locations where flowers were in fullest bloom. Nowadays most *corchos* are in the form of rectangular wooden boxes, usually brightly coloured.

Since the conquest of paradise, honey production has remained virtually unchanged on Tenerife where a cottage industry prevailed even after sugar replaced honey as a food sweetener, devastating the industry worldwide. It's believed honey continued to thrive on the Canary Islands because islanders used it as much for its medicinal qualities. A Canarian friend told us how his mother used to make a concoction similar to the Scottish hot toddy whenever he picked up a cold bug. As well as tasting like the food of the gods, it is well documented that honey helps soothe burns and heal wounds.

Tenerife's diversity of landscapes and flora combine to create a wide, and often surprising, range of flavours. Types of honey you can find on the island include *agave*, *retama* (white broom), *tajinaste, castaña* (chestnut), *aguacate* (avocado), *brezal* (tree heather), *hinojo* (fennel), *poleo* (minty pennyroyal), *malpico* (a type of thistle), *barrilla* (messembrryamthemum), *pitera* (another type of agave), *relinchon* (a mustard like plant), and *tedera* (bituminosa). There are also various multi-floral combinations as well as honeys from the highlands, hills and coastal areas. The best places for picking up a jar or two are at farmers' markets or shops specialising in local products where you can expect to pay around €4/5 for a 500g jar. Craft fairs are also good places, and there are usually a couple of varieties on sale at Tenerife's airports, but at hugely inflated prices.

The Casa de la Miel in El Sauzal, in the same location as the Wine Museum, has a visitors' centre where you can gain an insight into beekeeping traditions on the island, as well as stocking up on honey. *(+34) 922 562 711; La Baranda, El Sauzal; open 10.00-20.00 Tuesday to Saturday, 10.00-18.00 Sunday, closed Monday*

COCHINO NEGRO - CANARIAN BLACK PIG

Although pigs have been part of island life since the time of the Guanche, the prized *cochino negro* (black pig) didn't arrive until the conquest, when they were introduced by Spanish and Portuguese settlers from the Iberian Peninsula. Although a mainstay of islander's diet for centuries, Canarian *cochino negro* herds diminished over the years until the renaissance in Canarian gastronomy during the last decade brought old traditions and farming methods back into vogue. Various government and local council initiatives also encouraged farmers to invest their time in rearing and breeding the pigs. As a result, numbers rose and *tinerfenos* developed a taste for the black pig once again. On Tenerife you'll find some restaurants named after *cochino negro*; there have been tapas routes themed around it; and there's at least one *cochino negro* festival in the north of the island.

Black pig has more flavour than run of the mill pork, so tends to be a favourite with the new breed of Canarian restaurants on Tenerife. One of the most popular ways it appears on menus is as *carrillas* (cheeks). *Cochino negro* also turns up in chorizo, as burgers, *albondigas* (meatballs) and croquettes, and as creative tapas on *rutas de tapas*.

TENERIFE WINE

Souls of poets dead and gone,
What Elysium have ye known,
Happy field or mossy cavern,
Choicer than the Mermaid Tavern?
Have ye tippled drink more fine
Than mine host's Canary wine?
John Keats (1795–1821) Lines on the Mermaid Tavern

In its heyday, Canarian wine was widely accepted to be the best in the world and its fame spread through the writings of such literary bigwigs as Shakespeare (whose annual stipend included a barrel of Canarian Malmsey wine), Sir Walter Scott and John Keats.

Grape origins

It was the Conquistadores who first introduced vines to the Canary Islands in the 14th and 15th centuries. Largely made up of mercenaries from across Europe, the conquerors were given land in exchange for their fighting services and on it, they set about planting crops, including vines, for subsistence farming. Keen to see which root stock would grow best, varieties of vines were planted from Andalucia, Castilla, Navarra, Galicia and Catalonia as well as from Portugal, France and Genoa. Thus the Canary Islands found themselves with a greater variety of vincs than most other places in Europe. In the late 19th century when pylloxera swept through the vineyards of France and much of Europe, the vines of the Canary Islands escaped and many varieties lost to Europe survived. Even today, some of the root stock in the islands dates back hundreds of years.

Planting continued throughout the 16th, 17th and 18th centuries with the vines flourishing in their fertile new surroundings and the resultant wine being exported across Europe and the Americas. Two factors, more than anything else, contributed to the success of wines from the Canary Islands. Firstly, introduced in the second half of the 15th century, the Malvasía grape grew particularly well in the islands and produced a sweet, rich wine which not only suited the palates of Elizabethan England and her colonies very nicely but it also travelled very well. Secondly, the Canary Islands, and Tenerife in particular, were perfectly placed at the crossroads between the old world and the new, a focal point on all shipping routes which passed through the ports of Garachico, La Orotava (now Puerto de la Cruz) and Santa Cruz to make repairs and take supplies on board en route to and from Europe.

The wine monopoly

Merchants grew fat and wealthy on the earnings from wine and many of Tenerife's most noble families who settled in La Orotava, La Laguna and Garachico made their fortunes and built their fine mansions with its fruits. But by the mid 17th century, Canary wine's fortunes were about to change.

It was through the English that Tenerife's wines had flourished, their shipping channels distributing it across the globe to their colonies but in 1661, in an attempt to control the profits from the trade, the Canary Company was formed in London which was given exclusive rights to the Canary Islands wine trade. The Canary Company quickly began to exploit their power, manipulating prices and exploiting the producers. This stranglehold on the trade led to the Garachico Wine Rebellion of 1666 in which *bodega* owners broke into the warehouses holding the wine ready for export and smashed all the barrels causing the streets of the wealthy town to 'run with wine' according to one local historian.

With London prices for Malvasía spiralling out of control, the English monarch, Charles II, inadvertently supplied a second nail for the wine's coffin by marrying the Portuguese Catherine of Braganza. Queen Catherine expressed a preference for the wines of her homeland, specifically those of Madeira. Since Portugal had long since freed herself from the clutches of Spanish control, her merchants were easily able to undercut the now exorbitant Canary wine and to flood the English market where the nobility were quick to emulate their new Queen's tippling practices. Sadly depleted, by the mid 19th century when first plague and then mildew hit the crops, the trade all but disappeared.

Reviving wine fortunes

'Canary' wine has enjoyed something of a renaissance over the last 15 years and today has found its way onto the prize winners' platforms of international awards and onto the tables of wine connoisseurs worldwide. More than 10% of the total surface area of the Canarian Archipelago is given over to the commercial production of wine covering every island except Fuerteventura. Taking pole position in both quality and quantity of wine production are the islands of Tenerife, Lanzarote and La Palma with Tenerife being the largest producer.

There are at least 70 *bodegas* on Tenerife and five DOs (*Denominación de Origen* – recognised and accredited wine-growing regions):

Tacoronte Acentejo: The largest wine-growing area stretches along Tenerife's north coast. Most award-winning reds come from this area.

Valle de Güímar: The Güímar Valley in the east of Tenerife is particularly sunny, making it good for producing young white wines (dry, semi-dry and fruity).

Valle de Orotava: Even though it's next to the Tacoronte Acentejo area and also on the north coast, the Orotava Valley produces as many good white wines as reds.

Ycoden Daute Isora: The vineyards in the north west of Tenerife were originally cultivated by the Portuguese, Flemish and Genoese. It's an area famous for its distinctive white wines.

Abona: Tenerife's main southern wine growing area produces some excellent whites, and the occasional good red. Some vines are cultivated at 1700 metres above sea level, the highest altitude for vines in the EU.

Due to the diversity of terrain and variations in climate, there are a few difference in how vines are grown. In some parts they are planted in low-lying rows and held up by forks. In others, vines are supported by wide frames. Sometimes vines are tied to wires or are cut back to form a small bush. The most attractive method is when vines are plaited together, creating long, gnarled, natural supports.

Where to buy the best Tenerife wines

Wines bought direct from the *bodega* seem to always taste better. But there aren't many vineyards on Tenerife where you can just turn up and have a tour. Quite a few *bodegas* do offer tours and tastings, but prior arrangement is required. Saying that, Canarios can be a very accommodating bunch, so if you happen across a *bodega*, it's worth asking if you can have a look round.

Most supermarkets stock some local wines. Al Campo in La Laguna and La Orotava have an extensive selection of Canarian wines at some of the best prices you'll find. Canary Island wines are more expensive than their mainland equivalents, starting at around €5 a bottle. *Vinotecas*, found in bigger traditional towns, are great little wine shops where you can try before you buy and enjoy some tapas into the bargain. If feeling adventurous, look out for '*se vende vino*' signs when out exploring. The old roads above the north coast are a good hunting ground for finding these small producers selling their own wine direct from their casas. It won't win any awards but it's surprisingly easy (and sometimes potent) to quaff.

In most restaurants across the island now you can expect to see at least one locally-produced white and one red on wine menus while top restaurants in hotels and outside the resorts will offer a more comprehensive selection. As yields are low, prices are generally higher than Spanish mainland brands but by ordering a bottle, you're helping to re-establish what was once the darling of three continents.

Favourites of ours include anything (but especially Calius and Balcón Canario) from Bodegas CHP in La Matanza and the Güímar Valley, and the El Lomo, Brezal and Monje Tradicional, all from the Tacoronte-Acentejo DO. As red wine drinkers we're not best for recommending white wines, but you could do worse than those from Bodega Reverón.

CRAFT BEER

For those who prefer beer to wine, Tenerife has some tasty craft beers to seek out.

The first to recognise the rising demand for beers brewed in micro breweries was Tacoa, between El Sauzal and Tacoronte, where they brew the beer on the premises. This creation of a German/Spanish couple is known for its craft beers and an interesting fusion of Spanish and German cuisine. Their golden ales, porters, IPAs, and bocks slip down particularly well when accompanied by a challenging metre-long sausage. Tacoa regularly add to their beer menu, experimenting with beers which have a distinctly local flavour such as florally *tajinaste* honey.

The bad boys of local craft beers are Chutney, whose range of pale ale, stout and London brown beer sport gangsters' names – Willie Sutton, Albert Spaggiari and Ronnie Biggs. These are possibly the coolest looking craft beers in the Canary Islands.

Our favourite Tenerife craft beer is Tierra de Perros, Land of Dogs – a reference to how the Canary Islands got their name.

BARRAQUITO - TENERIFE'S SPECTACULAR SPECIALITY COFFEE

In the middle of the 20th century in the cool and shady interior of the Imperial, an unexceptional bar next to the bullring in Santa Cruz de Tenerife, a regular known to the waiting staff as '*El Barraco*' grabs a seat at the bar's counter mid-morning and orders his favourite *bocadillo*, *pollo* (chicken). To help wash down the dry crusty bread, he requests a concoction of his own making – espresso coffee, milk, condensed milk, and Liquor 43 layered in a tall glass. The striped drink is finished off with a sprinkling of cinnamon and a tiny slice of lemon zest. It is such an eye-catching drink other customers are keen to try it, instantly giving the curious coffee a thumbs up after doing so. Its popularity catches on rapidly and a half century or so later, the '*barraquito*' becomes known as the specialist coffee of Tenerife and the Canary Islands. It is one of the world's great speciality coffees. In recent years *barraquitos* have nearly become as well known as *papas arrugadas*, but there are pitfalls to be wary off. For a start, it's somewhat of a controversial drink, with endless debates on social media among Canarios who disagree passionately on what exactly is and isn't an authentic *barraquito*. In some parts of the north the drink described above is known as a *zaperoco*. Ask for a *barraquito* and you might be told, "you mean a *zaperoco*." In other areas of the island it's necessary to ask for a *barraquito especial* to ensure that essential shot of Licor 43 is included as what's known as a *barraquito* is more of a *leche y leche* made with condensed milk and milk. There can also be confusion around how it should be imbibed. It seems a crime to ruin the pretty pattern but, before that first sip is sipped, *barraquitos* should be rigorously stirred to blend all those colours and, more importantly, flavours.

Although they originated on Tenerife, *barraquitos* are now common on the other Canary Islands. In some bars on La Palma a dollop of cream is added, but the original remains the best in our view.

Top: Bodega Monje, bottom left: barraquito, bottom right: Tacoa beer

Tenerife Shopping

Having VAT-free status, the Canary Islands are a great place to pick up cheap cigarettes, booze and perfume. Every decent-sized resort town has a proliferation of perfume shops, and every supermarket offers a large selection of cigarettes and brand name local spirits. In some coastal resorts of the south, it's not unusual to see small supermarkets with four aisles of booze and one of everything else. But then, there are a lot of resort destinations around Europe where visitors can pick up cheap booze and fags etc. so it's hardly unique and, additionally, it's all a bit 'travel shopping 1980s.'

There are far more interesting things to pick up which have more or a local flavour, and browsing for these items gives a greater insight into the shopping habits of the local population.

Food

The north of the island is served by a vast network of supermarkets where, depending on the strength of the pound to the Euro, the weekly shopping bill can come in a lot cheaper than in the UK. Even the smallest towns will have at least one, and often two or three of the main supermarket chains of Mercadona, HiperTrébol, HiperDino, Lidl and Altesa; each of whom has aisles full of yoghurt, olives, biscuits and Serrano hams as well as fruit and vegetables and a fresh fish counter where a bewildering range of sea creatures are cleaned and gutted to order. Most also have their own butchery and bakery.

The island's hypermarkets are Al Campo (Santa Cruz, La Laguna, La Orotava) and Carrefour (Santa Cruz) where you can buy everything from beds to baked beans. Al Campo is especially good for picking up ingredients from other countries e.g. Greek feta, curry paste, British cheddar. For enthusiastic cooks you live on the island, access to a range of ingredients which aren't just Spanish makes culinary life far more interesting.

In recent years the main supermarkets have opened branches in or near the southern resorts. So holidaymakers and ex-pats no longer have to travel too far to find a decent shopping centre or supermarket. Some still make a weekly trip to places like Las Chafiras or CC La Laguna shopping complex where Decathlon, Ikea, Leroy Merlin and Al Campo all have hypermarket outlets.

Top of Tenerife's local produce to take home is wine. Vineyards are the best places to sample and pick up local wines, but arranging visits isn't always easy. Most supermarkets sell a selection of the most well known Tenerife wines but Al Campo stocks a far more expansive range than other supermarkets – a whole aisle is devoted to local wines – and has wines from less well known bodegas. Tenerife honey is also superb; 15 types are produced from the island's flowers, including the *tajinaste* where mobile hives are taken into the crater in spring so

85

that the bees can collect the pollen. Look out for the authentic '*Miel de Tenerife*' label. Equally good is the La Gomera produced *Miel/Sirope de Palma;* a rich, dark, toffee-flavoured natural honey-like syrup produced from palm sap. It's delicious in Greek yoghurt, drizzled over smoked goats' cheese, porridge or ice cream or added to dressings. And while on the subject of goats' cheese, Arico smoked was voted one of the world's top twelve cheeses and should make it onto every visitor's shopping list. Supermarkets are also good for stocking up on *mojos* (Tenerife sauces).

Clothes

Large commercial centres have Spanish outlets such as Women's Secret, Punta Roma and Zara as well as its sister shops Stradivarius and Bershka. In Playa de Las Américas and Costa Adeje, upmarket centres like Siam Mall, Safari and Plaza Del Duque are brimming with brand name outlets aimed at the wallets and purses of the 'more discerning' visitor that the resorts are now attracting. Santa Cruz has one of Europe's largest open air shopping zones and several commercial centres with Spanish and UK high street favourites as well as a good selection of independents. The Spanish version of Selfridges; El Corte Inglés is also in the capital, conveniently positioned right alongside the bus station.

Leather is still a good buy and for shoes, look out for the cheap and cheerful Carolina Boix or, for more unique and expensive footwear, the fabulously stylish Pécas.

Nowadays, as many shopping centres across Europe feature much of the same brand names, there's an uninspiring, homogeneous element to shopping for clothes in many European towns and cities. La Laguna is good for finding independent shops (such as local designer Caca de la Vaca); however, the town mainland Spanish head to, to find designer labels from Milan, Madrid, Paris etc. at surprisingly low prices might come as a surprise - it's Icod de los Vinos.

MARKETS ON TENERIFE

People enjoy strolling around local markets when they're on holiday, we know we do. Whenever we visit a new destination we usually end up browsing a market or two at some point. However, on Tenerife finding out where the nearest market is doesn't necessarily mean you'll end up browsing stalls brimming with local foods or unique handicrafts. In some areas you could end up surrounded by fake designer handbags and football shirts.

Markets on Tenerife come in a variety of guises, so it helps to be crystal clear about what sort of market it is you're seeking.

The Rastro

These are our least favourite type of market on Tenerife and are most commonly found around tourist resorts. *Rastros* are flea markets, places where you can find junk or gems ranging from second hand goods to brand new items. Most resorts and many towns will have a *rastro* at least once a week. Costa Adeje, Puerto de la Cruz, Santa Cruz, Los Cristianos, Playa San Juan, Alcalá and Los Abrigos all have *rastros*.

Artisan Markets

Artisan markets are a completely different kettle of creative fish. These are markets where stallholders are artists who create unique handicrafts, ranging from jewellery to clothes and leather goods to retro toys. There are all sorts of treasures and curios to be uncovered at artisan markets (e.g. a goat-shaped wine cask where you pour the wine from its bottom) They're not as easy to find as the regular *rastros* and tend to pop up as part of festivals like La Laguna and Puerto de la Cruz's *Noche en Blanco* or as Christmas markets in traditional Tenerife towns. The huge Pinolere Craft Fair in the Orotava Valley in early September is a fabulous hunting ground for unusual presents. Farmer's markets, such as the one in Tegueste, occasionally have handicraft stalls.

Farmers' Markets

Farmers' markets on Tenerife come in a couple of forms. There are those which take place at a specific time each week, usually during mornings and early afternoon at weekends. These are great places for picking up the best local produce – fruit, veg, meat, cheeses, honeys, herbs, wine and all manner of culinary goodies. If you're a foodie staying self-catering, farmer's markets are bliss.

You can find them all across Tenerife; although, you're unlikely to find a farmers' market in a purpose-built resort as they're aimed at the local population. But there should be one relatively close by. As a rule, the bigger markets are in the north with Tacoronte being the best example of its kind on the island.

The other type of farmers' market to be found on Tenerife is the one where you can find stalls selling the type of goods found in weekend markets every day of the week. The Our Lady of Africa Market (La Recova) in Santa Cruz is the best example of this type of agricultural market, followed by the market at Plaza del Cristo in La Laguna. Many traditional towns on Tenerife have smaller versions. For example the first floor of the Municipal Market in Puerto de la Cruz is good for fruit, veg and fish whereas El Sauzal has a decent little indoor market.

List of Farmers' Markets on Tenerife

Adeje: Beside Makro on Calle Archara; number of stalls: 50; Saturday and Sunday 08:00-14:00; and 16:00-20:00 on Wednesday; probably the most accessible for the majority of tourists.

Anaga Mountains: Cruz del Carmen; number of stalls: 12-18; Saturday 09:00-14:30 & Sunday 10:00-14:30; great location; enjoy one of the best walking areas on Tenerife, then stock up on some local goodies.

Arico: Calle Benitez de Lijo, 1; number of stalls: 23; Sunday 08:00-13:.00; a small affair worth visiting only if you happen to be in the area.

El Rosario: Plaza del Ayuntamiento; number of stalls: varies; Saturday & Sunday from 08:00-16:00; only worth visiting if you're in the area.

El Sauzal: Calle Constitución, 3; number of stalls: 17; Monday to Thursday 08:30-13:00 & 17:00-19:30; Friday 08:30-13:30 & 16:30-19:30; Saturday & Sunday from 08:00-14:00;Worth a look if you're in the town.

Güímar: Plaza del Ayuntamiento; number of stalls: 53; Saturday from 08:00-13:00; nice location in the town of the pyramids.

La Guancha: Conveniently located on the main road between Icod and Puerto; number of stalls: 53; Saturday & Sunday from 08:00-15:00; has a café/restaurant attached that's open 24 hours a day.

La Laguna: Plaza San Francisco; number of stalls: 103; daily 07:00-15:00 & also 17:00-20:00 Thursdays; this is one of Tenerife's biggies – salt cod piled high like books, vibrant spices, and the occasional skinned goat.

La Matanza: TF217 – the old road linking the northern hill towns; number of stalls: 60-100; Saturday & Sunday 08:00-15:00; another big, buzzing market which sells handicrafts and books as well.

La Orotava: Calle Educadora Lucía Mesa; number of stalls: 44; Saturday 08:00-13:00; an alternative to the permanent daily market above the Mercado Municipal in Puerto de la Cruz.

Puerto de la Cruz: First floor of the Mercado Municipal on the road leading down to Playa Jardín; number of stalls: varies; open daily except Sunday; part of a shopping centre which means we never think of it as a farmers' market but there are fruit and veg, meat and fish stalls.

San Isidro: TF64 near the TF1 motorway; number of stalls: 83; Saturday & Sunday 08:00-14:00; one of the places to get good fruit and veg in the south of Tenerife even if the location isn't the most picturesque.

San Juan de la Rambla: Carretera General La Guancha-La Orotava; number of stalls: Varies; Tuesday to Sunday from 09:00; better waiting for the weekend and going to La Guancha.

San Miguel de Abona: Poligono Industrial Las Chafiras; number of stalls: 66; Wednesday 16:00-20:00; Saturday & Sunday 08:00-14:00; Another solid place for good fruit, veg and local produce in the south.

Nuestra Señora de Africa, Santa Cruz: Avenida San Sebastián; number of stalls: 200; daily 06:00-15:00; any visit to Santa Cruz should include an explore of this fabulous colonial-looking market. Some of the fruit and veg are a complete mystery.

Santiago del Teide: Town centre; number of stalls: 6-12; Saturday & Sunday 08:00-15:00; picturesque location but feels as though it's for passing tourists.

Tacoronte: Main road between Tacoronte and Valle Guerra; number of stalls: 82; Saturday & Sunday 08:00-14:00; another of Tenerife's big farmers' markets – no surprise as this is the greenhouse of Tenerife territory.

Tegueste: Behind the petrol station on the road leading from Tegueste to La Laguna; number of stalls: 38; Saturday & Sunday 08.30-14:00; a personal favourite. Tegueste farmers' market is a good size with a nice atmosphere and a mix of handicraft and food and wine stalls.

Teno: Near the centre of El Palmar; number of stalls: 6-11; Saturday 09:00-14:30; Sunday 10:00-14:30 (but not always – this is real rural Tenerife); possibly the most stunning location for a market on Tenerife – just don't expect it to be open when it should be.

TRANSPORT

With two international airports, flying to Tenerife from many destinations around Europe is relatively easy and not overly expensive. There are flights from most British airports to Reina Sofia airport (Tenerife Sur) in the south of the island, located only a short distance from the main resorts. Los Rodeos (Tenerife Norte), near La Laguna, is better placed for accessing the north and Santa Cruz and receives more traffic from mainland Spain as well as inter-island flights; Binter Airways (*bintercanarias.com*) fly daily to all the other Canary Islands, Spanish cities, and a selection of non-Spanish destinations including Madeira, Cape Verde, Lisbon, Dakar, and Banjul. Most flights are from Tenerife Norte but there are some throughout the week from Tenerife Sur. CanaryFly (*canaryfly.es*) also operate routes between Tenerife Norte and most of the islands.

Most of the island is served by an *autopista* (Tenerife's version of a motorway) ring road and construction of the final section between El Tanque and Santiago del Teide is under way. The TF1 connects the south with Santa Cruz, linking with the TF5 northern *autopista* at Santa Maria del Mar which continues to El Tanque. The journey from Puerto de la Cruz to Playa de Las Américas takes roughly an hour and a half via Santa Cruz. Attempt it on a Monday morning and you can double that time. The opening of the ring road in the west (*Anillo Insular*) means it's now as quick to travel south heading west from Puerto de la Cruz, it's also a far prettier drive.

The commuter motorway stretch between Santa Cruz and La Laguna is congested during morning rush hour (which seems to last till about 11am) and can test the nerves of the most confident driver. Two tram routes linking the two cities offer a cheap (€1.35 single journey, €1.10 with phone app) and more stress-free way to commute between the capital and La Laguna. A light railway connecting Santa Cruz with south and north coasts has been touted for many years, but this is no closer to fruition.

Although the *autopistas* are a practical way of getting from A to B quickly, country roads are a much more interesting and enjoyable way of getting around the island. Most roads are in decent condition with far less traffic. The main drawback for nervous drivers is that some roads twist and turn over precipitous drops. It adds a little spice to journeys, but it's worth it as views are spectacular. With over one hundred car rental firms on Tenerife, hiring a car isn't a problem. Most of the major names are reliable, cars are generally in good condition and at as little as €100 (£79) for a week's rental, it's economical. The longer the rental, the better the deal.

For non-drivers, Tenerife has an excellent public bus service, Titsa (*www. titsa.com*). Known as *guaguas* (pronounced *wahwahs*, some locals say because of the noise made by their horns when they were first introduced) buses are clean, comfortable and relatively punctual. Routes cover nearly every town and village on the island although the more rural the location, the more limited the service is likely to be. The best bases for exploring Tenerife by bus are Santa

Top: Tranvia, Santa Cruz, bottom left: TITSA bus, bottom right: Tenerife honey at market

Cruz, La Laguna, Puerto de la Cruz and to a lesser extent, Costa Adeje (formerly Playa de Las Américas bus station) and Los Cristianos. From September 2018 the Tenmas travel card replaced the green Bono card. It can be purchased at bus stations, various kiosks, and vending machines at some bus and tram stops. It costs €2 and can be topped up with amounts between €5 and €100. Register your card with tenmas.es to ensure all discounts are applied. The Tenmas card can be used on trams as well as buses.

It's still possible to arrive in Tenerife the old fashioned way, by boat. Trasmediterranea (*www.trasmediterranea.es*) operates a crossing from Cadiz which takes just over 2 days. Trasmediterranea, Naviera Armas (*www. navieraarmas.com*) and Fred Olson (*www.fredolsen.es*) also run ferries between Tenerife and the other Canary Islands departing from Santa Cruz and Los Cristianos. Naviera Armas operate a route between Santa Cruz de Tenerife and Huelva that runs once a week whereas Fred Olsen ferries also run between Santa Cruz and Huelva twice weekly, taking only around 36 hours.

ECONOMY ON TENERIFE

Unsurprisingly, tourism is the main industry on Tenerife, accounting for around 75% of its GDP. However, that's a relatively recent development. Until the 1970s, agriculture provided the main boost to the economy. Now around only 10% of the island is farmed (bananas, vines, potatoes, tomatoes being the main crops) although the export of tropical fruits (mangoes, pineapples, avocados, etc.) is on the increase. The industry sector (water, oil refinery, energy) is also growing, but still only accounts for around 8% of the GDP (source: *Cabildo de Tenerife* website 2020).

Overall, unemployment in Tenerife generally tends to be higher than the national average for Spain, but that doesn't necessarily paint an accurate picture of job prospects.

With tourism being the main industry, the job market is very much a transient one and, in the southern resorts especially, there are many 'casual' jobs which don't make it onto the official radar and subsequently are never included in employment statistics.

That's not the only problem. Taxation systems on Tenerife, and in Spain, don't support SMEs (small and medium enterprises). Quite the opposite, they can cripple small businesses. Subsequently some people are forced onto the black market in order to survive. Nobody knows exactly how big Spain's black market is and it's a bit of an elephant in the room, rarely mentioned. But it means official unemployment figures are not exactly reliable in painting a picture of how many people aren't actually working.

Employment Market

Because the job market in resorts is such a transient one, with people taking bar work to finance extended holidays, there are always jobs available for waiters, bar staff, sales, PRs (those individuals who try to get you into bars and restaurants) and gardeners. Anyone that can hold a tune and play an instrument should also find work relatively easily as there are always places looking for entertainers.

The paradox however, is that most of these are located in the purpose-built tourist resorts in the south of the island, so anyone seeking to experience the true culture of Tenerife, and therefore basing themselves outside of the main resorts, may encounter more difficulties in finding employment. Whilst establishments in the north of the island also regularly display '*se falta camarero/a*' (waiter/tress required) notices; being able to speak Spanish is generally a prerequisite.

In terms of the types of jobs found in the average big town and city in Europe, generally speaking it can be difficult for foreigners to find employment in sectors they may have had experience in before they moved to Tenerife. We can think of some examples, but it's rare to see non-Canarios/Spanish in administrative positions etc. When we think back to our time in the British Civil Service, we worked in areas where the nationalities of our colleagues reflected the residents who lived in the immediate area, this included Spanish. You don't tend to find this on Tenerife. Not that the Canarios have it easy, a significant amount of people working in the tourism sector in the south come from the Spanish mainland or South America. This is partly because they tend to be more accomplished at speaking English. There have been various proposals put forward to try to even the playing field. The most obvious being to try to improve the levels of English among younger Canarios. The most outrageous was the politician who returned from Brussels saying he had a document which exempted Tenerife from EU legislation, so businesses on the island would be encouraged to show bias in favour of employing Canarios over incomers. It was complete fabrication and was exposed as such within hours of him making the announcement.

In general, English language forums and Tenerife Facebook groups are the best way to find out about English language job opportunities in resort areas whilst anyone looking for positions outside of resort areas should conduct their searches online in Spanish. Where possible, it's worth checking whether prospective employers are reliable payers; a lackadaisical approach to coughing up wages is not uncommon.

For people looking to start their own business, there are still plenty of opportunities to be found on Tenerife.

Housing

The housing market is disparate in relation to prices in the north and south of the island. Property can cost up to 30% more in southern areas, especially those considered fashionable. For the price of a two-bedroom apartment in Adeje you could have a three- or even four-bedroom one in Los Realejos. The same formula can be applied to long-term rentals.

Estate agents attribute this to the guarantee of more sunshine on the south coast, the Holy Grail for many; although cynics would say that these areas also invariably attract expatriates who are willing to pay more than Canarios.

Prices decrease with the temperature; the further inland you go, and therefore uphill, the more you get for your money and there are still some very good bargains to be had on Tenerife's hillsides.

Businesses in resort areas especially can come and go overnight in Tenerife, sometimes taking clients' hard earned money with them, so choosing the right *inmobiliaria* (estate agent) is essential. The safest bet is to opt for one which has been established for some time. It's common practice for the same property to be advertised in various *inmobiliarias*, often with different asking prices. Even then, advertised prices are little more than guidelines. Tell an estate agent that you like a property, but the price is way too high and in response they might pick up a piece of scrap paper, unconvincingly scribble some figures on it and then knock twenty thousand euros off the asking price. It's always worthwhile trying to haggle.

The real Tenerife

Part 2

Guide to areas, towns & resorts

NORTH TENERIFE

"...Under the torrid zone I found sites where nature is more majestic and richer in the display of organic forms; but after having traversed the banks of the Orinoco, the Cordilleras of Peru, and the most beautiful valleys of Mexico, I own that I have never beheld a prospect more varied, more attractive, more harmonious in the distribution of the masses of verdure and rocks, than the western coast of Teneriffe."
Alexander von Humboldt June 1799

When he uttered these words, Von Humboldt was gazing from Tacoronte across the La Orotava Valley and what today is referred to as the northern coast. And although two centuries of development would probably prevent him from considering the view today as the best he had ever seen, he would surely agree that it is still the most beautiful in Tenerife.

A few degrees cooler and receiving more rainfall than the rest of the island in a climate referred to as 'eternal spring', from the most westerly town of Buenavista to the north-eastern point of Punta del Hidalgo, Tenerife's north coast is lush, fertile and green. Banana plantations, vines and palm groves carpet the cultivated landscape which falls down to the Atlantic, carved by deep *barrancos* where the indigenous flora thrives.

From the north, without a crater wall to mask it, the true magnitude and beauty of Mount Teide dominates the horizon, acting as a constant reminder that you're at the foot of Europe's largest volcano and Spain's highest mountain.
Puerto de la Cruz is the area's main tourist resort while in the valley above it lies the colonial town of La Orotava, generally agreed to be the most sophisticatedof all Tenerife's towns. Further to the west are the historic and picturesque port of Garachico with its volcanic rock pools, and the busy town of Icod de los Vinos, home to the famous Millennium Drago Tree.

The former capital city of La Laguna forms part of a necklace of towns, strung above the north motorway; gems that many of the millions of visitors to Tenerife never see.

A thousand miles away from the busy beaches of the south, this is where you'll find the true Tenerife; its food, culture, history and people; where English is not widely spoken and you have only to step outside of your door to know that you are in a foreign country.

Top, Anaga coast; bottom left, caballero, La Matanza; bottom right, Garachico lava pools

ANAGA MOUNTAINS

What's it like?

Seven million years in the making, covering a huge swathe of Tenerife's north eastern tip, Anaga is the most beautiful part of the island and also the least explored.

It's a sign of the times that what was once the most populated area of Tenerife, due to its fertile soil, is now one of the least populated; the modern settler preferring the promise of sunshine over good farming country. The TF12 road traverses a ridge dissecting contrasting micro-climates. Arid slopes descend on the eastern side towards the capital, Santa Cruz. On the northern side, ancient *laurisilva* (laurel) forests, the likes of which have been lost to most of the rest of the world, spread with a velvety consistency through deep ravines, their emerald slopes broken only by the speckled white dots of tiny hamlets tucked into their folds and perched on rocky outcrops.

Agriculture is the mainstay of the economy as it has been since pre-conquest times. In picturesque hamlets like Afur, Chinamada (where most of the inhabitants still live in caves – albeit ones with modern façades, internet connection and satellite TV), Taganana and La Cumbrilla (whose houses are linked by little more than goat trails), farming techniques have changed little over the centuries. The terrain is too steep for machinery, so crops are sown, tended and harvested by hand.

The whole area is a nature lover's adventure playground and the best way to explore it is on foot along one of the many old *caminos reales* (merchant trails) which were once the lifeline with the outside world. It can be cool in the mountains, so layers are essential.

What's the story?

Anaga is an area of farmers and fishermen; from the Guanche who originally inhabited its lush ravines to the settlers who made it their home following the conquest. It was the most easterly of Tenerife's nine kingdoms and still retains the name given to it by the Guanche. The biggest settlement in the area is Taganana which was founded in 1501 when Hispanic settlers realised how fertile the land was, with sugar cane and then vines being cultivated on terraced slopes. In the 17th and 18th centuries, at Roque de las Bodegas, barrels of wine would be floated out to waiting merchant ships bound for mainland Europe. Trading on land wasn't quite so easy. Women would have to carry goods on their heads across the ravines to markets in Santa Cruz and La Laguna. Rising into the forest from Taganana is the Camino Real de las Vueltas, a twisting trail which is said to have as many bends as there are days in the year. We've walked it, but lost count of the bends so can't confirm whether this is true. In many ways, times haven't changed so much in Anaga. You can still see farmers tending the land in much the way they always have done. This sustainable relationship with the land has earned Anaga UNESCO Biosphere Reserve status.

Who'd want to stay here?

Anaga is a hiker's paradise. We've hiked across Europe and it's right up there with the places which have wowed us the most. It's not easy hiking, so not for everyone. It would also suit anyone wanting to get away from it all for a short while.

The food scene

Outside of the stops on excursion routes (Taganana, Roque de las Bodegas), there aren't that many places to eat in these remote mountains. In the hills the emphasis is on hearty, traditional fare consisting mainly of meat-based, dishes such as *pucheros* (stews) and *cabra* (goat). Roque de las Bodegas on the coast below Taganana is good for simple fish and seafood, but time it badly and you could find yourself sharing a restaurant with a tour group. Casa Africa gets touted in some travel guides and articles, but we avoid it because it's popular with coach excursions. Continue on to Benijo to escape the crowd. We haven't included El Mirador above Playa Almáciga in Benijo in our 'where we'd eat' section as it has a tendency to change hands regularly, but it is in a super spot and far too small to accommodate large groups.

Where we'd eat

Traditional - Cruz del Carmen Restaurant is perfectly placed for some post-hike food and a cosy sanctuary if the low cloud is swirling through the trees. The restaurant specialises in traditional, hearty Canarian cuisine. It's worth checking out some of the posters on the wall which have information about local produce. Also good for local produce and a coffee and cake is La Gangochera below the Cruz del Carmen car park opposite. *Carretera General Las Mercedes; +34 922 250 062; open 10:00-20:00, closed Thursday; average cost of a main meal is €9.*

Traditional - It's appropriate that a troglodyte village has a restaurant in a cave. In truth only part of **La Cueva** is inside a cave, but it's still a wonderfully unusual place to eat a tapas lunch. *Escaldón* (meat or fish stock with gofio) is their speciality and is cheap and filling, but not to everyone's taste. At weekends tables can be filled by an odd mix of dusty hikers and sharp-dressed city dwellers from Santa Cruz. *Chinamada, cave 14A ; +34 922 690 076; open 11:00-19:00 Wednesday, Thursday & Sunday; 11:00-22:00 Friday & Saturday; closed Monday & Tuesday; average cost of a main meal is €8.*

Why visit

Because it is the most stunning part of Tenerife, in a way even more surprising than Teide National Park. The biggest attraction is the mountains themselves and wherever you venture, you'll be assaulted by 'stop you in your tracks' scenery, the ultimate being the 360° panorama at the Pico del Inglés mirador.

The roads are in good condition and comfortably wide enough for two vehicles so driving through the mountains can be spectacular but the best way to really discover this ancient and little known region of Tenerife is undoubtedly on foot. There are myriad trails snaking their way up and down steep *barrancos* and through dense rain forest and you can walk from a couple of hours to a full day. But this is not suitable walking territory for the faint-hearted or for those who ordinarily stroll rather than walk. These mountains are unforgiving if you underestimate them and folks have been known to get lost for hours, and even days on end in their multiple trails, particularly if the *bruma* (fog) descends. Be sure you're properly prepared and kitted out before setting off. Cruz del Carmen is an ideal base for long and short walks; there's a good restaurant and a visitors' centre with free walking maps which are better used as 'guidelines' as they tend to have a *más o menos* (more or less) approach to detailed directions. You can walk anywhere in Anaga, except for the protected area at El Pijaral in the far north east. There are some endangered plant species here so a permit is required before entering. The Real Tenerife series of guides includes both walking and driving guides for the Anaga Mountains, see p279.

On the beach

As a visitor, you wouldn't really come to Anaga just for a beach; accessibility is not easy and facilities are few and far between. Saying that, Playa Almáciga beyond Taganana is one of the most photographed beaches on the island, and a favourite with fashion photographers. It's not only the landscape which is bare at the black sand beach of Las Gaviotas on the eastern coast; it's where the *santacruceros* come for an all-over tan. There's a café above the beach where you can have a beer in the buff. The small beach and harbour at Roque de Bermejo lies beside the hamlet of the same name, and is the most remote on Tenerife. The only way to reach it is by boat, or a three hour trek from Chamorga.

Where we'd stay

Forget about hotels, the only accommodation you'll find in the mountains are hostels (frequently occupied by youth groups) and privately-owned rural houses. A basic, but convenient base for hiking is the Montes de Anaga Hostel (*+34 922 822 056; www.alberguestenerife.net*) near El Bailadero in the heart of the Anagas with views down both flanks, to east and west. There's a cafeteria for breakfast and dinner, beds are of the bunk variety and only one room (a double) has its own en suite bathroom but if you wish to rent the unoccupied beds in a four person room, you're free to do so.

Best time to visit

Anaga is a feast for the eyes at any time of the year, unless the *bruma* descends. But without a doubt it is at its most glorious during the spring.

BAJAMAR/PUNTA DEL HIDALGO

What's it like?

Almost on the northernmost tip, the twin towns of Bajamar and Punta del Hidalgo are Tenerife's forgotten resorts, developed ostensibly as second home coastal getaways for *laguneros* (residents of La Laguna). Their setting, a stunning Anaga Mountain backdrop, makes the sight of the unattractive concrete apartment blocks which greet visitors on arrival, all the more depressing. Favoured by health tourists, although first impressions of both Bajamar and Punta del Hidalgo conjure tired 70s resorts, work is in progress to upgrade them. The promenades in both centres have been given a makeover and the sea front in Bajamar has been developed to incorporate smart wooden decking and tubular aluminium seating around the sea water pools which give the resort a more contemporary feel. In Punta del Hidalgo a wide, palm tree-lined walkway leads past an open air pool to a tiny sheltered harbour; a reminder of the simpler place this must have been before unimaginative architects left their mark on the landscape. Between July and September, the area buzzes with *laguneros*; the rest of the year it's popular with mainly German visitors who use it as a health resort and a convenient base for exploring the Anaga Mountains.

What's the story?

Originally a small agricultural farming and fishing community, the area was developed in the 1930s as a summer retreat for residents from La Laguna. When mass tourism took off in the late 1960s, a clutch of high rise hotels and apartments were constructed; however, the opening of the south airport put paid to its chances of making a real impact on the tourist market and the area fell into decline. Today its fortunes are back on an upward trend as the healthy quality of its air and ozone attract the spa crowd.

Who'd want to stay here?

This area has its own micro-climate and is generally sunnier and more humid than other parts of the north coast, making it one of the best sections on the north coast for sun-seekers. As well as a magnet for spa lovers, as it lies at the foot of Anaga, it's also a decent base for hiking.

The food scene

As you might expect, fish and seafood are the best things to enjoy here. The two centres both have a good selection of restaurants from which to choose. But when it comes to simple, fresh fish cooked straight from the nets we're fans of *cofradias* (fishermen's guilds). *Morena frita* (fried moray eel) is a speciality of this area. It can be a bony fish, but we've eaten ones which have been more like meaty chops.

Where we'd eat

Fish & seafood - Punta del Hidalgo's **Cofradía de Pescadores** is located beside its small harbour; so close fishermen could throw their catch from boat straight to plate. The proximity does mean you might sometimes have to watch a fisherman clubbing a moray eel to death on the jetty. It is a basic place, and very Canarian, so expect a casual approach to service. *Camino Puertito s/n; Bajamar; +34 922 590 092; open from lunchtime (vagueness is due to timings seeming to vary whenever we visit); average cost of a main meal is €9.*

Why visit

This stretch of northern coastline gets more than its fair share of sunshine and warmth which accounts for its year-round attraction as a natural health spa. The man-made rock pools, and outdoor pools attract swimmers and sunbathers in their droves, as do the natural pools further along the coast towards the lighthouse where, on summer weekends, families pitch their vans and tents for uninterrupted beach time.

At early morning, follow the coastal path beyond Punta del Hidalgo's artistic lighthouse to the viewpoint at the small *ermita* (chapel) of San Juanita. The vista, as the sun bathes the rugged Tolkienesque coastline with shafts of light, is mythical. The more energetic can follow a trail up into the mountains to the troglodyte village at Chinamada. For those who want to enjoy the same views but without the walking, the Mirador Punta del Hidalgo at the end of the TF-13 has views along the most rugged section of coastline to Roque de Tierra and Roque de Fuera jutting out of the sea. Along this road is also a quirky folly, a mock version of La Gomera's Torre del Conde.

On the beach

The coastline is rocky, that's not to say there aren't plenty of places for swimming. Man-made pools in Punta del Hidalgo, Bajamar and Charco de la Arena beyond the lighthouse blend nicely into the basaltic rock and offer protection from the Atlantic rollers. There's a small imported golden sand beach in Bajamar's sheltered harbour although most people prefer the wooden decking for sunbathing. A rocky beach links the two resorts, but unless you're accomplished on a surfboard (competitions are held here), it's probably better to stick to the safety of the pools.

After dark

There are few low-key bars, and there's quite a lively cultural/traditional scene in Bajamar. Time it right and there can be all sorts going on; from fishermen's fiestas (July) to drag queen competitions.

Where we'd stay

The choice is limited and the best are definitely those aimed at the German health market, **Océano Aparthotel** in Punta del Hidalgo (*C/Océanico Pacifico, 1; +34 922 156 000; www.oceano.de*) probably being the best. Very firmly aimed at those wanting a health regime, the price includes yoga sessions and exercises but it's also a great base for hiking in the Anagas.

Best time to visit

It's popular with German visitors in winter, when it can feel rather subdued. However, it's a completely different scene in summer when the *laguneros* descend bringing vibrancy and a joi de vivre to both Bajamar and Punta del Hidalgo.

BUENAVISTA DEL NORTE

"There's the library," pointed the man from outside the bar as we got out of the car in Buenavista del Norte. "And around the corner is the church. That's it, you've seen all there is to see." So advised a local on our first ever visit. He was kidding of course … just.

What's it like?

Capital of the Isla Baja region that hugs the north west corner of Tenerife, Buenavista feels like the place you pass through en route to the golf course or the lighthouse, the place where there seems to be constant construction work, despite the fact that it looks devoid of people or life. In reality, it has a very nice old quarter around Plaza de Nuestra Señora de Los Remedios tucked away behind the main road and is in fact one of the oldest settlements on Tenerife. But its more modern face is bereft of character and sprawls its way beyond the old plaza to the coast and ever further westwards towards Punta de Teno.

What's the story?

Buenavista's development began in parallel with the conquest of Tenerife. The first conquistadors, drawn to its fertile soil, ample forests and adequate rainfall, settled in the area from 1497. Lands were first distributed by Alonso Fernández de Lugo to Diego de Cala in 1498 in settlement for part-financing the conquest, and then sold on to Juan Méndez 'El Viejo' in 1502. El Viejo's residence of Hacienda de La Fuente borders the Buenavista Golf Course. Many of the first settlers who came to the area between 1502 and 1513 were from Andalucía and Portugal, influences which can still be seen in the architecture of the old quarter. Thanks to sugar cane and vines, Buenavista grew prosperous during the 17th century but the price of fortune included much of the forest that covered the Teno Massif and earned the town its name (Buenavista means beautiful views), which was consumed as fuel for the hungry sugar refineries. As elsewhere in Tenerife, the 18th and 19th centuries saw a decline in fortunes due to world conflicts, economic recession and, in the case of Buenavista, plagues of locusts (there's a locust statue at the western edge of the town). By the beginning of the 20th century, its citizens were returning to Buenavista and re-introducing agriculture, livestock and all the old crafts of wicker, cane and wood working that have survived to the present day.

Who'd want to stay here?

With its Seve Ballesteros-designed golf course, golfers seem the obvious answer. But, apart from that, it's not really golfing territory. We like it because it's very traditional, and is also a great launch pad for getting into the Teno Massif where there are some of our favourite walking routes on the island.

The food scene

Oddly for such a traditional town, restaurants are fairly conspicuous by their absence in Buenavista. Within the town itself you'll find only a handful of basic cafeteria/bars to eat, plus there are a handful of good traditional places on the outskirts of town near the bus station. Buenavista does, however, boast a restaurant which is in one of the best positions on the island.

Where we'd eat

Fish & Seafood - Perched on the headland where the beach reaches the golf course, **El Burgado**'s terrace is one of the quaintest you'll find on Tenerife, all billowing fishing nets and storm lamps. It's a superb spot to enjoy a lunch or sunset dinner of traditional Canarian cuisine such as *lapas a la plancha* (limpets drizzled with mojo) or the popular *cherne* (stonebass/wreckfish). P*laya de las Arenas; +34 922 127 831; open midday to 21:00; average cost of a main meal is €12.*

Coffee Break – It's difficult to pass the island's most famous confectioners, **El Aderno**, without popping in. The cafe/shop in the centre of the town which fronts the factory is tiny, but inside you'll find imaginative cakes and chocolates ranging from mojito-flavoured cakes and ones shaped like Mount Teide to gofio-sprinkled chocolates. *Calle de la Alhóndiga; +34 922 127 368; open 0900 to 20:30pm daily.*

Traditional – head into the Teno Massif and you'll find one of the best Canarian restaurants in the area. **Mesón del Norte** specialises in grilled meat, so steaks are a good option as is the *cabra* (goat) and *conejo* (rabbit). But it has a menu to suit many palates. The *menú del día* is usually generous and good value at around €12. *C/ General masca, 1, Las Portelas; +34 635 046 029; open midday - 17:00 Tuesday to Thursday and Sunday, midday - 17:00 and 18:30 – 22:30 Friday and Saturday, closed Monday; average cost of a main meal is €10.*

Why visit

Buenavista Golf Course (*www.buenavistagolf.es*) has the best location of all Tenerife's gold courses. Designed by Seve Ballesteros, it's an 18 hole, par 72 course with stunning views inland to the Teno Massif and over the ocean toward La Palma. Some shots look as if you're about to drive straight into the sea and if your aim is as good as mine, that's probably what you'll do.

Drivers have limited access to the most westerly point of the island, Punta de Teno, where an old stone lighthouse lies at the end of a tunnel roughly hewn through the seven million year old Teno Mountains. The 369 bus runs from Buenavista bus station every hour and takes around 20 minutes, taking you through the tunnel to reach this unspoilt spot, frequently emerging into a different climate zone and beneath blue skies. You'll find a small beach with views to Los Gigantes and crystal clear waters which seduce swimmers and divers alike. What you won't find, is anywhere to buy lunch. In heavy rain the tunnel is closed to all but essential traffic as there is real danger of rockfall.

A gentle and pleasant coastal path from Playa de las Arenas leads to the foot of the Teno mountains in one direction and beyond the golf course to a fishermen's cove in the other. Highlights include a 'secret', infinity pool and lots of side paths leading to viewing platforms and hidden rock pools. There are lots of free parking spaces at the beach.

On the beach

Follow signs for the Buenavista Golf Course to get to Playa de las Arenas, a black sand and pebble beach adorned by rock pools and extremely popular in summer. The beach has no facilities save for a kiosk selling ice creams and sweets, and El Burgado restaurant.

After dark

Outside of fiesta times, it's very typical of a small, traditional, Canarian town. The Ikko bar at the Hacienda del Conde is such a great-looking bar (like a converted church) that nothing for miles comes close to luring guests away.

Where we'd stay

About as prevalent as its restaurants, accommodation in Buenavista is hard to find but what it lacks in quantity it makes up for in quality and there's one place we would happily stay in time and time again. One of our favourite Tenerife hotels, **Meliá Hacienda Del Conde** is a boutique, five star, adults-only hotel situated right on the golf course with views across the Atlantic and the greens. Stylish and luxurious with expansive rooms, a beautiful spa and an excellent à la carte restaurant, it's the choice for anyone who wants to enjoy this unspoilt, verdant corner of Tenerife, whether you're a golfer or not (*Calle La Finca, s/n; +34 922 061 700; www.melia.com*).

Best time to visit

If you're in Buenavista at the same time as 1,500 head of cattle driven through the main street along with horses, goats, sheep and an assortment of pets including rabbit hutches on wheels and the occasional iguana or turkey on a lead … it must be around 15th January and the fiesta of San Antonio Abad. Surreal at times; always chaotic and unmissable if you happen to be in the area. Make sure you wander all around the town to see everything that's going on.

Outside of animal crackers time, summer is best if sunshine is the goal. The beach at las Arenas doesn't really show itself until the summer months. If hiking is the plan, then any time from autumn through to spring is good.

EL SAUZAL

What's it like?

Perched on the cliffs above the north coast, El Sauzal is home to some enchanting treasure troves. It also boasts some of the best views of Mount Teide you'll find on Tenerife.

El Sauzal possesses a different character to most of the other towns in the Acentejo group of municipalities; it has greater charm, a range of interesting and quirky features, historic pockets, a couple of markets, and more obvious

centres than the drawn-out enclaves of La Matanza and La Victoria. But apart
from the eye-catching church opposite the town hall's trickling fountains, its
most picturesque corners aren't immediately obvious. El Sauzal tends to be
overlooked by many visitors. Even some of those who do pause awhile only see
a fraction of what El Sauzal has to offer.

What's the story?
    Prior to the Spanish conquest, it was the King of Portugal who first sent
an emissary to the town in the form of Pedro de Oporto, and it was he and his
fellow artisans who first settled the area and planted the sugar cane that brought
its first wealth post-conquest. Vestiges of that Portuguese influence remain in the
town today, in the Byzantine dome of the Iglesia de San Pedro Apóstol and in the
mudejar ceiling of the Palacio de Salazar
    Despite its diminutive size, the town played an important role in the history
of the island. When the bubonic plague arrived on the island in 1582, carried
in carpets imported from Flanders, it ravaged La Laguna and Santa Cruz, seats
of the island's government. Consequently, the ruling council fled to El Sauzal,
governing Tenerife from the Iglesia de San Pedro Apóstol. By the end of the
outbreak, an estimated 5,000 to 9,000 people out of a population of just 20,000,
had perished. Remarkably, the disease never reached El Sauzal.
    From the 17th century, boats departing from and arriving at a small pier at
Punta del Puertito on the coast linked the town with the island of La Palma.
During the first quarter of the 18th century hundreds of people from other
Canary Islands disembarked here, seeking an escape from poverty and hunger in
their home islands.
    In the 19th century, due to a new road being constructed, the town was the
last stop on the stage coach route which transported travellers between the
capital and La Orotava. Waiting in El Sauzal for transport to take them to La
Orotava, Isabel Lady Burton, wife of adventurer Sir Richard Burton, proclaimed
her time there as "the happiest moment in my life".

Who'd want to stay here?
    El Sauzal would suit anyone who wants to stay in an off-the-beaten-track
traditional town which has a good gastronomic scene, is deep in the wine
heartlands of the Tacoronte-Acentejo region, and is handy for exploring both the
Orotava Valley and the likes of La Laguna and Santa Cruz.

The food scene
    The old road between El Sauzal and Tacoronte is renowned for having some
of the best traditional restaurants on Tenerife. But there's more than run-of-the-
mill, traditional restaurants to be discovered along this stretch of road that few

visitors venture along.

Where we'd eat

Spanish/German fusion – It's an unusual pairing for Tenerife, but Canarios love their grilled meats and sausages so the Spanish/German offerings on the menu at **Cerveceria Tacoa** is a marriage made in heaven. If feeling particularly ravenous, try the metre-long sausage which comes with a mountain of fried potatoes. The best bit about the place, especially for real ale fans, is that owner Jochen brews speciality beers on the premises. *Carretera General del Norte 122; +34 922 564 173; open Wednesday and Thursday 14:00-22:00, Friday 14:00-23:00, Saturday 13:30-23:00, Sunday 13:00-21:00, closed Monday & Tuesday; average cost of a main meal is €9.*

Contemporary Canarian/international - Visit on a sunny day and the views of the north west coast and Mount Teide from **Terrazas del Sauzal** are phenomenal. Located in the grounds of a colonial mansion, it is one of those special Tenerife places to dine. The menu has Canarian/Spanish roots, but when the first thing you spot on it is banana gazpacho you know you're in for something different. They also do a decadent brunch on Saturdays and Sundays (10am to midday). *Pasaje Sierva de Díos 9; +34 922 571 491; open 12:30-23:00 Wednesday to Friday, 10:00-23:00 Saturday & Sunday, closed Monday and Tuesday; average cost of a main meal is €14.*

Why visit

Many of the people who do stop at El Sauzal do so to visit La Baranda Wine Museum (*signposted from the El Sauzal exit on the TF5, +34 922 572 535; www. tenerife.es/Casa-vino.htm*). Tenerife's wine and honey museum is housed in the outbuildings of the appropriately rosé coloured Casa del Vino 'La Baranda'. Most of the exhibits are in Spanish, but even if your grasp of the language doesn't stretch much beyond *hola*, La Baranda's photogenic rustic buildings and courtyards are a classic example of colonial architecture and worth a visit in their own right. Besides, there's a good tapas restaurant with more of those views to enjoy and lots of wines to taste and buy. The island's honey museum also forms part of the complex.

Even better is a visit to a proper vineyard. Bodegas Monje (*Camino Cruz de Leandro, 36*) is located in the hills above El Sauzal and is one of the few *bodegas* on Tenerife where there are daily guided tours (*11:00, 13:00, 15:00, and 17:00*). There's a wide choice of tasting options, including wine and tapas, and a restaurant with terrace which is open from 10:00-18:00 every day except Monday. Bodegas Monje gets pushed in just about every travel article written about Tenerife which references wine, with most other wineries left ignored. But the wine is good, and it's fun to drink your way through the various bottles, all with different coloured corks.

Somewhat of a Tenerife quirk is the Museo Casa de La Sierva de Díos (*Calle Sierva de Díos, 34, 38360 El Sauzal; +34 922 573 492; open Wed 15:00-18:00, Thurs-Sat 11:00-18:00, Sun 10:00-13:00, closed Mon & Tues; entrance free*). Born in this house in 1643, Sister Maria de Jesús was a fervent Dominican nun who, when she died an old lady in 1731, her body never decomposed. Housed in a glass coffin in the Convento de Santa Catalina in La Laguna, the corpse is now one of the most revered religious relics in the Canary Islands and every year on the 15th February thousands of pilgrims travel from across the world to see it when it's taken from its tomb. The house where she was born has been beautifully restored and is still the way it would have been when Sister Maria was born. Alongside is a museum, and outside stands a statue of the little nun who was known as The Servant of God (*La Sierva de Díos*).

One of the jewels in El Sauzal's crown is Parque Los Lavaderos, a former communal washing area below the church which has been turned into enchanting wild gardens with trickling springs. There may or may not be (ownership can change hands regularly) a small cafeteria in the depths of the garden, overlooking the most magical area of the landscape. If it's open, it's a delightful spot for a drink and a snack.

Signposted from the northern edge of town, Mirador La Garañona is a small park with walkways through tropical foliage and panoramic views of the cliffs and the north coast.

There are also excellent views from Mirador de Las Breñas, tucked away in a residential area above the cliffs to the west of the town centre. However, the views aren't the best bit. A zig-zagging path leads from the viewpoint down to the coast and a peach of a path which meanders along the coast.

After dark

El Sauzal Auditorio beside the town hall has a surprisingly varied programme which ranges from contemporary theatre and dance to rock bands and classical concerts. As for the general bar scene, El Sauzal can offer something quite special. The Terrazas del Sauzal is also a cocktail bar, possibly the best placed one on Tenerife. There's an extensive range of cocktails to choose from, including nine different types of mojitos. You can also occasionally find quite the most bizarre-sounding nocturnal entertainment in El Sauzal, Bodegas Monje's famous (infamous) Wine & Sex nights which are held at various times throughout the year. They're not quite as scandalous as they sound, more burlesque show with food and wine.

Top: Icod de los Vinos, bottom left: lighthouse, Bajamar, bottom right: Garachico

Where we'd stay

We haven't stayed here, but the villas at Linaje del Pago (*linajedelpago.com*) would be where we'd choose. Why? The contemporary style helps, but the fact it's also a *bodega* seals the deal.

Best time to visit

Between June and September is always livelier in traditional areas, and there tends to be more fiestas – six in El Sauzal in this period. Its position above the coast can make it slightly cooler in winter than the likes of Puerto de la Cruz which is at sea level. Summer nights are also definitely friendlier for enjoying the sunset scene at the Terrazas del Sauzal.

GARACHICO

Where is it and what's it like?

Garachico encapsulates Tenerife's boom and bust fortunes. Occupying a semi-circular promontory on the north west coast it has been the victim of plague, floods, fires and pestilence yet it retains a unique character and charm which make it one of the island's most picturesque and most visited towns. In its halcyon days, the town was home to wealthy merchants, bankers, artists, musicians and religious orders from Spain, Italy and Portugal. Their legacy is quaint cobbled streets lined with an eclectic mix of smart town houses, churches, monasteries, convents and fishermen's cottages with terracotta and amber façades.

The town's main hub of activity - Plaza de la Libertad - is arguably Tenerife's prettiest square. The bandstand kiosk and café, shaded by Indian laurels and complete with ubiquitous domino-playing locals, is perfectly placed to soak up architectural delights such as the 16th century Moorish styled Iglesia de Nuestra Señora de Los Ángeles; the neoclassical town hall, and the Iglesia de Santa Ana. A statue of a fellow in an oversized pith helmet on the town's northern edge pays homage to the night in 1666 when the townsfolk, weary of the English monopoly over the control of wine prices, broke into the wine cellars and smashed the lot, turning Garachico's streets red.

What's the story?

Founded at the end of the 15th century by a Genoese banker named Cristóbal de Ponte, Garachico quickly grew very wealthy due to its natural deep harbour which was the best in Tenerife and which placed Garachico at the centre of trade between Europe and the New World. Sugar, leather, wine, tar and silk for fine fabrics from England and France; works of art from Flanders; gold and silver from America; spices from the Far East and slaves from Africa all found their way through Garachico and the town soon became Tenerife's wealthiest. The rich and powerful of Europe made their way to Garachico to build mansions with lookout towers from which a wary eye could be kept on the horizon for passing pirates. As news of Garachico's wealth spread, artists, musicians, bankers and religious orders took up residence and the gap between the 'haves' and 'have-nots' widened to such a degree that it's rumoured there was even an entire street constructed of marble which the poor were only allowed to walk down one day a week in order to beg for alms. By the end of the 17th century there were two churches, a hospital, a castle, five convents, several hermitages and numerous mansions.

But money didn't protect Garachico from all manner of misfortunes. In 1601 the bubonic plague arrived on two ships bringing cargo from the Spanish mainland. Over the next five years the pestilence devastated the town and surrounding areas, taking thousands of lives and bringing trade to its knees, finally abating in 1606. Even as its economy rallied, Mother Nature had more in her store of surprises for Garachico that century. In December 1645 heavy rains dislodged great swathes of earth from the cliffs behind the town and a landslide of sludge destroyed more than 80 houses in the town and sank 14 ships that were anchored in the harbour; over a hundred people lost their lives and the economic ruin was severe. As if having to deal with the elements wasn't enough, in 1659 a plague of African locusts destroyed the town's crops lending a biblical aspect to the whole sorry century which refused to leave before it had once again wreaked havoc on the prosperous but fated Garachico. In 1692 and again in 1697, great fires rampaged through the narrow streets and timbered houses of the town claiming a hundred and nine dwellings in total and razing the San Agustino convent to the ground.

However it was one fateful day in 1706 that finally toppled Garachico when, not long after midnight, the ground began to shake, shock waves travelling underground from nearby Montaña Negra. By 3am the volcano was billowing smoke and sending waves of molten lava and burning rocks creeping inexorably towards the coast where the residents of Garachico lay sleeping. Alerted by the thunder, residents packed up their most precious possessions and fled before the twin rivers of destruction cascading down the cliff face (today still clearly visible behind the town) engulfed them. One river poured into the harbour, the lava solidifying on contact with the sea, filling the depths with rock; the other enveloped a third of the town, destroying everything in its wake, including old convents whose buildings were said to be more spacious and numerous than the Gibraltar Barracks and more enduring than the spires of Oxford, crumbling beneath the molten destruction. It took nine days for the lava to stop flowing and when it did, Garachico lay in ruins.

Considered to be one of the most catastrophic communities in the world, each time fate dealt Garachico a blow, its inhabitants responded by re-building and re-investing, always determined to recover what they had painstakingly built up. Unfortunately, the damage to the harbour could never be reversed and the town lost its pole trading position, first to Puerto de la Cruz and later to Santa Cruz. In a complete reversal of fortunes, the economy turned from feverish trade and the creation of vast wealth to subsistence farming and fishing. Two world wars took their toll on trade and with money and food becoming scarce, the 19th and 20th centuries saw much of the population emigrating to the Americas to seek work.

The town's motto is: '*Glorioso en su Adversidad*' (Glorious in its Adversity) and by the beginning of the 20th century, banana production brought a degree of stability to the economy enabling Garachico to rebuild itself. True to its nature, it turned disadvantage to advantage by carving rock pools from solidified lava to create a summer playground for the townsfolk and a magnet for summer visitors who brought a new kind of wealth to the town – tourism.

Who'd want to stay here?
It's one of the most picturesque towns in the Canary Islands, the streets are full of history, there's a good restaurant scene, and it has the best boutique, colonial hotels on Tenerife, Basically that means it's the perfect choice for travellers who want to immerse themselves in local culture, enjoy great traditional food, and have a stylish and comfortable place in which to chill out at the end of the day.

The food scene
When it comes to eateries, Garachico punches above its weight. You can find several excellent dining options within the town. Unfortunately, a few are also resting on their tourism laurels and seem content to serve inferior quality to passing tourists whom they know will never return. If only they knew about Tripadvisor …
Most restaurants and cafés are situated along the town's seafront and because of their vantage point, prices can be higher than those found in the streets behind the town's main façade.

Where we'd eat
Contemporary Canarian - Mirador de Garachico is our favourite Garachico restaurant because it's friendly and professional, with dining areas which include a light and airy covered terrace, a stylish interior or a more formal and intimate lower level dining room. Most importantly, the food is wonderful with an imaginative menu that includes updated classic Canarian favourites. We've enjoyed some great nights there, once turning up during a *fiesta de flores*

when many dishes had a flower theme. Despite the name, there's no view; it's a reference to the owner's father's restaurant in the hills above Garachico. *Calle Francisco Martínez de Fuentes 17; (0034) 922 83 11 98; open 13:00-17:00 and 18:30-22:30 Thursday to Sunday, closed Monday to Wednesday; average cost of a main meal is €14.*

Italian - The best pizzas we've eaten on Tenerife were at **Pizzeria Rugantino**. It's so popular with locals there's often a queue to get a table. A secret of their success is the chef likes to explore the hills looking for herbs and ingredients to add extra oomph to the food. If the inclusion of a pizzeria in a traditional town seems odd, this is no ordinary Italian restaurant. Its fame has spread to such an extent even visiting Michelin star chefs eat here. There are no frills and families love it (children get to practice making their own pizza bases). *Esteban De Ponte 44; open 19:00-23:45 Tuesday, Friday & Saturday, 18:00-23:45 Sunday, closed the rest of the week; average cost of a pizza is €8.*

Why visit

The biggest draw in Garachico are the El Caletón rock pools which run most of the length of the seafront. These are a series of natural pools and channels hewn from solidified lava; some are suitable for paddling, some deep enough for the town's *muchachos* to plunge into from great heights ... about 10 feet. A concrete path laid into the lava leads to secret corners and more pools. Be warned - if you go off exploring barefoot, that lava can get exceedingly hot!

In Parque Puerta Tierra, built around an old toll gate (the only survivor of the original harbour), shaded paths wind through palm, fig and laurel trees. Hidden amongst the undergrowth are 'poet's corner' (good luck trying to find anything that rhymes with 'there was a young man from Garachico ...'), a traditional wooden *lagar* (wine press) and busts of eminent townspeople. The park culminates at a vantage point with views across the town's red-tiled rooftops and of the two slate-coloured lava streams which forged Garachico's destiny.

Castillo de San Miguel (*open Mon-Sat 10:00-16:00; entrance €2*) dates from 1575 and was built to defend the town from marauding pirates. Inside you'll find detailed displays about Garachico's chequered history and there are good views from the ramparts.

Ultimately Garachico is the sort of town where the greatest pleasure lies in simply wandering its old streets, and relaxing with a *barraquito* on Plaza de la Libertad.

On the beach

There is a small pebble beach beside the harbour which doesn't have any facilities (cafes and restaurants are nearby) and isn't the most comfortable for sunbathing, but its aquamarine waters are sheltered, attracting Spanish families who virtually camp on the beach at weekends during the summer months.

After dark

There's no nightlife to speak of. The few bars are mostly very traditional, small and full of local men, or low-key tascas. On the other hand, there are a lot of fiestas and cultural events which liven up the nocturnal scene now and again.

Where we'd stay

Garachico is blessed with two of the most stylish rural hotels on Tenerife and we love staying in both of them.

La Quinta Roja (*Glorieta de San Francisco, 2; +34 922 133 377; www. quintaroja.com*); The sandstone walls of Quinta Roja conceal two storeys of pure colonial elegance set around a patio garden on the lovely plaza in Garachico. Wide wooden walkways, mudejar ceilings and a lounge in a lookout tower provide traditional charm while the owner and staff provide genuine warmth and home made jams for breakfast.

San Roque Hotel (*C/Esteban de Ponte, 32; +34 922 133 435; www. hotelsanroque.com*) This is the most stylish and luxurious boutique hotel on the island. Effortlessly combining its original, 18th century fixtures and fittings with contemporary art fittings and Josef Hoffmann and Rennie Mackintosh furniture, this is the perfect romantic retreat for those with the taste, and the wallet, to enjoy it. Their restaurant's excellent too.

Best time to visit

Garachico's streets flow with wine again during the Romería de San Roque on the 16th August, but that's partly because so much gets spilled. Ox drawn carts trundle through the narrow streets followed by donkeys, goats and traditional musicians. Lads and lassies in traditional costume hand out *gofio cakes, papas arrugadas*, skewers of *pinchos morunos* and steaks as well as gallons of wine from plastic flagons. If arriving by car, park as soon as you see other people parking theirs. Even though you might be a couple of kilometres from your destination it's a sign that from here on in, spaces are at a premium.

One of the most spectacular and bizarre events on Tenerife takes place during the *Fiestas Lustrales* at the beginning of August when, in a re-enactment of the time lava flowed through the streets, fireballs are launched from the hills above the harbour. It's an incredible sight to witness and draws thousands of people. However, it only happens every five years. The next should be in 2025.

ICOD DE LOS VINOS

Where is it and what's it like?

Located on steep slopes above the north west coast, the town of Icod de los Vinos sits beneath the spectacular profiles of Mount Teide and Pico Viejo in a lush valley embroidered with the vines from which the town derived its name five centuries ago and bordered to the west by a steep *barranco* (ravine). Today, it's the Millennium Drago Tree, the oldest drago tree in the Canarian Archipelago and a magnificent specimen aged somewhere between 650 and 1,000 years, that brings most visitors to Icod, arriving on tour buses and spilling into the pretty plaza of San Marcos. After dark the town reverts to its *tinerfeño* self and few tourists actually stay here which is a pity because it has one of the most spectacular views of Mount Teide to be seen on Tenerife. Every year, around San Andrés at the end of November, the wine once again takes centre stage in Icod as the new harvest is enjoyed, along with roasted chestnuts, while local youths careen down the town's steepest streets on polished wooden boards, emulating the precarious journey wine barrels took in the town in days of yore.

What's the story?

Prior to the Conquest in 1496, Icod was one of the most important centres for the Guanche, Tenerife's original inhabitants, due to its abundance of woodland and water. Following the conquest, it was chosen by Alonso Fernández de Lugo as the ideal site for a sugar mill and for the cultivation of sugar cane. In 1501 the first church was built, dedicated to San Marcos and the first priest to hold mass there was a Portuguese named Ruy Blas who had been given lands in the area in return for his role as chaplain during the conquest. The area owned by Ruy Blas still bears his name today. As sugar cane took easily to the slopes of Icod and grew well, so the centre's wealth grew and it took just 13 years for the area to be recognised as a parish and its first parish priest to be appointed. With the presence of the sugar mill, Icod's importance as a centre quickly rivalled that of Garachico and La Laguna. The population first began to grow around the area of the Caforiño *barranco* which was known as 'the river of Icod' due to the year-round presence of water. The opportunity to make money attracted immigrants to Icod from across Europe, mainly Portuguese, as well as many Canarios from the neighbouring islands of Gran Canaria and La Gomera, many of them inter-marrying with the Guanche population. It wasn't until the collapse of the sugar trade in 1542 that the first vines were planted in the area; a trend started by Ruy Blas and quickly emulated by the rest of the population. That's when '*de los Vinos*' became part of the name, and wine became a way of life for the valley dwellers.

By 1585 Icod had begun to rival Garachico in terms of size of population and residencies, the quality and quantity of its vines far exceeding those of its wealthy neighbouring town. As the wine trade grew, so too did Icod, largely due to the popularity of the Malvasia whose grapes grew well on its slopes, producing wines beloved by both Great Britain and Portugal. As a result of the income brought to the town by the export of its Malvasia, great mansions and churches were constructed and the population continued to grow so that by 1676 it was the fourth largest centre on the island after La Laguna, La Orotava and Garachico.

On May 2nd 1798 a fire began in a cell in the Bernardas Convent and it quickly spread, reducing houses, including the Mayor's office, to ash and rubble within just two and a half hours. The town was rebuilt in 1803 to a design by Antonio Guillermo Rodriguez and Luís Madero; the Bernardas Convent however, was not rebuilt and two centuries later, the Andrés de Lorenzo Cáceres Park was constructed on its site.

When the wine trade collapsed in the latter part of the seventeenth century, like so many places across the Canary Islands, the male inhabitants of Icod fled to the Americas -mainly Cuba and Venezuela- to seek work, leaving the womenfolk to fend for themselves until their husbands sent money. It was at this time that silk stockings became one of the area's main exports and more than 70 silk looms were in operation in Icod in 1770. Icod's fortunes took a short-lived turn for the better at the beginning of the 20th century as France blocked trade between the UK and North America, opening the opportunity for wine to once more bring wealth. When the bottom fell out of the market shortly afterwards, it was to banana production that Icod turned. Today, its income is still largely derived from agriculture as well as from the tourism which its drago tree brings in.

Who'd want to stay here?

Icod is a traditional Tenerife town which attracts a lot of day-trippers, many of whom don't venture far from the main attraction. It's a different place after they leave, and staying here gives a true taste of Canarian life. But there are a couple of other reasons for considering Icod. It's in a good location for exploring Isla Baja; there's a nice little beach nearby; it's on the doorstep of very good walking country; and, with the *anillo insular* (ring road) now mostly connecting the north west coast with the south west coast, if the weather's gloomy you can be on the sunny south west coast in no time.

The food scene

Most restaurants in and around Icod de los Vinos are of the traditional Canarian variety. They're good enough restaurants but no different from hundreds of others around the island.

118

Where we'd eat

Contemporary traditional - Breaking the mould is **El Mortero** where the food is a modern take on the traditional, so you get the likes of raviolis in an *almogrote* sauce or *carrilleras de cerdo ibérico* (ibérico cheeks cooked in red wine). It might be more contemporary than other restaurants in town, but it's still very much traditional fare which also means big portions at reasonable prices. *Camino Guayadil 1; +34 922 814 955; open 09:00-23:00 Tuesday to Saturday, closed Monday & Sunday. Average cost of a main course is €13.*

Why visit

The thing that draws most people to Icod is the *Drago Milenario* tree. This impressive specimen, now shored up by concrete to counter the effects of the vibration caused by its proximity to the road, stands in the centre of landscaped gardens (*open every day 20:30-18:30; entrance €5, €3 over-65s*) which include a picnic zone. Whilst it's an impressive collection of indigenous plants for gardeners and a pleasant enough stroll for everyone else, the best view of the tree is actually from the main square of San Marcos which overlooks it and which won't cost you anything. Despite its name, the drago tree is not actually a tree at all, rather a plant, of the same family as the asparagus, which makes it virtually impossible to age accurately. Crowned by a dense canopy of twisted limbs and leathery leaves, the tree has become a symbol, not just of Icod but of the enduring nature of the Canarios themselves. Whatever its real age, there's no denying it's a magnificent sight.

The most attractive part of town is the old quarter which begins at the jacaranda-shaded plaza beside the 16th century Iglesia de San Marcos which has a small museum adjoining it in which you'll find a priceless collection of processional silverware, including a 48 kilo Cuban Cross, the largest of its kind in the world. Continuing eastwards along Calle San Sebastián takes you past souvenir and wine shops, artisan shops and pavement cafés to the traditional Canarian style Town Hall flanked by the Convent of San Agustín with its triple bell tower.

To the south of Iglesia de San Marcos, the pretty little Plaza de la Pila has a seven-branched palm tree and a fountain at its heart and surrounded by 16th, 17th and 18th century houses with carved wooden balconies, including the Casa Lorenzo-Cáceres music academy where a small inner courtyard has Tuscan columns supporting an upper gallery- all of them funded by profits from Icod's wine trade. From here, climbing steeply along C/San Antonio rewards with a second ancient drago, this one tethered at the neck and standing in splendid solitary confinement, all eyes on its bigger and older cousin.

El Mariposario (*www.mariposario.com*) is a wonderful butterfly garden whose owners are committed to conservation and creating the perfect

119

environment for their flamboyant '*mariposas*' to thrive. Stand still long enough and you might find yourself acquiring a rather splendid overcoat of colourful butterflies.

If claustrophobia isn't a problem take a trip to the dark side with a two hour guided exploration of La Cueva del Viento (*www.cuevadelviento.net*). The 17km volcanic tube is the longest in Europe and until you've switched your torch off while in its interior, you haven't really experienced the term 'pitch dark'.

Other curios are the Malvasia Museum on Plaza de la Pila, perfect for trying the tipple that inspired Shakespeare, and the quirky ARTLandya Doll Museum (*www.artlandya.com*) on Camino de Moleiro.

On the beach

Black sand Playa San Marcos on Icod's coast is set in a sheltered bay and backed on one side by unattractive apartment blocks. It's favoured by locals and has a couple of restaurants where you can partake of the local white wine with fried sea bass.

After dark

Much the same as other historic towns on Tenerife, there are plenty of bars in Icod, but they are of the quite basic, traditional type. Not the sort of places to hang out in your most chic outfits.

Where we'd stay

Accommodation in and around Icod de los Vinos is largely in rural houses but there are two small, colonial hotels within the town itself, and we're suckers for small hotels in historic buildings. **Hotel Emblemático San Marcos** (*Calle Hércules 11; +34 922 816 509; www.sanmarcos-hotel.es*) and **Hotel San Agustín** (*San Agustín 18; +34 922 813 194; www.hotelsanagustin.es*), are both beautifully restored 18th century manor houses.

Best time to visit

On the 29th November the new wines are ready for quaffing and *bodegas* throw open the doors of their wine cellars. In the past wine barrels were transported by wooden sleds drawn by oxen from the upper town to be washed in the sea. As streets are almost vertical, this was a precarious business. Nowadays the tradition is commemorated in an extreme sport. The '*arrastre de las tablas*' involves the town's two steepest streets being barricaded with mountains of old tyres into which local lads crash, having hurtled down them on polished wooden sleds at breakneck speed. C/del Plano is a the place to enjoy the best of the mayhem.

A Dragon's Tale

The drago tree (*Dracaena draco*) is more than just a Tenerife icon, some of its number are amongst the oldest living members of the plant kingdom and its history has as many facets as the tree has crowns; a tangled tale of idolatry, exploitation and magic.

Twenty million years ago the giant drago tree was prevalent throughout the Mediterranean, stretching all the way to the shores of Southern Russia. Acre by acre, the lands where the drago tree grew became covered in ice and the frozen carpet spread ever more south, killing everything in its wake, until only the Canary Islands, Madeira and Cape Verde remained free of the Ice Age. Painfully slow growing, mature specimens are still as highly prized and venerated today as they have always been, and rightly so, for this is a tree born of a legend.

Enter the Dragon

In Greek mythology, Atlas the giant had three daughters; Egle, Eritia and Aretusa, known collectively as the Hespérides. These three women lived in the most westerly land in the world; an Eden in the Atlantic Ocean where the weather was always mild and golden apples grew on trees guarded by a hundred headed dragon called Ladon. The land was known as the Garden of Hespérides. Tasked with the Twelve Labours of Hercules, the eponymous strong man had reached number eleven on his list; to steal the apples from the Garden of Hespérides. Knowing he would likely be barbecued by Ladon, he decided to ask Atlas to undertake the task for him; the dragon knew Atlas and wouldn't suspect him of being a thief. But Atlas was busy. Condemned by Zeus to hold up the sky for all eternity, when Hercules asked Atlas to do him a favour in exchange for which, Hercules would take his place holding the sky, Atlas jumped at the chance for a change of scenery and a rest for his weary shoulders. The plan worked. Atlas stole the apples and slew Ladon before returning to Hercules who tricked him into once again taking up his burden. Back in the Garden of Hespérides, Ladon's blood spilled throughout the garden and for every drop, a tree sprang up, its massive trunk sprouting a complex tangle of crowns like the hundred heads of Ladon. When the tree was cut, blood ran from it, as it had run from the scales of the dragon.

Today, we know the Garden of Hespérides as Tenerife, and the tree that was spawned from the dragon's blood, as *Dracaena draco*; the drago tree.

First Blood

Oblivious to its mythological beginnings, the earliest known inhabitants of Tenerife, the Guanches, revered the drago tree as a source of magic, knowledge, fertility and divination. Believing the tree imparted wisdom, the elders and *menceys* (kings) of the island held court and performed sacred ceremonies to retain its good will. Known as 'dragon's blood', the sap of the drago tree was recognised by the Guanche for its curative properties and was used by them to heal sores and ulcers and in the process of mummifying their dead, helping to slow down oxidation of the body. If the tree had a good blossom one year, the Guanche believed it prophesied a good harvest and so they tended the tree with care, ensuring long life and full fruiting. Under their auspices, the tree was able to reach ever greater ages, one specimen in the La Orotava Valley reputedly attaining a height of 25 metres with a girth of 15 metres.

Following the Spanish conquest of Tenerife, the drago became so prized that its export to Europe became liable to tax and Spanish and Portuguese sailors carved their names into the trunk of mature specimens to identify ownership. The popularity of dragon's blood for all manner of uses reached its zenith during the eighteenth century. Among the most notable of its applications, was its alleged use as a component part of the varnish used by Italian violin makers, including the renowned Stradivari. Many people claim the varnish was a contributory factor, not only to the beauty and strength of the wood, but also to the resonance of the finished instrument. The translucent quality of the dye also ensured its presence in the workshops of Florentine masons who, by rubbing dry, pure dragon's blood onto heated marble produced a fine red tint that penetrated deep into the stone. In cosmetic terms, Venetian noble women used it to dye their hair golden; a lengthy process involving the application of a mixture of oriental crocus, dragon's blood and henna which was left for three days before being washed off; a good reason to be grateful for the advancements made by L'Oreal et al. Hernia sufferers were taken at daybreak to a drago tree at a crossroads where they were hoisted up horizontally and the outline of their feet was drawn onto the trunk with a knife, doing neither the patient nor the tree any discernible good whatsoever. If the cuts on the tree healed over, the hernia would be healed within a year, if not, the operation would be repeated the following year. Other uses chronicled include putting dragon's blood under the pillow to cure impotency and burning the sap by an open window for seven nights to bring back a straying lover.

When the superstition and bad hairdressing are stripped away, what you're left with is the magnificent *Dracaena draco*, the sap and bark of which do indeed have both antiseptic and anti-oxidising properties. The oldest surviving specimen in the Canary Islands stands within its own gardens in the town of Icod de los Vinos and is thought to be somewhere between 600 and 1000 years old but no-one is entirely sure. The drago tree defies accurate ageing by refusing to form annual circles, choosing instead to throw out new branched crowns every ten years or so which then intermingle with the existing crowns and cause havoc on the arboriculturalist's abacus, thus preserving the aura of mystery and magic that still surrounds the drago tree today.

Drago Milenario, Icod de los
Vinos

La Laguna

Where is it and what's it like?

One of the Canary Island's most interesting cities, San Cristóbal de La Laguna is often overlooked by visitors; probably because it doesn't have a beach and, from the northern TF5 motorway which runs parallel to the city, it looks like an unattractive concrete jungle. But the urban 20th century façade hides a corker of an historic city centre. The first city to be built following the conquest and the first Spanish overseas territory, its unique grid layout was conceived as a model town for Spain's new era of peace and became a blueprint for many Latin American cities, including Havana. Perfectly preserved streets and squares are lined with colonial 16th, 17th and 18th century mansions designed by Genoese, French, Portuguese, Castilian and Flemish architects; earning it UNESCO World Heritage status and providing a living museum which combines European and Islamic elements and has played a pivotal role in the development of architecture in the Spanish New World.

Situated inland 600 metres above sea level (making it considerably cooler than coastal communities) in the Aguere Valley, poised at the gateway to the Anaga Mountains, La Laguna is a city for travellers rather than casual tourists and the best way to get to know it is to pick up a *mapa turístico* from the tourist information office in the Casa de los Capitanes (C/Obispo Rey, beside Plaza del Adelantado) or purchase our La Laguna Town Walk on PDF (see p279) which takes you to all the best bits, including exploring its cobbled streets lined by smart mansions and convents with towers whose latticed wooden balconies enabled cloistered nuns to see without being seen. Detours into churches and inviting doorways reveal tranquil leafy courtyards and curios like the baptismal font used to baptise the Guanche in the Iglesia de la Concepción, or the skull and crossbones of the tomb of the notorious pirate, Amaro Pargo, engraved into the stone floor of the Iglesia de Santo Domingo.

Having a university lends the city a cosmopolitan air of young sophistication, and stylish students share cobble space with old men in fedoras and nuns in slate grey habits. Shops are similarly contrasting; musty bookshops, barbers with lumbering antique chairs and tabacs whose walls are steeped with the aroma of tobacco leaf, all sit comfortably beside chic shops displaying the latest fashions, and in the run-up to Lent, some of the best places on Tenerife to buy yourself a carnaval outfit.

Plaza del Adelantado was once the focal point of the old city, but since the relocation of the agricultural market (great place for spices, salted fish and exhibition-worthy vegetables) to Plaza del Cristo, the plaza has lost some of its vibrancy; however the benches around its wonderful Carrara marble fountain are still an unbeatable spot for soaking up the charm of this living, open air museum.

What's the story?

Originally founded in 1496 by Alonso Fernández de Lugo, leader of the
Spanish conquistadores, San Cristóbal de La Laguna was chosen for its elevated,
inland position which made it a clear vantage site and safe from the attentions of
sea-faring brigands. The city was named after a nearby lagoon which supplied
its water source. Immediately following the conquest, building was random and
unplanned with the Conquistadores effectively given free reign to build in what
was conceived as a 'balanced space with no walls or fortresses, within which
its citizens could live peaceably together'. As a result, most houses sprang up
around the Iglesia de la Concepción. With disorder looming, a plan was drawn
up, based on plans by Leonardo da Vinci for the city of Imole. Alonso Fernández
de Lugo had the plans adapted to fit the area between his official residence and
the church. Long, wide main streets known as Calles Reales linked open spaces
and formed a grid into which smaller streets were inserted.

Building continued at a pace during the early part of the 16th century,
attracting the island's ruling classes and by 1515 there were already more
than 1000 inhabitants. The eclectic styles of architecture reflected the many
nationalities of the carpenters, architects and builders who constructed
them - Portuguese, Genoese, Flemish, French and Castilian – many of them
Conquistadores who now chose to settle on the island. With wealth came religion
and where the money went, so did religious orders and in a period of just
seven years, a further church, a monastery and two hospices were constructed.
La Laguna had become the archipelago's ecclesiastical centre. In 1521 the
Municipal Council brought water to the city and the first public buildings were
constructed in 1525. As La Laguna's population expanded to 6000 inhabitants,
by far the largest city in the archipelago, in order to reduce the risk of fire, the
Council ordered all cane buildings to be destroyed in 1554.

Throughout the 17th and 18th centuries La Laguna remained the dominant
political, religious and commercial centre of the Canary Islands, status which is
reflected in the magnificent buildings which still stand today. In 1821, following
the destruction of Garachico, the port of Santa Cruz became the economic centre
of the island and with it, the political power shifted. Santa Cruz became the
capital of the Canary Islands and San Cristóbal de La Laguna began to decline,
retaining only its ecclesiastical status. In 1742 the University of La Laguna was
founded and the city derived a new status, that of learning and culture.

As for the lagoon from which it took its name, all the demands of farming
around the rapidly expanding city choked the natural seasonal supply of rain,
causing the lagoon to become stagnant and a source of pestilence. It was finally
drained in 1837.

Who'd want to stay here?

La Laguna is good for a city break. The old quarter is compact, full of interesting architecture, independent shops, and loads of atmospheric restaurants. In term time there's also a youthful buzz to the place thanks to the student population. It's also the best place on the island for accessing Anaga, so ideal for anyone who wants to combine city strolling with hiking in one of the most stunning parts of Tenerife.

The food scene

La Laguna is rich in restaurants offering both traditional and contemporary dining in irresistibly inviting old buildings. Every time we visit, new places have appeared, whilst others have disappeared. It's difficult to go wrong gastronomically in La Laguna and, due to its student population, there are good vegetarian choices.

Where we'd eat

Creative cuisine – We're fans of having our taste-buds surprised and wowed, so **Nub** inside the La Laguna Gran Hotel is right up our perfectly-preserved, historic street. One of Tenerife's Michelin star restaurants, the avant-garde food features a blend of Chilean, Italian, and Canarian influences – the first two because of the nationalities of chefs Andrea Bernardi and Fernanda Fuentes. Starters may include a mix of small dishes like horseradish in white chocolate; tiny *sopapillas*; miniature carrots with tangerine; and clam on a *gofio* biscuit all served on a 'cloud'. *Calle Nava y Grimon, 18; +34 922 07 76 06; open 19:30-21:30 Wednesday & Thursday, 13:30-14:30 and 20:00-22:00 Friday & Saturday, 13:30-14:30 Sunday, closed Monday & Tuesday; tasting menu is €110.*

Canarian/international – The menu is small, the dining area is cosy and it's got a great name – **El Jinete Sin Cabeza** (the Headless Horseman). There are many, many good traditional restaurants in La Laguna but El Jinete encapsulates the feel of this learned city for us; it's got a relaxed, friendly atmosphere and is kind of cool in a casual way. Plus the food is very good; the select menu swinging from steak tartar to snails in sauce, and a selection of Canarian specialities to a platter of smoked fish. *Calle Bencomo, 23; +34 622 88 62 88; open 20:00-22:45 Tuesday to Thursday, 13:30-16:00 and 20:00-22:45 Friday & Saturday, closed Sunday & Monday; average cost of a main course is €10.*

Why visit

It's a UNESCO World Heritage, need we say anything else? There's much to explore on those old streets.

The Iglesia de Nuestra Señora de la Concepción dates from the beginning of the 16th century and was the first church built on Tenerife. Climb the tower for impressive views over the Aguere valley to the airport and over the roofs of the city.

La Laguna's Neoclassical Cathedral of San Cristóbal underwent extensive renovation at the beginning of this century and is now suitably splendid inside too.

The extensive daily market (mornings only) housed on Plaza Cristo is a cook's dream in terms of fresh ingredients and you'll find pristine displays of fresh vegetables and exotic fruits adorning stalls. It's also a great place to buy cheeses, spices, local wines, fresh fish, meat, breads and pastries. There's a lovely flower stall outside too for some tropical flora to brighten your day.

The Instituto Cabrero Pinto (*C/San Agustín, 48*) is a perfect example of La Laguna's seamless integration of the contemporary with the historic. The former 16th century convent now houses art galleries with avant garde 21st century exhibitions. Its profuse courtyard garden underneath a carved, tea wood balcony is a perfect spot for contemplation (i.e. trying to figure out what the exhibits actually mean).

Displays and information at the History Museum (*+34 922 825 949; C/San Agustín, 22*) might be on the 'abridged' side, but it's another beautiful building worth exploring.

Nature and science are the themes at the Museum of Science and the Cosmos (*+34 922 315 265; www.museosdetenerife.org*) where 100 interactive exhibits turn potentially dry subjects into family-friendly ones (entrance to museums on Tenerife is free on Sundays).

After dark

Being a university city means you can be sure of one thing; a vibrant nightlife. You wouldn't know it during the day, but by midnight, the triangle of streets known as El Cuadrilatero in the newer part of the city between the Central Campus and Plaza San Cristóbal explode into life. Groups of students, blessed with that Spanish knack of effortlessly looking cool, down a couple of *combinados* on their wrought-iron balconies, before heading to the throng of bars below, where House, Latino and jazz vibes vie for dominance. Bars in the old quarter are much more sedate and spread out; a mix of traditional haunts with narrow Andalusian doorways and comfortably bohemian café bars which look as though they could be someone's living room. Throughout the year, concerts featuring international as well as Spanish bands are held in the plaza in front of the University Campus.

Alternatively, a slice of culture in an old fashioned grandiose setting can be experienced at the lovingly restored Teatro Leal (*+34 922 265 433; www. teatroleal.com*) which stages theatre, dance and concerts.

Where we'd stay

It's interesting to note that in the mid 19th century there were 6 inns in La Laguna. Today, when the number of annual visitors to Tenerife reaches into the millions, there are only three (Hotel Aguere, Hotel Nivaria & Hotel La Laguna Gran), all of them good but the cream of the crop is the La Laguna Gran Hotel.

La Laguna Gran Hotel (*Calle Nava y Grimon 18; (+34) 922 108 080; www.lalagunagranhotel.com*) is a fabulously stylish boutique hotel in the heart of the city. A converted 18th century manor house and former tobacco drying warehouse, the original features of tea wood balconies and stone floors have been beautifully paired with contemporary design and comfort. The best bits are the breakfast, the rooftop swimming pool, the lobby courtyard and bar, and the Michelin-starred Nub restaurant. The hotel restaurant is also very good value for money.

Best time to visit

Still the ecclesiastic centre of the Canary Islands, Easter represents the most important and solemn event on the city's calendar. Although the conical, hooded gowns which are worn by penitents during the Semana Santa (Easter) processions were corrupted by the Ku Klux Klan, they authentically derive from devout Catholicism and are worn to disguise the identities of those who wear them lest they glean any pride from their participation. The two main processions are the 'Magna' and the 'Silent Procession' at 17.00 and 21.00 respectively on Viernes Santos (Good Friday) when brotherhood after brotherhood solemnly parade through the old streets, some carrying full-sized crucifixes. The afternoon procession is best for photographs, but the candlelit 'Silent Procession' probably shades it in terms of atmosphere. It might be Tenerife's quietest celebrations, but it's the most evocative; once witnessed, never forgotten.

Held on the Sunday following Corpus Christi, the flower carpets of La Laguna are less ornate than those of La Orotava but are more numerous and for spectators, the event is a far more laid-back affair. Covering the streets emanating from Iglesia de la Concepción, the carpets are constructed the night before with *alfombristas* working through the night. The designs are simpler but still visually stunning and given the wider streets of La Laguna, are generally larger and bolder than those in La Orotava.

Being a UNESCO World Heritage Site means La Laguna is an interesting place to visit at any time of the year, but it is considerably cooler during winter months.

LA MATANZA

"The havoc the Guanches caused among the conquistadors will be an eternal memory among the people living in our islands and the name of La Matanza de Acentejo a monument of the bloody battle."
Jose de Viera y Clavijo – Historia de Canarias

What's it like?

When Mencey Bencomo led the Guanche warriors in a war against the Spanish invaders in the spring of 1494, he set the tone for the character of the town that was to grow up around the site of his victory. The banners that draped the coastal hamlet of El Caletón when 75 houses were threatened with demolition because of the *Ley de Costas* left visitors in no doubt as to the level of resolve the *matanceros* (La Matanza inhabitants) hold when it comes to preserving their culture and their way of life. We wandered into this odd little place one summer when it was bustling with Canarios and many protesting banners hung from many buildings. Over a decade later and the houses still stand.

Much of the *matancero* way of life comes from the cultivation of grapes, potatoes, and chestnut trees. Drive just ten minutes into the hills behind the main town and you find yourself deep in a rural landscape where acres of vines hang heavy with the fruit that goes to produce some of the finest wines coming out of Tenerife.

Like many of the other workaday Acentejo hill towns, La Matanza isn't a picturesque place; it's not even easy to pinpoint a centre as such, as its buildings meander along the hillside seemingly without much purpose, but there are pockets of interest, and it is resolutely Canarian. For those who want to delve deeper, there are numerous *ermitas*, many examples of traditional architecture, a profusion of drago trees and some excellent traditional restaurants, including *guachinches*.

What's the story?

La Matanza is named after the Battle of Acentejo, May 1494. Meaning 'slaughter' or 'massacre', it refers to the heavy losses sustained by the Spanish conquistadores when they met Guanche resistance in the ravine that today marks the boundary between La Matanza and the neighbouring municipality of La Victoria.

Alonso Fernández De Lugo led his army westwards to take the territory of Taoro, which was held by Mencey Bencomo; the strongest of the nine ruling *menceys* of Tenerife. At the same time, Tinguaro, Bencomo's brother, was leading his men to meet the invaders.

The two armies met in the Acentejo Ravine where, with the advantage of terrain on their side, the Guanche warriors rained down spears and stones on the unguarded troops below. The invaders were resolutely defeated and fled for their lives.

Against steel and cannon, the stone of the Guanche had beaten the mighty conquistadores; the victory wasn't to prove decisive in the long term but, on that day, David had slain Goliath.

Entering the town from the north east, it's quite clear which side the locals favoured in the battle which gave the town and municipality its name – a mural depicts a proud Guanche blowing into a conch shell whilst at his feet lies a stricken knight.

Who'd want to stay here?

Although well placed for accessing the north coast, the only compelling reason to choose La Matanza as a base over other, more charming, northern towns is if you desire a more off the beaten track location which also gives a flavour of authentic life in those Tenerife hills.

The food scene

The northern hillside is the place to find absolutely loads of Canarian restaurants, this is also *guachinche* country. If it's good local fare in an authentic setting you're looking for, you can't really go wrong. When we eat in La Matanza it tends to be the likes of fried rabbit, or *pinchos morunos*, from stalls at fiestas but there is one place we particularly like which is quite different from the other restaurants in La Matanza.

Where we'd eat

Contemporary Canarian - La Cuadra de San Diego's setting is the charming courtyard of a 400 year old hacienda. Outside of the *hacienda*'s faded lemon walls, La Cuadra's own vines flow down the hillside. The menu features an interesting mix of traditional offerings, some with unusual twists (e.g. green *almogrote*), and international dishes with a local flavour – wontons filled with ham and cheese. *(+34) 922 578 385; Calle Botello, 2; average cost of a main course €10; open 13.00-16.00 & 19.30-23.00, closed Sunday evening & all day Monday.*

Why visit

There are no *stand-out* attractions as such in La Matanza, the centre of San Antonio, where the San Antonio Abad fiesta is held, has some fine examples of the sort of buildings found in a traditional Canarian agricultural hamlet. A short drive inland through a landscape of orderly rows of vines and neat agricultural terraces will take you to Mirador de La Vica, a recreational zone on the edge of the forest which has expansive views along the north coast, as long as the foliage around the viewpoint hasn't grown to the extent it obscures the view. As many walking routes pass through here, it's a good base for exploring dappled forest paths filled with the sensual scent of pine and eucalyptus, before roasting any chestnuts you've gathered on your meanders at one of the *zona recreativa*'s barbecues.

More of a pleasant little spot than an attraction is la Fuente del Pino (the fountain of the pine). Accessed from the point where Calle Real joins Calle Canales, a volcanic shingle path leads to a trickling emerald pool beside a poignant lone cross. In bygone days, local people used to do their laundry here and, if it was especially hot, slip into the cool spring water themselves.

Definitely worth a visit if in the vicinity is the Mercadillo del Agricultor, Vino y Artesanía (*Carretera General Avenida de Tinguaro, 20; open 08.00-15.00 every Saturday, and 08.00-14.00 Sunday*) where a wide selection of locally grown fruit, vegetables, herbs and nursery plants sits alongside a range of local handicrafts including pottery, furniture and jewellery. It's also good for picking up wines from local vineyards.

On the beach
You don't go to La Matanza to sunbathe; although, El Caletón does get crowded with Canarian sun & sea lovers during summer months. Parts of the coast are good for an explore on foot, with old coastal paths such as the Sendero el Jagre winding above the rocky cliffs.

Where we'd stay
If you want to stay in La Matanza, the choices fall into two categories – plush villas overlooking the coast, or traditional houses further inland (given its steep slopes, there might be even better views than from those closer to the coast).

Best time to visit
La Matanza's main fiesta, and one of the oldest of its type in the Canary Islands, is dedicated to San Antonio Abad. For three consecutive Sundays in January, livestock farmers from all over the island flock to the traditional *barrio* of San Antonio where rows of empty agricultural pens await their annual visitors. The second Sunday, Octava Ganadera, is the main day of celebration when the streets around the small church are packed with people and all manner of animals – as well as agricultural livestock there can be snakes and birds of prey – in this lively and noisy farmyard fiesta.

Top: harbour, Puerto de la Cruz, bottom left: La Orotava, bottom right: El Sauzal

LA OROTAVA

What's it like?

Arrive at the bus station or drive in from the TF5 and you'll find yourself in the middle of a busy, unappealing sprawl of spare parts outlets and hardware shops wondering why on earth anyone would recommend this place.

But make your way to the primrose walls of the 17th century Iglesia de San Agustín on Carrera de Escultor Estevez and you're at the start of the old quarter where beautifully preserved 16th, 17th and 18th century mansions line elegant cobbled streets and the trees outnumber the lamp posts.

La Orotava is the jewel in Tenerife's crown. Following the Spanish conquest, La Orotava quickly established itself as home to the island's landed gentry and still maintains its aristocratic air today. The atmosphere in the heart of the old town is that of quiet sophistication and affluence with chic tascas tucked into leafy courtyards and upmarket independent shops selling books, antiques and ornaments. Unsurprisingly, for a town set into the sides of a valley, its streets are steep, and wandering around for a day will make itself known to your calves. It's also a bustling working town, so outside of siesta hours, roads are constantly busy and crossing them can be a dodgy business. At this height above sea level the air is a good bit chillier than at the coast, so in winter bring something warm to put on.

What's the story?

La Orotava is located 335 metres above sea level in the valley that was once described by the German explorer and naturalist, Alexander Von Humboldt, as "that charming country, of which travellers of every nation have spoken with rapturous enthusiasm."

Before the Spanish conquest of Tenerife, this was the Guanche kingdom of Taoro, the most fertile and sought-after land on the island. It was the most powerful of the island's nine kingdoms, ruled over by the mighty *mencey* Bencomo, considered the greatest and bravest of the island's kings. The conquest of the Canaries ended in Taoro (in 1496 Taoro stretched as far as present day La Matanza to the east and Los Realejos to the west) when Bencomo's son, Bentor, leapt to his death from the Tigaiga ridge after being defeated by the Spanish troops, his father having been slain in the fighting. Following the conquest, the land was distributed among *hidalgos* (noblemen) favoured by Alonso Fernandez de Lugo and by those who had invested in the conquest. The wealthy settlers who came here following the conquest planted its slopes with sugar cane and built their homes alongside the sawmills and *gofio* mills of the small settlement that had begun to grow around the church of Nuestra Señora de La Concepción.

Due to the demand for sugar cane at the time, the area rapidly prospered and

133

La Orotava was established as a township. In the space of a couple of decades the population rose from under 100 to over 2,500; the wealthiest residents living in grand colonial houses in the lower town (Villa de Abajo) whilst the craftspeople and labourers who worked for them occupied more modest abodes in Villa de Arriba (the upper town).

In the second half of the 16th century wine production took over from sugar and by the 17th century the valley was almost entirely devoted to the cultivation of vines; wines destined for Europe departing from the port of Garachico and the port of La Orotava (now Puerto de la Cruz) where there was a British settlement. It was through these ports that the wealthiest travellers from Europe arrived on Tenerife, bringing with them culture and sophistication as well as money; setting a trend which defined La Orotava's personality.

Towards the end of the 19th century, banana plantations were introduced to the Orotava Valley, British companies Fyffes and the Yeoward Brothers being the drivers behind a business initiative which spread across the Canary Islands and which generated more wealth for the entrepreneurs of the Orotava Valley.

As its historic centre remains virtually preserved, a stroll around the streets of Tenerife's "Very Noble and Loyal Town" (a title bestowed upon it in 1905 by King Alfonso XIII) is like architecturally time-travelling; styles ranging from colonial and Baroque to Renaissance and neo-Gothic all reflect the fruit of a series of economic booms that stretch all the way back to the conquest.

Who'd want to stay here?

La Orotava is suited to travellers who want to dip into the life of a colonial and sophisticated Canarian town life for a while. It's not off the beaten track as its charms attract plenty of day-trippers. But like many of the popular traditional towns, it's a very different scene once the day visitors depart. That's when to really get a feel for the place. It's also a good base for heading up to Teide National Park, walking in the pine forest, or dropping down the hill to Puerto de la Cruz and the beaches of this part of the north coast.

The food scene

As befits a town with a noble past and a stylish present, there's a satisfying choice of restaurants in and around La Orotava, ranging from traditional tascas and simple *guachinches* to some of the best creative Canarian cuisine you'll find on Tenerife.

Where we'd eat

Contemporary Canarian - Located in an elegant old building (formerly Lucas Maes) on the slip road to the TF5, **Restaurant Haydée** is ideal for people like us who relish creative traditional cuisine which has been given a

134

contemporary reboot – we've enjoyed the likes of bau buns with *cochino negro*, and *almogrote* risotto. Anyone who likes Michelin dining should appreciate the food. We recommend putting yourself in their hands and opting for one of the *degustación* (taster) menus (from €60). *Barranco La Arena, 53 (Slip road onto the TF5 motorway); +34 822 902 159539; open 19:30-22:30 Thursday and Friday;13.30pm-16:00 & 19:30-22:30 Saturday; 10:00-16:00 Sunday; average cost of a main course is €23.*

Traditional - For a cheap and cheerful traditional Canarian restaurant, **La Duquesa** in a lopsided cottage below the Iglesia de la Concepción is a cosy place to enjoy hearty local food at low prices. It's more a lunchtime venue and whilst the wooden decking terrace beside the church is a nice place to sit, we like the atmospheric hustle and bustle of dining inside its crooked embrace. *Plaza Patricio Garcia 6; +34 922 253 282; open 07:00-16:00 Monday to Friday, 08:00-15:00 Saturday; average cost of a main meal is €8.*

Even more traditional - Located beside the TF324 at **La Perdoma** (good *guachinche* hunting territory) just outside La Orotava, Guachinche San Antonio, located in a colonial building just off the main road, has the tag attached to its name, but it's a bit more like a traditional rustic restaurant than many *guachinches*. In that respect it's a good place for *guachinche* virgins to have their first experience of what is the most authentic types of home-cooking on Tenerife. Dishes include *ropa vieja* (old clothes), *escaldón* (gofio paste), and *huevos al estampido* (basically egg and chips). *Carretera Gral. 324; open midday-midnight daily, but it is a guachinche so expect hours to be flexible; average cost of a ration is €5.*

Coffee break - It's not always easy to get a seat but **Relieve**, opposite the town hall, is stylish, sweet, small and unbelievably cheap. The coffee is like a shot of adrenalin but the home-made cakes are sublime. Perfect for taking time out from exploring the town. *Carrera del Escultor Estevez; +34 922 326 326; open 07:00-21.30 daily.*

Why visit

La Orotava is one of the best preserved Canarian towns in the archipelago. Anyone looking for ready made things 'to do' wouldn't be suited to the town; this is a place where the rewards come from strolling the historic streets, soaking up the atmosphere and enjoying centuries worth of architecture ranging from elegant town houses to old *gofio* mills which still supply residents with the Canaries' favourite toasted flour.

Most popular of the old buildings are the Casas de Los Balcones on Calle

San Francisco. These are the finest examples of traditional balconied houses to be found on Tenerife and so attract large numbers of tour groups. Luckily, the groups tend to confine themselves to the Casa del Turista (1590) which is really just a front for souvenir selling.

Across the road is the infinitely lovelier and slightly quieter Casa Méndez-Fonseca (1657). Head inside to its charming courtyard and fork out the pittance entrance fee to explore the quirky museum upstairs. Next door is the Alfombras Art Centre, a small exhibition dedicated to the town's flower carpets. Leave the tour groups behind altogether and drop down Calle Colegio to find Casa Lercaro with its beautiful exterior and its pretty, balconied interior courtyard cafeteria.

Just a few steps further down Calle Colegio takes you to the Iglesia de la Concepción, an icon of La Orotava's skyline; an 18th century Baroque masterpiece with a rainbow-coloured dome and twin towers.

For nature lovers the 18th century formal Italian Victoria Gardens are pristine and are graced with a marble mausoleum which exists as a snub to the Catholic Church after it refused to allow the Marquis of Quinta Roja to be buried in a graveyard because he was a Freemason. The mausoleum was commissioned by his mother so her son's final resting place could be seen from all over the town, including the church. The gardens are worth seeing at dusk when up-lighting adds a completely different aspect. On the wilder side, the Botanical Gardens behind the Town Hall are little sister to the one in Puerto de la Cruz and feature a mini jungle of exotic plant life with a mystical drago tree and public toilets at its centre.

Drop down the hill from the old centre along Calle Tomás Zerolo to find the Iberoamerican Museum of Art inside the 17th century Convent of the Dominicans. It might sound a tad dry, but the exhibits are fascinating and often quite bizarre. Also in the lower town on Callle Leonor Monteverde is the Telesforo Bravo Visitor Centre which is free and full of information about Teide National Park. There's a lot more to discover in La Orotava which is why we've created a detailed Town & Cities guide (see p279).

On the beach
Head inland and the municipality of La Orotava stretches to the slopes overlooking the south side of the island (Teide National Park falls into La Orotava). Toward the coast, Puerto de la Cruz hogs the view, but tucked away to the east, and falling under La Orotava jurisdiction, are the three attractively wild black sand beaches of Bollullo, Patos, and El Ancón. The further east the beach is, the more likelihood you'll find sunbathers *sin ropas* (naked), and the more difficult it is to actually reach the sand. There are plans to improve access, but those may take a while to come to fruition.

After dark

As well as a handful of decent *cervecerías*, there are usually a couple of venues to enjoy live music ranging from folk to rock at the weekends. Añepa (*www.pubañepa.es*) on Calle Rosales is an intimate courtyard corner with art exhibitions and regular concerts. The liveliest scene tends to be on Plaza del Quinto, above the San Pedro car park.

Where we'd stay

You won't find any modern, high rise hotels in La Orotava. Here the discerning traveller disappears behind an unassuming exterior to emerge into the tranquil courtyard of a rural hotel where traditional carved wooden balconies and 17th century tiles abound and their idea of facilities is a telephone in your room.

Hotel Alhambra (*C/Nicandro González Borges, 19; +34 922 320 434; www. alhambra-teneriffa.com*).

North Africa meets colonial Tenerife in this 18th century mansion restored in Arabic style with just 5 individually styled double rooms each with exquisite en suite bathrooms. Fabulous style and comfort, eclectic art and good breakfasts.

Hotel Rural Orotava (*Calle Escultor Estevez, 17; +34 922 322 793; www. saborcanario.net*);

Big on history and character but small on natural light, this 16th century traditional Canarian mansion also boasts a traditional restaurant in a courtyard. Rooms are nicely refurbished with plenty of floor space but breakfast is nothing to write home about.

Hotel Rural Victoria (*Hermano Apolinar, 8; +34 922 331 683; www. hotelruralvictoria.com*)

Right in the heart of the old town and offering style, elegance and very good cuisine in a 300 year old mansion. Beautiful tiled walls, a lovely interior courtyard and a roof terrace with views across the La Orotava Valley.

Best time to visit

Any time is good for visiting a historic town, but May/June when it's Corpus Christi is particularly good as you get fun, fiestas and, usually, good weather.

The Flower Carpets of Corpus Christi are exquisite, transient works of art which only exist for a few short hours and should be on every respectable traveller's list of 'must sees'.

On the Thursday after the feast of Corpus Christi the town takes on a carnival atmosphere as the streets around Iglesia de la Concepción are decorated in elaborately designed carpets of petals. In the immense plaza that fronts the Town Hall, an 850sq metre tapestry is created from coloured soils and sand taken from the Teide National Park. The tapestry is the largest of its kind in the world and is nothing less than breathtaking in its intricacy and composition.

That same evening, the Corpus Christi procession walks over them all on its way to the church.

To get the best of the carpets, arrive around midday on the day, late enough so that designs will be well under way but early enough to give yourself time for at least a couple of circuits.

At the Town Hall, go inside and upstairs to one of the balconies that overlook the plaza for a perfect shot. And if you really want to see something special, go along to the Town Hall the day before to see the master *alfombristas* at work, it's like watching Michelangelo paint the Sistine Chapel ... well, it's brilliant anyway.

The Romería de San Isidro is one of the biggest and best *romerías* on Tenerife and takes place on the Sunday following the flower carpets. The entire town dresses in traditional *mago* (country folk) costumes and takes to the streets in a procession to celebrate their saint's feast day.

Beginning with camels ridden by the Romería Queens, the old town's narrow main street witnesses no less than 70 decorated carts pulled by oxen, each one packed to the gunwales with laughing people, a barbecue on which an assortment of prime cuts are being roasted and a couple of barrels of *vino del país*, or country wine. Accompanying the carts are bands of musicians (*parrandas*) and troupes of traditional dancers.

This is a boisterous, three to four hour marathon that involves a great deal of standing around so 'sensible' shoes are well, sensible. The idea is to share in the town's bountiful harvest by accepting the food and wine being handed down to you from the carts, it's positively rude to refuse. Buy yourself a small glass which hangs in a leather pouch around your neck (on sale from *vaso* vendors on the day) and enjoy. Who says there's no such thing as a free lunch?

The festive season is also a charming time to visit; the town is one of the best on Tenerife for Christmas decorations, there are *belén* routes, and the Reyes Magos (Three Kings) parade (5 January) is one of the most flamboyant on Tenerife.

LA VICTORIA

What's it like?

Of all the Acentejo hill towns, La Victoria probably has the least to offer the inquisitive traveller. For a start, it's not the easiest town to stop in if you arrive by car. We've driven through on countless occasions without stopping, partly because the main street is perpetually congested and partly because it doesn't offer anything much different from its neighbours, where parking is a bit easier ... but only a bit.

Like the municipalities around it, La Victoria is farming country, with cereal crops and vines traditionally characterising the upper slopes whilst banana plantations spread across the lower ones above the coast. It was known for its artisans, being a centre for pottery, lace-making, and carpentry - especially in making wine barrels, *lagars* (wine presses) and chairs. Ultimately though, La Victoria is a down-to-earth working town which kind of gets lost between Santa Úrsula and La Matanza.

What's the story?

La Victoria – the Victory – was named after the second battle of Acentejo when, in December 1495, the Spanish conquistadors exacted revenge for their humiliating defeat just along the hillside at La Matanza. Interestingly, there are no murals showing triumphant conquistadors standing over fallen Guanche here. The victory more or less signalling the beginning of the end of the conquest of the Canary Islands. To commemorate this, Alonso Fernández de Lugo ordered a church to be built in honour of Nuestra Señora de la Victoria and a series of small settlements were established which partly explains the drawn-out appearance to towns along this coast. That Christmas Day in 1495, a mass was said next to a pine tree which still stands today.

In 1906, King Afonso XII visited the town and was asked for a bridge to be built to cross the Barranco Hondo in order to unite the municipality with Santa Úrsula. Known as the Puente de Hierro (Iron Bridge), the bridge still unites the two boroughs. It might have been wide enough for horses to pass each other back in the early 1900s; it certainly wasn't designed for cars.

In 1922 the first telephone was installed and in 1932 the town received its first electric light.

Who'd want to stay here?

It's difficult to find a good reason to stay in La Victoria, other northern hill towns have more charm, restaurants, and better amenities. It is very Canarian, so anyone seeking a truly authentic experience on the northern slopes might enjoy its down-to-earth nature.

The food scene

La Victoria is another municipality where there are plenty of authentic restaurants serving traditional meat and fish dishes accompanied by local wines. It's also *guachinche* heartlands so a good place for seeking out these (sometimes) ramshackle establishments, if you've got a vehicle capable of tackling the ridiculously steep streets.

Adeje in the south is known for its *pollo al ajillo* (garlic chicken), but there's at least one restaurant in La Victoria which can rival the best of what Adeje has to offer.

Where we'd eat

Traditional - Located at the top of a steep street, **Casa Francisco** (los Garrafones) specialises in traditional Canarian cuisine, especially *carnes a la brasa* (grilled meats); although it does have vegetarian options. It's one of those all-purpose Canarian restaurants where locals hold birthday and wedding celebrations, karaoke parties etc. Don't let that put you off, these sort of restaurants are the ones which are truly authentic. Window tables have great views along the north coast, the ideal accompaniment for a plate of crispy, garlicky chicken. There's even a breathalyser in the restaurant, useful for drivers who want to check if they've drunk too much of the owner's own wine before setting off home. *(+34) 922 580 124; Calle Laureles, 2; average cost of a main course €9; open 12:30-16:30 Tuesday and Sunday, 12:30-16:30 & 20:00-23:00 Friday and Saturday, closed Monday, Wednesday & Thursday.*

Why visit

The most interesting spot in La Victoria is at the Iglesia de Nuestra Señora de la Encarnación (also known as the Church of La Victoria). This is the site where de Lugo's post-victory church was built and is an interesting religious building in its own right, as are the historic artefacts found within its walls. But it's the old pine outside the church which is of real interest, this Pino Centenario is said to be the one on which a bell was hung to be used a place of mass following the defeat of the Guanche in 1495. For anyone interested in traditional architecture, there are a few quite interesting religious buildings dotted around La Victoria, including tiny El Calvario tucked away on Calle Perez Diaz and the more impressive 17th century Convento de Santo Domingo on Calle Santo Domingo.

Not particularly easy to find is the Mirador de la Sabina on the cliffs overlooking La Victoria's coast. It's reached via a track leading from a road running parallel to the TF5 beside the Barranco de Acentejo, the ravine where the Spanish took their revenge on the indigenous islanders.

Where we'd stay

It is exactly like its neighbour, La Matanza, accommodation in La Victoria falls into two categories – modern villas overlooking the coast, or traditional houses. There's no standout place, but that doesn't mean there aren't some nice houses to call home for a short while.

Best time to visit

The second half of August sees the town's *fiestas patronales* taking place. This means you get live music, a *romería*, *verbena* (open air dances), dinners with everyone in traditional dress, processions, fiesta queens, and fireworks.

Los Realejos

Where is it and what's it like?

Nestling into the western folds of the Orotava Valley below the Tigaiga ridge and on the edge of the Corona Forestal, Los Realejos has two centres; Bajo near the TF5 motorway and Alto, a few hundred, muscle-torturing metres higher up the valley. Whilst many of its older buildings were destroyed by fire over the centuries, there are still enough historic corners to warrant a visit. Tenerife's oldest church, the Iglesia de Santiago Apóstal in Realejos Alto, has a spire straight out of Hans Christian Anderson. Fernández de Lugo's former abode, the Hacienda de los Principes, can be found in Realejos Bajo near an unusual pair of drago trees, Los Gemelos (the twins).

Exploring Los Realejos can be frustrating; parking is almost impossible and the one-way system can be bewildering, yet the town exudes a bustling charm.

In her book The Canary Islands (1911), the writer Florence Du Cane described Realejos Bajo as "...without doubt, the most picturesque village I ever saw in the Canaries."

It must have changed quite a bit since then, but it's still an interesting Canarian town which is overlooked by most visitors.

What's the story?

Having bravely defeated the invading Spanish conquistadors at La Matanza, the Guanche were subsequently defeated at The Battle of Aguere or Acentejo in November 1495. The powerful Bencomo, *mencey* of Taoro was slain at that battle and his eldest son, Bentor, was appointed his successor. During a second Battle of Acentejo in December 1495, the Guanche were decimated and their remaining numbers re-grouped on the slopes of the Tigaiga mountain from where, in February 1496, Bentor jumped to his death rather than surrender his father's kingdom to the Spanish. With their leader dead, the beleaguered Guanche surrendered and thus the conquest of Tenerife ended, in Los Realejos.

Encamped on either side of a deep *barranco*, the victorious conquistadores on the upper slopes known as Los Realejos Alto and the Guanche in the lower Los Realejos Bajo, on the morning of July 25th 1496, five Guanche *menceys* crossed the ravine to the Spanish side where they surrendered to Fernández de Lugo and were ceremoniously baptised into Christianity. The font used to baptise them is still in existence today and can be seen in the Apóstal Santiago church in Realejos Alto.

Here, below the lush forested slopes of the Tigaiga Mountain range, Fernández de Lugo, made his home. The two settlements of Los Realejos continued to exist as separate entities until 1954 when a formal merger was finally ratified and the town became known as Los Realejos.

141

As well as its place in the history books as being where the Conquest ended and Tenerife was ceded to Spain, Los Realejos is known for being the birthplace of one of Tenerife's most eminent sons; the naturalist, writer and historian José Viera y Clavijo, born in the town in 1730. Most influential of his extensive works is his Historia de Canarias (History of the Canary Islands).

Who'd want to stay here?

Where Puerto de la Cruz is the north's main tourist resort and La Orotava attracts many day-trippers and coach excursions, Los Realejos remains below the tourism radar. Parts, like the Rambla del Castro have become better known in the last decade, but much of it is still not very well known making it a good option for people who want a historic base in the Orotava Valley which is still off the beaten track.

The food scene

The heights of Los Realejos are known for producing excellent potatoes, especially ancient varieties such as *papas bonitas*, of which there are nearly thirty varieties. It's also *cochino negro* (black pig) country. Unlike much of the rest of the northern side of the island, the area is better known for distinctive white wines than its reds. Although the, mainly Canarian, restaurants found in Los Realejos are dependably good, we've never found any which particularly stands out. In fact our favourite restaurants in the municipality are to be found outside the town, and we like them as much for their other attributes as we do for the food served.

Where we'd eat

Traditional - El Monasterio is not really a converted monastery as is the popular belief, more an *ermita* which has been lovingly and beautifully expanded into a series of restaurants with a religious theme. Located on a volcanic cone overlooking the Orotava Valley, El Monasterio is a treat for the eyes and worth a visit in its own right. As well as its restaurants, all with differing specialities, there are gardens and an animal enclosure. The food in some restaurants can be hit and miss, but the experience of dining there is quite unique. We would end visits from family and friends with a cava breakfast at the Mirador restaurant. It's an extra special, but not expensive, way to round off a trip to Tenerife. *Montaña de los Frailes; +34 922 340 707; open 09:00-midnight daily (restaurants within El Monasterio close on different days). Menu prices vary from restaurant to restaurant.*

Contemporary traditional - One of our favourite spots on Tenerife is to sit at a wine barrel table looking along the subtropical coast from the Mirador

San Pedro. There's always been a decent restaurant there, but in recent years it's upped its game with a menu which features Canarian dishes which have been perked up so that the *croquetas* are Canarian black pig; the tortilla is made with avocado, prawns, and black garlic *alioli*; and the tuna is flavoured by teriyaki vinegar and comes with new potato puree. *Mirador San Pedro; +34 922 34 08 75; open 10:00-23:00 daily, average cost of a main course is €13.*

Why visit

El Monasterio is worth a visit for the views, setting, the mock religious buildings, and assorted wild life even if you don't choose to eat there.

La Rambla del Castro is a former merchants' trail on the coast below Los Realejos. A path leads from the San Pedro Mirador past banana plantations, haciendas, secret coves and palm groves to a tiny fort, where soldiers used to keep a vigil for pirates. It's an absolutely delightful spot that feels more Caribbean than Canary Islands.

For superb views of the Orotava Valley, the TF-342 heading west from the town passes the Mirador de El Lance where, as well as valley vistas, an impressively proportioned statue of Guanche Mencey Bentor shakes his fists angrily at the gods. The PR41 trail from Playa Socorro passes the viewpoint before climbing to the Tigaiga Ridge and Mount Teide beyond.

On the beach

El Socorro, a few kilometres from town, is a beautiful black sand beach with lifeguard, toilet facilities, a wifi zone and a little fish restaurant. The beach shelves gently into waves which reach a height of five metres in winter, making it a favourite spot with surfers as well as sunbathers. It's one of the Tenerife beaches whose sand can disappear in winter months, replaced by boulders, before magically appearing in the summer again.

After dark

A few quiet bars and no clubs, but with 80 fiestas, short film seasons, jazz weekends, world music festivals and cinema on the beach in summer, who needs them?

Where we'd stay

Most of the hotels in Los Realejos are in the more modern urban developments of El Toscal and Longuera on the other side of the TF5. They're handy for the coast and getting to Puerto de la Cruz, but it's a very different vibe there from the town of Los Realejos.

Which is why we'd opt for **Hotel Rural Bentor** (*Calle del Cantillo de Abajo, 6; +34 922 353 458; www.hotelruralbentor.com*), a beautifully restored 17th century town house and courtyard in the heart of the older town which has 19 spacious rooms. Furniture is in keeping with the age of the house, decor and bathrooms fittings are contemporary and stylish, and floors and ceilings are polished tea wood.

The area is also good for staying in a *finca*.

Best time to visit

Los Realejos claims to celebrate more fiestas than any other place in Spain. It's home to the Toste Brothers' pyrotechnics factory, suppliers of fireworks all over the Canary Islands, which might explain why there's such a penchant for fiestas.

The most explosive is celebrated on 3rd May when crosses throughout the town are elaborately decorated and a three hour firework display lights up the skies above the town.

The plaza in front of the town hall is a good spot to enjoy the spectacle, which starts from around 10pm. The display isn't continuous and it can be a bit nippy; a jacket is essential.

LOS SILOS

Where is it and what's it like?

A stranger to many guide books, the low rise white buildings and icing sugar-coated spire of the church of Los Silos snuggle in a fertile green carpet known as Isla Baja at the foot of the Teno Mountains on Tenerife's north west coast.

Los Silos has two contrasting faces. At the coast is Puertito de los Silos, where a 16 metre, 20 tonne skeleton of a whale serves as a monument to man's relationship with the sea and is a coastal landmark beneath which eco festivals attract tie-dies and dreadlocks. The main town of Los Silos lies slightly inland, at its heart, a laurel shaded, Art Nouveau-styled plaza plays host to architecture spanning four centuries, a church whose name, La Iglesia de La Luz (Church of the Light) is a descriptor as well as a title, and a beautifully restored 17th century former convent.

It's a picturesque town which seems to attract gentle neo-hippies and German ex-pats who renovate its traditional houses and maintain its historic beauty. Protected from the attentions of tour groups by virtue of its narrow streets which prohibit access by coaches, Los Silos is content to be overshadowed by near-neighbour Garachico in exchange for its tranquil and unassuming way of life.

What's the story?

Pre-conquest, Los Silos was part of the Guanche kingdom of Daute, one of the most powerful kingdoms on the island and one that sided with Bencomo

Top: La Giganta, Santa Ursula, bottom left: La Laguna, bottom right: Rambla de Castro, Los Realejos

in order to fight the Spanish conquistadores to the death. After the Battle of Aguere, the kingdom of Daute fell, along with the powerful Taoro, and Tenerife was ceded to the Castilian crown. The area of Los Silos was quickly recognised as being a potential source of wealth due to its rich soil, abundant rainfall and strong harvest, particularly of cereals which grew well on its slopes. During the 16th century, centres of population formed which were made up of Castilians, Catalans, Portuguese and Genoese as well as an influx of islanders from La Gomera, El Hierro and Gran Canaria.

Wealthy Portuguese landowner, Gonzalo Yanes, is credited with founding the town; it was he who oversaw the construction of a sugar refinery and of the grain silos which gave the town its name in 1509. As well as the grain, sugar plantations were created which grew so well that sugar refineries were constructed. By the middle of the century Los Silos had 100 inhabitants, and a convent established on the estate of Gonzalo Yanes.

The growth of Los Silos was a spin off from the fortunes of its neighbour, Garachico; as Garachico's port grew and flourished, so the population of Los Silos grew to produce the grain, sugar and wine to meet export demands. By the beginning of the 17th century and despite a plague epidemic, Los Silos doubled its population and began to construct fine houses and sculptures to showcase its burgeoning wealth, prosperity which continued into the 18th century.

By the 19th century, there were already well established routes linking Los Silos to Garachico and to Buenavista but in 1883 communications took a leap forward when the underwater cable from Tenerife to La Palma was laid and was connected at Los Silos. The small telegraph station erected for the East India Rubber Company of London still stands today, as indeed does the sugar refinery, now a banana storage depot, on the headland at San José. Another surge of prosperity came towards the end of the 19th century when banana cultivation was expanded and cattle-rearing increased. The 20th century saw the arrival of Mariano Estanga to the town. A leading proponent of urban renewal, Estanga brought Arte Nouveau and Gothic revival style to Los Silos.

Today the town's tradition of agriculture continues and the area is one of the main suppliers of organic produce on the island.

Who'd want to stay here?

Although on the coast, and one of Tenerife's prettier towns, the gastronomic scene lets it down so it's not ideal for those wanting to mix historic surroundings with a choice of good dining options. It is, however, well placed for hiking, with one of the best walks in the north west starting from the town and some more of our favourite walking routes on the island within easy travelling distance.

146

The food scene
It's difficult to define Los Silos gastronomically as restaurants in the town are either basic affairs that don't stand out or they simply don't last. La Escuela on Calle la Estrella is a prime example; the former schoolhouse is located in a lovely old building but it changes hands on a regular basis. Sometimes it's open as a restaurant, other times not. With Los Silos, it's always a case of let's see what there is this time.

Where we'd eat
Despite giving up eating anything substantial in Los Silos, anytime we're in the town we stop at **El Kiosko** on Plaza de la Luz for a coffee/*cerveza* as it's such a lovely spot ... irrespective of who actually is running the kiosk. Last time they stocked homemade cakes and tarts, including a yummy fresh fig tart. But it's probably changed hands again by now.

Why visit
Basically, it's a nice, historic Canarian town which too often gets overlooked. A wander through the streets reveals pastel cottages, narrow lanes, and a main plaza surrounded by historic buildings including the former Convent of San Sebastián, now the town's cultural centre.

On the outskirts of town is a good little picnic zone with a kiosk, whilst on the coast are a handful of curios; the whale sculpture, old lime kilns, the little building which marks the spot where the Atlantic telegraph cable reached Tenerife – to a fanfare welcome by all accounts. You never know what you'll find when you explore Los Silos. Last time we encountered a giant seagull made from rubbish.

A rather lovely legacy of the town's Storytelling Festival is the Calzones Literarios; four narrow alleys around the centre where visiting tale weavers have left their mark with a few words and little plaques.

Beside the main car park is a metal sculpture of *Canarina Canariensis* – the Canary Island Bellflower, a symbol of the town and found in abundance in the hills which rise above the town. All of which leads to the main reason many people choose to stay here - hiking. Paths opposite the bellflower sculpture lead into the Teno hills, climbing past the Cuevas Negras and abandoned hamlets to venture deep into the *laurisilva* forest of the Monte del Agua.

On the beach
El Puertito's little, sand and pebble beach that hugs the coast in the shadow of the whale skeleton is nothing to write home about, which is why most sun-worshippers head for the El Piscina complex with its Olympic-sized swimming pool, sun-bathing terraces and kiddies play area. But there are also rock pools big

enough to swim in, and the coastal path west leads to some interesting curios, such as Buenavista del Norte's unusual lighthouse and a large rock arch.

After dark
There's not a lot going on, a handful of low-key local bars with life revolving around the plaza.

Where we'd stay
Apart from apartments and traditional houses there are a couple of contrasting hotel options in, or close to Los Silos.

Luz Del Mar (*Avenida Sibora 10; +34 922 841 623; www.luzdelmar.de*) Located at the coast in Puertito and frequented predominantly by German hikers, this four star hotel has mini apartments and rooms and a heated swimming pool. A small spa and gym, both included in the room price, have massages available at extra cost. Good for a quiet getaway, but you might get bored if you book in for a week.

Casa Amarilla (*La Caleta de Interián; +34 607 468 445; www. fincacasamarilla.com*) The 18th century former home of the sugar refinery manager set in a sea of banana plants at the foot of the Teno Mountains in La Caleta, is rustically charming and provides an elegant base from which to explore the area. Furniture and furnishings are in period style and only suites have a TV set. Tranquillity dominates.

Best time to visit
Early December sees fairytale figures, giant spiders and various 'Grimm' characters decorating the Plaza and the Convent of San Sebastián as Los Silos plays host to one of Tenerife's most unusual festivals. The Festival Internacional Del Cuento (International Storytelling Festival) attracts children from across the island to lend their ears and their imaginations to storytellers from all corners of the globe. After dark, the tales grow more eerie and erotic as the adult folk stories unfold to tickle the goosebumps … and the parts other stories cannot reach.

Late September is probably the best time of all. It still feels like summer, but with fewer people around once the Spanish summer holidays are over (mid September). It's also when the Boreal International Festival is held at Puertito de Los Silos. This celebration of sustainability and the relationship with the sea brings cultural events, live music, artisan stalls, and a lot of neo-hippies to this small town in the north west.

PUERTO DE LA CRUZ

Where is it and what's it like?

Puerto de la Cruz, on the north coast, is the only town on Tenerife which has all the amenities of a tourist resort yet is resolutely Canarian in character.

For centuries its location at the foot of the Orotava Valley attracted scientists, explorers and authors (Agatha Christie set her short story 'The Man from the Sea' in Puerto). Nowadays Northern Europeans escaping dreary winters and seeking a dose of culture as well as warm weather, boost the population between November and April. During the summer months, Spanish mainlanders descend en masse adding a 24/7 joie de vivre to the town's streets.

On the coast, Puerto is split into two halves. The area stretching east from Punta del Viento on Calle de Zamoro to Playa de Martiánez is the newer part of town. But Puerto's heart lies in the squares and cobbled streets of the old town to the west of Punta del Viento. Wander along the harbour during early morning as fishermen bring their catches ashore and elderly gents in fedoras play cards loudly, through Plaza del Charco at dusk when families from grandmothers to toddlers congregate to socialise, or along the narrow streets of the fishermen's quarter, and it won't take long to discover what sets Puerto apart from other resorts.

What's the story?

Prior to the Spanish conquest of Tenerife, a small community of Guanche occupied caves in the cliffs of Martiánez on the eastern edge of the harbour and archaeological remains suggest the existence of a necropolis. In 1502 life revolved around the harbour which was frequented by maritime traffic but the population was centred around La Orotava and the port was known as the Port of Orotava. By 1588 it was being referred to as Puerto de la Cruz and in 1603 a church was constructed on the headland, establishing Puerto as a centre in its own right. It took almost fifty more years before Puerto was able to extricate itself from the control of La Orotava and it became independent in May 1651. At one point it was known as a British settlement and two of its mayors were actually Irish.

Although already an important port for the export of sugar to European markets and the import of manufactured goods, in the second half of the 16th century the cultivation and export of wine began to gain economic importance, nudging sugar from the top spot and placing Puerto, from where the top quality wines of La Orotava were exported, at the forefront of the new prosperity. Now a tempting target for pirates, the coastal defences were augmented and the San Felipe fortress and Santa Bárbara battery were constructed.

The destruction of Garachico's harbour in 1706 served to strengthen Puerto's position even more and although the General Command moved to Santa Cruz in 1723 and instigated a programme of prioritising maritime traffic through that port instead, evidence suggests Puerto remained the busier port for a further 25 years. As the century unfolded, a decline in the wine market in England which had cast aside Canary wine in favour of the Portuguese newcomer, coupled with restrictions on maritime traffic to anywhere other than Santa Cruz, led to a recession which prevailed until the 1860s when new markets emerged in bananas and cochineal. Although cochineal's success was short-lived as synthetic dyes were developed, the trade in bananas has continue to the present day.

The 1880s saw the emergence of Tenerife's first steps into the world of tourism and Puerto de la Cruz really does deserve the title of Tenerife's first tourist resort as scientists, botanists and explorers began to arrive, as well as the elite of Victorian England who over-wintered in the newly built Gran Hotel Taoro which was quickly followed by the Marquesa, Monopol, Tremearne and Turnbull hotels as well as numerous inns.

The opening of the Los Rodeos airport in 1946 opened the way for a tourism boom throughout the 1950s and 60s. When the Reina Sofia airport opened in 1978, siphoning mass tourism south, Puerto retained a core of loyal return visitors.

Who'd want to stay here?

Whether families or couples, Puerto de la Cruz should suit visitors who want to stay in a traditional Canarian town but also want many of the amenities associated with a holiday resort. It is possible to have very different holiday experiences in Puerto. Those who follow the local patterns of dining later at every meal time, staying out late and getting up late, will experience a very different town from those who don't.

The food scene

With over three hundred restaurants to choose from, there's almost too much choice in Puerto de la Cruz. Canarian restaurants dominate, but there are plenty of other interesting gastronomic options as well. If you don't eat meat, Puerto de la Cruz is one of the best places for vegetarians on Tenerife. There's been a rise in contemporary Canarian restaurants over the last decade and now the streets of La Ranilla (the fishermen's quarter) to the west of Plaza del Charco are home to some excellent modern Canarian restaurants as well as dependable, traditional ones.

Where we'd eat

Contemporary Canarian - Up there with the best restaurants on the island, **El Taller Seve Diaz** is for foodies who like to experience new taste sensations rather than be comforted by old favourites. The food is inventive rather than avant-garde, so not too 'out there'. We've enjoyed the likes of pig cheeks on mushroom and pumpkin risotto, and salmon coated in poppy seeds served with El Hierro pineapple, fennel and celeriac. Best option for a full range of flavours is the tasting menu. *Calle San Felipe 32; +34 822 25 75 38; open 19:30-23:00 Wednesday to Friday, 13:30-15:00 and 19:30-23:00 Saturday, 13:30-15:00 and 19:30-22:30 Sunday, closed Monday & Tuesday; average cost of a main meal is €17.*

Contemporary Canarian - Run by a sweet young couple, **Tasca Ihuey** is a rising star of Puerto's restaurant district, La Ranilla. The menu is select which is just as well as everything on it (e.g. mushrooms in prawn ravioli) sounds delicious. The dishes we've tried have always exceeded expectation. *Calle San Felipe 34; 0034 922 984 773; open 19:00-22:30 Thursday & Friday, 13:00-15:00 and 19:00-22.30 Saturday & Sunday, closed Monday to Wednesday; average cost of a main meal is €12.*

Fish & seafood - Fishermen's guild restaurants tend to be *the* places on Tenerife to try the freshest local fish and seafood. Puerto's **Cofradía de Pescadores** is the poshest on the island with lovely views over the town harbour. Don't expect anything fancy; the fish usually comes with head and tail intact, which actually makes it easier to identify. Their mixed fish grill is good value. *Calle Las Lonjas, 5; +34 922 383 409; open 13:00-23:00 daily; average cost of a main meal is €10.*

Traditional - **Meson Los Gemelos** is a bit of a rare breed, a Canarian restaurant in the centre of Puerto de la Cruz which is as popular with locals as it is with visitors. The formula for its success is good quality, basic, traditional meat and fish dishes at low prices. As they don't take reservations, expect to have to queue for a table. *Calle el Peño, 4; +34 922 370 133; open daily midday-23:00, closed Wednesday; average cost of a main meal is €10.*

Contemporary Canarian - Located inside a 17th century mansion, **Tito's Bodeguita** is one of the most exquisite looking restaurants in Puerto de la Cruz. It's situated on the border with La Orotava, so a taxi ride or long walk is required to reach it, but it's worth the effort. The food, contemporary traditional, is as wonderful as the surrounding. The *capricho de pollo* (crispy chicken in an almond sauce) is many people's favourite, us included.
Camino del Durazno 1; +34 647 933 433; open 12.30-23:00, closed Sunday; average cost of a main meal is €14.

Why visit

Originally called the Jardín de Aclimatación de La Orotava, the Jardín Botánico in La Paz (*open 09:00-18:00; small entrance fee*) was originally established in 1788 as an acclimatisation garden for specimens en route to the royal gardens in Madrid. Unfortunately, for Madrid but not Tenerife, many plants weren't suited to the climate on the Spanish mainland, and so the gardens blossomed in their own right. This is a lush 'Lost World' of giant strelitzias, emerald foliage, leafy paths leading past lily ponds, and exotic plants like the 'drunken' and 'sausage' trees. It's a tranquil oasis to while away a few relaxing hours, but watch out for the enormous, ancient Moreton Bay fig which is said to eat tourists after dark.

Designed by César Manrique, Costa Martiánez (*open 10:00-19:00 daily; the entrance fee includes sun lounger and mattress, parasol extra*) is one part open air art gallery, three parts swimming pool complex. Abstract sculptures add a unique style to the plunge pools, Jacuzzi, children's and lake-sized swimming pools below towering palms which run almost the entire length of the town's promenade. After dark the town's casino, under the main pool, opens its doors for would-be James Bonds.

One of Tenerife's most enduring tourist attractions is Loro Parque (*www. loroparque.com*). Set in tropical gardens, animal enclosures are mostly spacious and designed to replicate their inhabitant's natural environment, although the parrots which first brought fame to the park have been somewhat relegated to a sideshow. Nowadays the main draws are the ethically dodgy orca, dolphin and sea lion shows, and Planet Penguin; a simulated iceberg where it actually snows. The topic of orcas, and other animals, being held in captivity is somewhat of a hot potato, with varying views and opinions for and against. We personally wouldn't visit the park now, although we did on a number of occasions in the past, but neither are we comfortable with some of the questionable reports criticising the treatment of animals there. In the end, do the research and decide for yourself.

On the beach

The César Manrique-designed black sand beach of Playa Jardín stretches from the Castillo San Felipe to Punta Brava. Brits and Germans use the sunbeds at the rear of the beach while Spanish and Italians decamp on the sand closer to the shoreline. Waves here can pack a punch; great fun for fearless swimmers, less so if you lack confidence in the water.

At the eastern end of town, Playa Martiánez is a smaller black sand beach mostly favoured by surfers.

In between is the harbour beach, a pebbly affair used mostly by locals and Spanish mainlanders in summer. There's another sheltered, pebble beach at Playa San Telmo beside the Costa Martiánez swimming pool complex. Again, this is more popular with locals, especially in summer when rock pools are exposed.

After dark

Plaza Charco is the place to chill early evening; it's a hive of bustling activity and the bars surrounding the plaza couldn't be better positioned for those with a passion for people-watching.

Many locals don't come out to play until midnight when bars in the streets of the old town, especially around Calle Iriarte and along Calle La Hoya, fill to near bursting point. The pick of these is Blanco Bar, a sleek, chic, live music venue; and Limbo, a lively rooftop bar further along Calle Blanco from Blanco Bar, with good music, occasional live bands and drinks promotions.

Where we'd stay

Puerto's hotels simply don't match the new breed of affordable, luxury hotels in the south. There are good hotels for varying budgets, and hotels we like, but none that we really get excited about.

Hotel Botanico (*C/ Richard Yeoward 1; +34 902 080 000; www. hotelbotanico.com*) offers old fashioned luxury and top notch service in one of the north's finest hotels. Situated in the La Paz district alongside the botanical gardens, with views across the fertile La Orotava Valley, Thai themed décor within leads to magnificent gardens and an elegant pool outside. Lots of dining choices on the doorstep as well as very good on-site restaurants. Fabulous spa facilities consistently rated amongst the best in Europe.

Hotel Tigaiga (*Parque Taoro, +34 922 383 500; www.tigaiga.com*) is located above the town in Puerto de la Cruz, alongside the former Hotel Taoro and in the lovely park of the same name. A quiet, family owned, elegantly styled and environmentally friendly hotel with that rarest of pleasures – waiter service at dinner. Fabulous views, gorgeous gardens and excellent staff.

Best time to visit

With fiestas of one sort or another taking place every month, from contemporary to celebrations steeped in Guanche tradition, Puerto lays claim to being the fiesta capital of Tenerife. The embarkation of the Virgen del Carmen during the July Fiestas and the beach party and goat bathing of the Fiestas of San Juan in June provide some of the most colourful pageants, but it's the town's carnival (Feb/March) which is the main extravaganza of the year.

A whirlwind week of flamboyant processions and surreal events includes the 'Burial of the Sardine' and the 'Mascarita Ponte Tacon' (an outrageous drag marathon not for the easily offended). The soul of carnival lies in the street parties which take place nightly around Plaza Charco. From midnight to dawn, thousands of revellers in fancy dress salsa their way through the streets. To really experience carnival, it's essential to dress up; it makes the world of difference.

Our favourite time is the summer months when the Spanish descend and bring an extra buzz to the town. Winter months, apart from carnival, tend to be quieter, with the local population boosted by mainly more mature Northern European visitors.

SAN JUAN DE LA RAMBLA

Where is it and what's it like?

The village of San Juan de la Rambla, halfway between Icod de los Vinos and Puerto de la Cruz, is one of the very few places left on Tenerife's coast that is completely unspoiled by tourism. That's not by design, judging by the political slogans that adorned walls and occasionally streets in the past, but rather by negligence and a lack of funds on the part of the local town hall. Adding to its woes is the fact that you can't rejoin the TF42 from the Puerto de la Cruz end of the village, well, not without risking a collision, thus making it a sort of cul de sac.

The pretty plaza surrounding the Church of San Juan de Bautista is lined with 16th and 17th century examples of traditional Canarian architecture with carved wood balconies. Unfortunately, many of them are in a state of decay and in need of restoration. Apart from that, there's nothing other than the church to detain you in the plaza, no café tables and chairs from which to contemplate life and the locals.

But head down the hill at the Puerto de la Cruz side of town and you'll find yourself in the cove of Las Aguas which has no less than two restaurants of island-wide acclaim for their speciality rice dishes.

What's the story?

Following the Spanish conquest, the municipality is credited with being founded by Martín Rodríguez, a Portuguese settler who, in 1530, built the first church here, dedicated to San Juan Bautista (St John the Baptist). Rodriguez' family and descendants settled the rich agricultural lands around the church and, along with several other families attracted by the quality of the soil and the temperate climate, formed the nucleus of the first population in what was known as San Juan del Malpaís.

In the 16th century the lowlands were used to cultivate vines, the highlands to cultivate wheat, both crops so important to the economy that wills written here often included a clause requiring an offering of one or both at the funeral. By the middle of that century, the main coastal population centres of San Juan and La Rambla de los Caballos became known collectively as San Juan de la Rambla.

In 1925, King Alfonso XIII granted the area the title of Villa de San Juan de la Rambla.

Who'd want to stay here?

Anyone who wants a very tranquil base in one of the most scenic parts of Tenerife's north coast.

The food scene

Generally speaking San Juan de la Rambla is not a place where people would go to seek out restaurants, but the Las Aguas part of town on the coast is. Thanks to one restaurant in particular, Las Aguas has become known for *los arroces* (rice) and *cazuelas* (casseroles).

Where we'd eat

Speciality Fish & seafood - The owners of **Las Aguas**, in the coastal *barrio* of the same name, believe that a table without rice is like "a mass without a sermon, or a woman without love." Their signature dish of *calduset* (rice with seafood) has brought customers flocking to them for twenty years. There is a range of *arroces* and *cazuelas* to choose from, each for two people. *Calle La Destila 20; +34 922 360 428; open 13:00-15:30 daily, and also 19:30-22:00 Wednesday to Saturday; average cost of arroces for two is €22.*

Fish & seafood - **La Escuela**, Las Aguas' charming former schoolhouse, also specialises in rice and casserole dishes, but has a wider range of fish and seafood dishes. Its outdoor terrace has been widened making the restaurant perfect for people who like good views with their seafood. *Camino de los Alenes, s/n; +34 922 360 438; open 12:30-20:00 Wednesday & Thursday, 12:30-22:00 Friday & Saturday, 12:30-18:00 Sunday, closed Monday & Tuesday; average cost of a main meal is €12.*

Why visit

As well as having some fine examples of 17th and 18th century colonial buildings, San Juan is the starting point for a great little coastal walk which passes old *haciendas* before arriving at the quirky little hamlet of El Rosario. Head briefly inland from El Rosario and you reach the Barranco de Ruiz *zona recreative,* which is the starting point for a hiking route which ascends the lush ravine. On the western edge of the ravine is the Mirador de Mazapé, a white elephant of a viewpoint due to it's remote position. Since it was built in 2005, three restaurants have tried and failed. In 2018 it was announced the Mirador would be turned into an *albergue*, a hostel for hikers. The hostel was due to be finished in 2020 ... as long as nothing went wrong. We all know what happened next.

On the beach
The pebble beaches at Las Aguas are unremarkable, and uncomfortable. More charming is the Charco de la Laja, a natural rock swimming pool with concrete sunbathing area on the western edge of town.

After dark
It's quiet enough during the day, after dark ...

Where we'd stay
Accommodation in San Juan de la Rambla is extremely limited, so we wouldn't stay. There is a hostel in the town for anyone who wants budget. Apart from that, there's the **Finca San Juan** (*Mazapé, 3; +34 922 694 078; www. finca-san-juan.com*) in the hills above the town.

Best time to visit
The town's big celebrations are during the fiesta de San Juan Bautista towards the end of June. Houses are decorated in preparation for the week-long festivities which include the usual processions accompanied by local bands. The end of the fiesta is marked by the 'Papada's day', when all the townspeople get together in the main square for a grand community feast. The most magical feature of the fiesta is when little bonfires are lit all the way along the path leading up the hill behind the town and balls of straw are set alight and rolled down the hillside leaving a trail of burning embers. UK health and safety officers would have apoplexy.

SANTA ÚRSULA

Where is it and what's it like?
Set 300 metres above Tenerife's north coast a mere five minute drive from Puerto de la Cruz, Santa Úrsula is a small working town with a penchant for good food; the right soil and conditions for producing good wines, and a surprisingly large British ex-pat population.

As recently as 50 years ago, this area was covered in palm groves, vines, bananas and fruit trees with just the church, parochial house and a few farmers' cottages to mark the position of the village. Today the Carretera Provincial which runs through its centre, linking the historic hill towns of the north from the old capital of La Laguna to La Orotava and Teide, is lined with a healthy selection of shops, family-run restaurants and '*se vende vino*' (wine for sale) signs from the small harvests which occupy every inch of cultivated land.

The Santa Úrsula referenced in travel company blurb tends to be the housing development creeping across the headland at La Quinta. There are fabulous views above the north coast here, but it is mostly a characterless place. The real Santa Úrsula is the traditional town which lies immediately on the other side of the TF5 motorway, where roads climb steeply from behind the main street into the upper reaches of the municipality. Of all the Comarca de Acentejo towns (Tacoronte, El Sauzal, La Matanza, La Victoria) Santa Úrsula has the most thriving shopping and commercial centre, possibly because it has more of an obvious centre than some of the other towns. Like the others, as a working hill town, it isn't the prettiest but it is good for food and wine. Towards the coast there is a different face to Santa Úrsula; aside from the housing development, much of this part of the municipality remains untouched *malpaís*, like Barranco Hondo whose cliffs provide sanctuary for seabirds like the shearwater and whose valley floor is carpeted in the lush palm groves that were once prevalent throughout this area.

What's the story?

In pre-Hispanic times, this north westerly area of Tenerife was part of the most important Guanche kingdom on the island – Taoro – which was led by the powerful Mencey Bencomo. Archaeological remains show it to have been the home of Bencomo himself, the Cueva de Bencomo, or Cueva del Rey (King's Cave) is set high into the cliffs above the *barranco* making it difficult to access.

Not a particularly fertile area, following the Spanish conquest, the lands in Santa Úrsula were given to lower ranking contributors to the conquest and were used primarily for the cultivation of cereals and vines, the malvasia grapes growing particularly well, producing high quality wine for export to Britain. By the 17th century, potatoes had been introduced to the terraces and were also growing well.

The collapse of the wine trade led to severe hardship from the middle of the 17th century onwards, with crops of cereals and potatoes unable to sustain the population economically. With traditional livestock-rearing long since driven out by the need to plant more vines and, exacerbated by floods, tropical storms, and epidemics of plague, the population diminished throughout the 18th- and early 19th centuries. The introduction of cochineal in the mid 19th century helped to alleviate some effects of recession but its economic success was short-lived as synthetic dyes displaced it from the market.

It wasn't until bananas began to be cultivated at the end of the 19th century, followed by the arrival of tourism in the 20th century, that Santa Úrsula's fortunes rallied.

Historically being at the hub of transport, Santa Úrsula was an obligatory stop on the mid nineteenth century Santa Cruz to La Orotava horse-drawn carriage route; the horses were rested at Cuesta de la Villa, and in 1902 it was on the first bus route on the island which ran from La Laguna to La Orotava.

Who'd want to stay here?

If you want a quiet, traditional area and a good base for exploring the north coast then Santa Ursula ticks those boxes. The traditional part doesn't apply to La Quinta, but it does have great views along the coast.

The food scene

Santa Úrsula has a reputation on the island as being home to numerous good restaurants, especially around Cuesta de la Villa on the old road to La Orotava. The Torres family dominates this area, with three excellent restaurants (El Lagar de Mario, El Calderito de la Abuela, and La Bodeguita de Enfrente) offering different takes on traditional cuisine. Our favourites are La Bodeguita de Enfrente and El Calderito de la Abuela.

Where we'd eat

Traditional - La Bodeguita de Enfrente looks like a small cottage from the outside but is actually made up of a series of cosily attractive rooms, some with intimate little dining booths. The place positively buzzes at weekends, unsurprisingly as it's got a taste-bud teasing *picoteo* menu (basically big tapas) which includes such delights as *cherne* drizzled with *mojo rojo* and *mojo verde* on a bed of sweet potato. *Ctra Provincial del Norte 205; +34 922 302 760; open 18:00-22:30 Friday, 13:00-16:00 and 18:00-22:30 Saturday to Tuesday, closed Wednesday & Thursday; tapas cost around €7.50.*

Traditional - Another bustling restaurant, **El Calderito de la Abuela** is rammed with locals at weekends. Like other restaurants belonging to the family, the food is traditional Canarian with a bit more verve than usual. Apart from serving good looking, tasty local food, this is in an excellent position for sunset dining so be sure to reserve a window seat in advance. *Ctra Provincial del Norte 130, +34 922 301 918; open 13:00-16:30 and 18:00-22:30 Wednesday to Sunday, closed Monday & Tuesday; average cost of a main meal is €9.*

Why visit

When in 1799 Alexander von Humboldt was wowed as he looked over the La Orotava Valley, he noticed how the vegetation adapted to the conditions from coastal to upper levels and thus began the science of geo-botany. The vegetation today is largely covered by banana plantations and the valley's housing developments but Mirador de Humboldt is still a great vantage point. Although it is located in La Orotava, it's slightly closer to the centre of Santa Úrsula. The fiasco surrounding Humboldt's Mirador illustrates how business on Tenerife can be terribly frustrating. Millions of Euros (much of it funded by the EU) were invested in the project over a period of 11 years between 1999 and 2010 when the viewpoint, restaurant and cafe opened. By 2014 it was closed due to contractual irregularities on the part of the company managing it. It stayed closed for six years until all legal shenanigans were finally resolved. There are also plans to make the Cueva de Bencomo, just behind the *mirador*, more of a feature.

Although we're not fans of La Quinta, there are some stunning vistas from the cliffs there, especially from Mirador de la Quinta, which is just above a military bunker set into the cliffs. Our favourite attraction in Santa Úrsula is also to be found in La Quinta. La Giganta is a delightful and magical 4m tall stone and floral statue in el Jardín Social de La Quinta.

On the beach

Although there are ancient trails leading to unspoilt ravines and secluded coves along Santa Úrsula's coastline, recent urbanisation has meant that finding them can prove more taxing than cracking the Da Vinci Code. Two hundred yards before Café Vista Paraíso, a passage leads to a path which meanders through glorious countryside to La Orotava's trio of beaches. Beyond La Quinta Park Hotel, a woodland track dissecting a row of trees emerges at four wonderful mature drago trees. Across the bridge over the TF5 at the end of Camino Malpaís, one 'dead end' road from the roundabout leads to the historic Ermita of San Clemente, whilst on the other, a trail descends through the Barranco Hondo to a small beach; a perfect spot for appreciating why the Acentejo coastline was once considered to be one of the most beautiful natural areas of the island.

After dark

There are quite a few decent local bars to be found in Santa Úrsula, and some can be quite stylish and contemporary in design; great if you're seeking an authentic bar scene, but anyone hoping for a Brits abroad vibe should look elsewhere.

Where we'd stay

Like the other towns which form Acentejo, most accommodation is in apartments and villas/cottages, with those on the coastal side of the municipality being more villa-like whilst those further up the hill are more likely to be traditional. Unlike its neighbours, Santa Úrsula does at least have a hotel, **Spa**

Aparthotel La Quinta Park (*+34 922 300 266; Urbanizacion La Quinta s/n; www.laquintaparksuites.com*) but it's a trek to the actual town if you don't have a car.

Best time to visit

Given its position, spring and summer especially would be the best times to enjoy Santa Úrsula.

TACORONTE

Where is it and what's it like?

At 500 metres above Tenerife's north coast, Tacoronte has three main distinctions as far as Canarios are concerned; it's considered to have the island's best restaurants, its best wine and its worst weather. If it's cold or raining anywhere on Tenerife, it's likely to be in Tacoronte.

Constantly bustling, this historic Canarian town has more 'real' shops on its main street than there are in the whole of Playa de Las Américas and Costa Adeje. You can find just about anything you want or need in its proliferation of supermarkets, shops, furniture stores, extensive agricultural market and its *bodega* where they produce the award winning Viña Norte label.

Before the 20th century, Tacoronte was one of the stops on the stagecoach route for the north of Tenerife and anyone wishing to explore the island, including Alexander Von Humboldt and Richard Burton, passed through here. Today it's home to many Santa Cruz and La Laguna commuters whose large rambling houses hide behind leafy *avenidas* or cluster along the slopes above the coastline.

Exploring Tacoronte's unassuming, yet beautifully preserved old quarter via cobbled walkways uses just enough energy to justify lunch and a bottle of locally produced wine in one of its restaurants before heading down to its coast for an afternoon on the beach – the sort of day very few British visitors ever experience.

What's the story?

The municipality of Tacoronte was one of the original nine kingdoms of the Guanche, the natives who inhabited the island before its conquest in the fifteenth century. Their king, Acaymo, was known for his bravery and he aligned himself with five *menceys* (kings) who fought to protect the island from the Spanish invaders, led by Alonso Fernández de Lugo. Many of Tacoronte's citizens were involved in the defeat of the Spanish conquistadors at La Matanza de Acentejo in 1494.

The brave tradition of Tacoronte's people was again brought into service in the eighteenth century when the infantry regiment stationed in the town helped to repel the attack of Santa Cruz by the British Navy under the command of Admiral Nelson.

The settlement of modern day Tacoronte was founded by Sebastián Machado, a Portuguese mercenary who fought alongside Alonso de Lugo during the conquest and was rewarded with a large piece of land. In 1508 he founded the small Ermita of Santa Catalina Mártir around which the town grew.

Who'd want to stay here?

Tacoronte is one of Tenerife's unsung locations. The historic centre is more expansive than many realise. There are some very good restaurants, mostly frequented by Canarios, to both east and west of the town, and it has a nice little coastal route leading to an off-the-beaten-track, black sand beach. Most importantly, it's in the heart of Tenerife wine country, so a good base for wine and culture lovers.

The food scene

The stretch of road between Tacoronte and La Laguna is the area known as Los Naranjeros, an area known for good restaurants, but not amongst visitors. Even the former King of Spain, Juan Carlos, dined here during some visits. At the coast, food is as simple as it gets. Restaurants in El Pris serve mountains of small shrimps still in their shells – *camarones*.

Where we'd eat

Upmarket traditional – The choice for kings and queens is **Los Limoneros** whose upmarket menu of Spanish classics featured the most expensive starter (€115) we've seen in a restaurant on Tenerife. The prices of other dishes aren't quite as eyebrow raising but this is for people who like old-school elegant dining (think rose petals on white linen tablecloths). *Calle General Del Norte 432; +34 922 636 637; open 12:30-22:30, closed Sunday evening; average cost of a main course is €25.*

Traditional - At the other end of the scale is **El Calvario** (Casa Pepe) beside the little park and shrine of the same name. Dining here is more like a *guachinche*-type experience. There are no rose petals on the tablecloths, come to think of it, there are no tablecloths, but the food's good, plentiful and cheap. Meats from the grill are the speciality, especially chicken. They also like their kiwi fruit here, so you find it served with chicken as well as in salads. *Calle El Calvario 65; +34 922 563 734; open 10:00-22:00 Wednesday to Saturday, 10:00-18:00 Sunday, closed Monday & Tuesday), average for a main meal €8.*

Why visit

Move away from the workaday main street near the TF5 motorway and into the more tranquil lower town to discover an old quarter with some picturesque spots. Looking over the town's main plaza is the 17th century Santuario del Santísimo Cristo de los Dolores. This is where, during Corpus Christi, the best flower carpets after those of La Orotava and La Laguna are laid. From the plaza Calle de Jose Izquierdo descends through the Hamilton Gardens where you can see different ways vines are grown in the Canary Islands. The lane emerges at the 17th century Calvario (crucifixes) and former grain store of La Alhondiga which is now used as a cultural centre. For fans of religious architecture, head west along Calle del Calvario to reach the 16th century Iglesia de Santa Catalina, a church which rarely gets a mention in guidebooks but which is one of the best examples of religious architecture on the island.

Also to be spotted on the old streets are references to Tenerife's most famous artist Óscar Domínguez who, although born in La Laguna, spent his childhood in Tacoronte with his grandmother. The main example is found on Carretera Gral - a drago tree encased in metal featuring Domínguez's trademark use of a sardine can with rolled-back opener.

On the beach

On the coast below the town are the settlements of El Pris and Mesa del Mar with a nice, if brief, coastal walk linking the two.

Very much a fishing village, El Pris doesn't have any beach to speak of but it has a large open-air rock pool which is great for swimming, and two or three no-frills seafood restaurants serving excellent fish and seafood.

Along the coast, boardwalks and decking provide sunbathing areas around more rock pools and a large swimming pool at Mesa del Mar. Ugly, run down, high-rise apartment blocks dominate the front and spread along the promontory looking like the desolate end of the road. But head through the tunnel and you'll emerge onto the black sand bay of Playa de la Arena from where the concrete sprawl is pleasantly hidden. There are no facilities or lifeguard but there's a café at the back of the beach and a restaurant at the camp site on the hill.

After dark

Bars are of the very traditional Canarian variety with most being located around the modern centre of Tacoronte. Cultural events take place in the older part of town at the main plaza.

Where we'd stay

There's a choice of attractive old houses and cottages to rent in and around Tacoronte. It's not hotel territory, but there is one.

Hotel Emblemático Casa Casilda (*+34 660 345 633; Calle Calvario 53; www.canariasesverde.com/hotel-emblematico-casa-casilda*) is a boutique rural hotel in a 300 year old house located in Tacoronte's historic quarter. There are just five double bedrooms, each designed individually. Three are in traditional style, two are contemporary. The house also has lovely gardens, splendid views and vegetarian breakfast options.

Best time to visit

As this is very much wine country, the best time to visit is during the *vendimia* (wine harvest) which takes place during September. There is usually a programme of wine-themed events taking place during the month. September is also a lovely month on Tenerife, still very much the end of summer, and that can make all the difference somewhere like Tacoronte.

TEGUESTE

Where is it and what's it like?

An independent municipality, Tegueste is made up of two picturesque settlements, Tegueste and El Socorro. Sitting 200 metres above sea level in the humid Valle de Guerra it is an area known as Tenerife's greenhouse and is famed for its cultivation of tropical and ornamental plants. In this part of Tenerife are fields of bird of paradise flowers destined for the foyers of plush hotels in the south of the island.

Completely surrounded by the municipality of La Laguna, Tegueste is like an island, but without the sea, a factor which hasn't stopped it from being obsessed with boats. The volcanic soil and humid climate combine to produce delicious potatoes and plump, aromatic grapes which yield excellent wines. Hell-bent on preserving its agricultural heritage and its traditions, the municipality has a thriving agricultural market; a penchant for the national sport of *lucha canaria* wrestling and some of the most unusual and colourful fiestas on the island.

What's the story?

The name 'Tegueste' is the one given to the municipality by the Guanche, Tenerife's original inhabitants who originated from the Berber tribes of North Africa. The Guanche settlements in this area included a sizeable necropolis excavated into the walls of the Barranco Agua de Díos. Forming an alliance with their neighbours from Taoro, Tacoronte, Ycoden and Daute, the Tegueste Guanche fought against the Spanish invaders and, even after their resounding defeat in 1495 and the surrender of the island to the Spanish in 1496, Guanche rebels remained hidden in the mountains for more than 20 years.

Following the conquest, the invaders were given the rights to use land,

163

water and forests and there began a systematic conversion of the Guanche to Evangelism, baptising them into the Catholic faith and building churches across the island. This practice of allocating lands to foreigner investors continued for more than four centuries, creating lower status amongst the island's indigenous population. In Tegueste alone, only 20% of land was owned by *teguesteros* as late as 1862.

The first of Tegueste's settlements grew around the small church of San Marcus Evangelista in 1530 and, protected from the ravages of piracy and sea borne diseases due to its landlocked status, by 1629 the population had risen to 1307. In 1701 the little church of San Marcos was moved from its original site in El Llano, to its current location.

The town itself owes much of its development and traditions to one man, Prebendado Pacheco, the parish curate. Retiring to Tegueste in 1842, Pacheco spent the next sixteen years chronicling the culture, traditions and costumes of the community. When he wasn't penning its heritage, he was busy building Tegueste's Plaza de San Marcos, its first cemetery and his own house. And just to ensure his retirement was entirely null and void, he even set up a schoolroom in his home where he taught the village children to read and write, thus bringing literacy to the community.

Who'd want to stay here?

Tegueste offers more than it might seem at first glance. For a start you get the experience of staying in a traditional town in a scenic setting; the weather is good, hence the greenhouse tag; it's very convenient for visiting both La Laguna and Anaga; the coast is only a short drive away; and you get two towns for the price of one as Tegueste is virtually joined on to Tejina which, in August, has one of the most bizarre fiestas on the island – Corazones de Tejina (the Hearts of Tejina) where three giant hearts are made from fruit, vegetables, and pastry. Basically, Tegueste would suit those looking for culture, tradition, and hiking.

The food scene

Being the greenhouse of Tenerife you'd expect there to be a tasty gastronomic scene around Tegueste ... and there is. But there's a but. Every time we visit we find a restaurant we like. By the next time we visit it's gone; although there's always another interesting restaurant to be found. Currently there are great traditional restaurants and a couple of interesting contemporary ones. In twelve months time though ...

Where we'd eat

We've been accused in the past of overlooking Bodegón **Casa Tomas** located in El Portazuelo near the TF5 motorway. We don't overlook it, we simply don't understand why it's raved about. The food is traditional Canarian and good, but no different from countless other Canarian restaurants. For something different, it's worth checking if **Mesón El Drago** in El Socorro is still operating as a restaurant as it's located in an attractive colonial building. Also worth checking is the traditional house at Calle San Ignacio, 17. At the time of writing it's called **La Sandunga** and serves contemporary cuisine with a local flavour. Previously this was Casa Mi Suegra, so there's a legacy of very good food being found here ... whatever its name. There are also views right across the valley from the dining room.

Why visit

Tegueste is another of those historic Tenerife towns which remains below the radar of many visitors. It's worth a visit just to experience what is a pleasant traditional town in a rural setting.

There are three official walking routes which take in not only the historic parts of Tegueste, but also its rural surroundings; paths passing through palm groves and cane thickets; skirting orchards and vineyards; and following cobbled lanes such as the Camino de los Laureles which is lined by colonial houses. Unfortunately the trails aren't well marked so can be difficult to find.

The Mercado del Agricultor (*Avenida Asuncionistas, open 08:00-14:00 Saturday & Sunday*) is one of our favourite small markets on Tenerife. There are 34 stalls serving local produce and crafts. There are more impressive markets on Tenerife, but this one has more of a laid-back, friendly atmosphere to it.

One look at the neat rows of vines that carpet the hillsides in this area tells you you're not far from a spicy white or a smoky, vanilla red. Bodega El Lomo (*www.bodegaellomo.com*) produces wines from the Listán, Malvasia and Negromoll grapes from fresh whites to oak-aged reds. The *bodega* offers guided tours of the vines and the vaults, and various wine tasting options.

The Museo de Antropología de Tenerife (*MHAT; +34 900 546 300; www. museosdetenerife.org*) in nearby Valle de Guerra on the Tegueste to Tacoronte road has a fascinating and beautiful collection of artefacts chronicling 500 years of clothing and textiles, agriculture, ceramics, musical instruments and household objects set within an immaculately restored 18th century Manor House of Casa de Carta and its extensive grounds.

After dark

The nocturnal scene is the typically low-key affair found in small traditional towns, but being a wine area there are a handful of decent bars.

Where we'd stay

Like much of the north, accommodation is mostly in rural houses, apartments and villas. But there are some beautiful old houses to rent. For anyone seeking simple comforts, **Lagarto Backpackers House** (*Camino del Guincho, Valle de Guerra*) isn't too far from Tegueste.

Best time to visit

When, in the 17th century, bubonic plague infected the entire surrounding area, Tegueste remained disease-free; a 'miracle' credited to San Marcos. In thanks for his help, the town chose to build something that would require skills not hitherto held and thus, being landlocked, they built boats with billowing white sails. Every year on San Marcos' feast day (Sunday closest to 25 April) the town holds a *romería* in which the boats are pulled by oxen, along with carts ornately decorated with seeds and grain, the whole scene a sort of mobile work of art. The normally tranquil town becomes packed with Canarios in traditional dress for this lively and colourful fiesta.

Once every three years the *teguesteros* re-enact their part in keeping Santa Cruz safe from pirate attacks during the 17th century by staging a wonderfully colourful, night time pageant involving a full scale castle being erected in front of the Town Hall from which cannon and artillery defend the battlements against three galleons manned by pirates, Moors and the English. There are costumes, fireworks, animals and a very touching rendition of Ave Maria during which all the townsfolk hold aloft flaming torches and sparklers. The Librea is next due to be held in September 2023.

TEIDE NATIONAL PARK

Where is it and what's it like?

To the original inhabitants of Tenerife, the Guanche, it was the place where the earth held up the sky; to Columbus' crew of the Santa Maria in 1492, it was a bad omen, erupting as they passed it, but to 3.5 million people every year, Mount Teide represents the literal and symbolic highlight of their holiday.

Occupying the centre of the island, Teide National Park is largely above 2000m and is a stark, volcanic landscape. The unique rock formations resemble an almost lunar landscape and the colours of the rock run through almost all conceivable shades of red, brown and grey. This area is often above the cloud line and temperatures are generally lower in winter and higher at the height of summer.

The mid-zone includes the heavily forested slopes of Mount Teide. Here the landscape is changeable and thick forest is interspersed with volcanic landscapes, areas of black volcanic sand and deep valleys running down to the sea. This zone covers from around 1500m down to 500m and often the cloud line rests somewhere in this area. The weather here is changeable and mists can come in unexpectedly and rapidly causing a sudden drop in temperature and damp conditions underfoot.

An icon, not only of Tenerife but of the whole archipelago, Mount Teide stands in a 16 kilometre-wide crater known as Las Cañadas del Teide where, at 3718 metres above sea level, it's Spain's highest mountain and Europe's highest volcano. To most people, it's better known as Parque National del Teide (PN del Teide on road signs and maps) or Teide National Park. Owned by the municipality of La Orotava and so technically in the north, Las Cañadas del Teide is a surreal landscape of russet-coloured lava flows, orange volcanic cones, shiny black obsidian rivers, extraordinary rock formations standing proud above white pumice fields and towering crater walls beneath an iridescent blue sky. In winter snow covers the peak and lies in compacted ice on the crater floor and in spring Las Cañadas blossoms into a kaleidoscope of colour as the Teide violet, the white broom and the two metre-high crimson peaks of the *tajinaste* spikes come into flower.

Who'd want to stay here?

Anyone seeking an extra special experience will lap up spending a night or two in Teide National Park. It's an incredible place during the day, after dark when the crowds leave it is quite magical and humbling. We've stayed in the park a few times and each time find ourselves simply standing still, totally bewitched as darkness creeps across this volcanic world. Fellow guests at the Parador are mainly hikers and some of the world's top cycling teams.

167

Top: Roque Cinchado, bottom left: terrace at the Parador, bottom right: Minas de San Jose

The food scene

We're not the biggest fans of the food on offer inside Teide National Park save for that served in the restaurant of the **Parador de Las Cañadas del Teide** which is of a very good standard. The Los Roques café adjoining the Parador is a self-service style cafeteria and restaurant catering to an endless stream of coach parties and Lycra-clad cyclists clip-clopping over the flagstones in their cleated shoes. Prices here have you wondering why the staff aren't wearing stockings over their faces and the quality of what's on offer is inconsistent at best. Slightly better value and with equally spectacular views is the restaurant and bar/cafeteria of the cable car station which has a good range of offerings and the distinction of being Spain's highest eating establishment. There are other dining options near the northern end of the park, **Restaurant Papillon** and **Restaurant Teide**, but we have never had a drink at either, let alone eaten there as they are frequented by coach excursion after coach excursion.

Where we'd eat

Traditional - When we check our walking routes in the park, we tend to stay at the Parador and eat there. On day visits, our preferred stop for refreshments is **Restaurant Portillo** opposite the junction with the TF24 heading to La Laguna. It's still pricier than the average traditional bar/restaurant but it doesn't feel quite so much like a tourist processing centre.

Less crowded than restaurants (except at weekends), more wallet/purse friendly, and just an enjoyable thing to do if travelling by car is to bring a small picnic and enjoy it in the fragrant shade of the Chio or Las Lajas *zonas recreativas* (see p270).

Why visit

Because visiting this incredible UNESCO World Heritage Site is simply a travel 'must'.

Every tour company on the island offers the Teide experience which consists of taking the Cable Car to a height of 3555 metres above sea level; a rise of 1200 metres in eight minutes. It's not for serious vertigo sufferers but the rewards are breathtaking; views over the crater of Pico Viejo with Gran Canaria, La Palma, La Gomera and El Hierro floating on the horizon. You can walk to the summit of the mountain from the upper cable car station but you must have prior, written permission to do so. You can apply online for permission through the Teleférico website. The cable car operates between 09.00 and 17:00 and takes 7 minutes to ascend to the upper station from where you can walk north and south. Temperatures below the summit are cold even in summer so dress appropriately. On windy days the cable car will not operate, check the Teleférico website in advance to ensure it's running before you set off (*www.volcanoteide.com*). The cost of a return trip for non-residents is around €27.

For an extra special experience, take the cable car to witness sunset at 3555m above sea level. Restricted to 90 persons, the cable car will take you to the upper station where you will be met by a guide who will lead you to the Pico Viejo viewpoint to watch the sunset. Back at the cable car station you might just be in time to see the shadow of Mount Teide cast over the landscape below. Tickets cost around €50pp.

Second stop on the tour is the Roques de García (opposite the Parador at the southern end of the crater); spectacular volcanic dykes from which the wind has eroded the rock, leaving towering sculptures of solid magma that defy gravity by being skinny at the base and wide at the top. The stand-out, shillelagh-shaped, Roque Cinchado adorned the 1000 peseta note prior to the introduction of the Euro and is still the iconic image of the park. NB Theft from cars is a constant nuisance at Roques de Garcia, don't leave anything valuable in the car even for very short intervals.

Leave the crowds behind and head out on foot to explore this extraordinary landscape. Well signposted trails matrix Teide National Park and you can pick up a guide at the Visitor Centre at Portillo or buy our **Real Tenerife Island Walks** (*www.walkingtenerife.co.uk*) to download and print off at home.

For the ultimate challenge, set off from the base of Montaña Blanca to hike to Teide's summit for which you'll need a permit. It's a gruelling four and a half hour contest of you vs. altitude and fatigue to get to the Altavista Refuge and another hour and a half from there to the peak. By staying overnight at the refuge you eliminate the need for a permit provided you return from the peak before the first cable car at 09:00. Most climbers reach the peak for sunrise to watch Teide's shadow cast across the sea of clouds before catching the first cable car back down. Home comforts at the refuge run to a bunk bed, a table on which to rest your elbows, two toilets between 50 people and unless the temperature drops to minus seven or more, no heating. There are some parking spaces available in a small lay-by at the start of the walk to Montaña Blanca. Failing that, you might want to park at the cable car station so the car's there when you arrive back down next morning. Either way, it's a road trek between cable car and start of the walk.

After dark

Tenerife has been designated a Starlight Tourist Destination and a Starlight Reserve by the Starlight Foundation, a UNESCO supported body set up to protect the world's 'right to starlight'. The Starlight Reserve award is given to locations that successfully demonstrate a commitment to, and achievement of, low light pollution and clean skies which optimise our ability to see the night sky. The Starlight Tourist Destination award recognises locations that combine clean skies with good facilities for stargazing and its related cultural and scenic values - in short, places where you can enjoy the night sky while learning a little about what you're seeing as well as experiencing standout scenery and aspects of a location's culture.

An unforgettable way to experience both the drama of ascending Mount Teide and the beauty of the night sky is to take a Sunset & Tapas excursion which includes taking the cable car to 3555m to witness the sunset from Pico Viejo viewpoint followed by a guided stargazing session. Optional extras include a (meagre) picnic to be enjoyed back at cable car base level and pick-up from either the north or south of the island. Prices start from around €74 and can be booked online at *www.volcanoteide.com*

Where we'd stay

Camping within the boundaries of Teide National Park is strictly prohibited so for those who wish to enjoy the sunset, night skies and sunrise to themselves there are only three options: stay in Vilaflor and drive the short distance in and out of the park; stay at the Altavista Refuge (those who are climbing to Teide's summit) or stay at the Parador, the only hotel within the confines of the park.

Parador de Las Cañadas del Teide (*+34 922 38 64 15; www.parador.es/ en/paradores/parador-de-las-canadas-del-teide*) is quite possibly the hotel with the most unique location you will ever stay in, set at the foot of Alta Montaña, opposite the Roques de García and with Mount Teide at the bottom of the garden, well, metaphorically speaking. Lodge style hotel with a roaring log fire on winter nights, a nice bar and one of the clearest night skies on the planet. Rooms are clean and spacious if a tad unimaginative. The food is fab, the service is slow but who cares when you're staying here anyway, and the staff are friendly. It's not cheap, but neither is it outrageous for what is an 'out of this world' experience.

Best time to visit

Teide National Park WOWs every month of the year. It can be very, very cold in winter months, and very hot and dry in summer. There are two times we would avoid the park. The first is when the cloud is above Mount Teide's peak; the scenery doesn't have quite the same impact when the sky isn't intense blue. The second is immediately after snowfall. It is a winter wonderland when covered in snow, but the prospect of playing in the snow draws what seems like all the Canarios on the island and it gets absolutely manic. So much so, the government introduced a system which basically creates a one-way system in the park. You arrive by one road and have to leave by another. When you arrive from the north and have to return home via the south (or vice versa) it adds hours to the journey.

EAST TENERIFE

Arid, windy and sunny, the eastern side of the island is the least commercialised of Tenerife's coasts.

The busy TF1 motorway runs along its length from the island's capital city and port of Santa Cruz, to the southern coastal resorts of Los Cristianos and Playa de Las Américas. Around the motorway the landscape is characterised by *malpaís*; badlands of volcanic cones, pale pumice cliffs and dusty desert punctuated by industrial estates and power pylons. It's an ugly coast that for most visitors is only viewed from the window of a moving vehicle.

Motorway exits lead to the coastal towns of Candelaria and Puertito de Güímar, then to smaller settlements as the road travels further south. Outside of the vibrant, cosmopolitan Santa Cruz and the much quieter Candelaria, there are very few concessions to tourism along this coast. Around Eras, Poris and Abades characterless housing developments are springing up behind the windswept sand dunes with the occasional pizza restaurant and small supermarket but the area feels like a desolate construction site.

Beyond the rocky shore the outline of Gran Canaria shimmers on the horizon. Inland from the motorway, the white propellers of modern windmills bear testament to the near-constant winds that sweep this coast. Running parallel above the TF1, lining the old road that first joined north and south of the island, are now-forgotten rural settlements where people still till the soil by hand and store their products in caves, while in the upper reaches, virgin pine forests conceal a network of walking paths where you can amble all day without seeing another soul.

ARICO

Where is it and what's it like?

Located in the hills overlooking the south east coast, any route to Arico involves negotiating winding roads. Agriculture is the mainstay of the economy, predominantly potatoes and tomatoes grown in rows of neat *jable* terraces around the three towns of Villa de Arico, Arico Viejo and Arico Nuevo. Villa de Arico and Arico Viejo are typical of the farming communities found along the old road which linked Santa Cruz with the south of the island before the TF1 autopista was built in the early 70s. In Villa de Arico, the 18th century Iglesia de San Juan Bautista with its baroque façade and Portuguese-influenced bell dome towers is one of the most attractive churches on Tenerife; however neighbouring Arico Nuevo is the real surprise package in these hills. The tiny village is still

Left: Mencey statue,
Candelaria
173

something of a 'secret', and you get the impression that the locals are quite happy to keep it that way. It's a sleepy hollow built by wealthy landowners in the 18th century which still exudes an air of exclusivity.

It's easy to bypass the village as the old Carretera General barely skirts its boundaries. A narrow, cobbled road descends from the small car park at the top of the village, past whitewashed old houses with green window and door frames, to a quaint little square flanked by old buildings with lopsided roofs and the Iglesia de Nuestra Señora de la Luz. Narrow paths lead from the square beyond enticing wooden gates fronting leafy courtyards overlooked by rickety balconies. The only colour on many streets, apart from white and green, is provided by the luminescent petals of bougainvillea trailing over walls. Arico Nuevo is a perfectly preserved example of rural living in a bygone age.

What's the story?

Pre-conquest, Arico was part of the Abona *menceyate* (kingdom) of the island and the land was given over predominantly to the grazing of livestock while the Guanche lived in small cave villages in the barrancos of del Rio and Tamadaya from where they could easily access water.

After the conquest, the new colonists, consisting predominantly of Castilian and Portuguese along with some settlers from Gran Canaria, intermarried with the surviving Guanche and continued the legacy of livestock-rearing. At this time, the forests surrounding Arico underwent devastating deforestation in an attempt to meet the voracious appetites of house and ship-building and to supply resin for the production of tar. The port of Poris de Abona grew in importance as its role in the export of wood to other islands in the Archipelago and to the Peninsula grew.

Throughout the 18th and 19th centuries, the wealth created from its exports and an increase in the price of grain in the domestic market, resulted in the segregation of Arico's population, a minority of owners and large tenants monopolizing the large estates while the impoverished peasants struggled to access enough land for subsistence farming. As late as 1854, a quarter of the population still lived in caves.

Already forced to grow only those crops that needed little water, Arico's problems were further exacerbated in 1704 when the eruption of Siete Fuentes buried the area's main water spring. Farmers introduced cochineal production to the area in an effort to ward off the demise of their economy. The cochineal kept poverty at bay until the collapse of the market in 1870 when the consequent mass migration to Cuba in search of work decimated the local population, as it did in much of the archipelago.

The addition of potatoes and tomatoes to Arico's terraces brought renewed wealth as most production was bound for export. The annual temporary workforce required to harvest the new crops forced development of infrastructure in the region and a system of roads and trails was constructed to connect the central farming zones with the coast.

With economic progress hampered by the Civil War and then WWII, by the 1950s Arico had once again suffered mass emigration of its population, this time to Venezuela and to the Santa Cruz-La Laguna area in search of work. In the 1980s the emigration turned south, to the burgeoning tourist centres of Arona, Adeje and Granadilla but the opening of the TF1 motorway went some way to reversing the trend, allowing faster and easier commute and attracting people back to the coastal settlements of La Jaca, Tajao, Las Maretas and Las Eras.

Who'd want to stay here?

You get quite a good little package in and around Arico. It's Tenerife's second largest municipality even though many visitors have probably never heard of it. It has historic towns, good beaches, great cheese, and is mostly sunny. It is generally very quiet, and a car is essential. If that combination appeals then it might be the place for you.

The food scene

This area produces some of the tastiest cheeses in the world and that's official. Arico's goat cheeses, coated with paprika and *gofio*, have won gold medals at the World Cheese Awards. Deliciously smoky with a soft creamy texture and a hint of wild herbs, they're good enough to have Wallace and Gromit changing allegiance. Drizzled with fresh local honey, it's a case of love at first bite.

Restaurants around Arico (Arico Casco, Arico Nuevo, Arico Viejo) are simple, traditional affairs so there's not a lot to choose between most. Most of the best restaurants in the Arico municipality are to be found at the coast, especially fish restaurants in Tajao which has become known as the 'new' Los Abrigos amongst some of the British expat population. The most diverse choice of dining options is to be found at Abades where, as well as traditional, there are Italian restaurants, tapas, and even a vegetarian place.

Where we'd eat

Another of the restaurants whose name changes on a semi-regular basis, but whose location we love irrespective of whatever name it has at the time, is the one located in a lop-sided old building at the far end of Arico Nuevo's picturesque plaza. It's just such a lovely spot for lunch.

Why visit

Apart from Arico Nuevo arguably being the most picturesque small, inland town on Tenerife, and the lure of a people-free beach scene at the coast outside of summer months, part of Arico's attraction lies in the fact its three hillside towns are home to some of the island's most attractive churches.

Also of architectural and cultural interest is the hamlet of Icor located right beside the TF-28. It hasn't changed much since the 16th century and its honey-coloured buildings lay dormant for years, but there are signs of life returning to the old hamlet.

The abandoned leper colony at Abades is an eerie curio worth exploring, but maybe not after dark.

Arico has a wild side as well. The road leading into the mountains from Villa de Arico's church ends at a deep rift in the earth with plunging walls of golden rocks accentuated by ledges, chimneys and impossible looking overhangs. It's a natural theme park for rock climbers, considered one of the best areas for crag climbing in Europe.

On the beach

There are some lovely, quiet beaches and coves tucked away in the folds of the coastline which runs east toward Santa Cruz. Some like those at Tajao, Abades, and Punta de Abona are easy to find. Others lie hidden by rather unattractive small coastal villages; places which can be like ghost towns in winter months but come summer, they burst into life.

After dark

Much the same as similar small town areas on Tenerife; quiet and laid-back.

Where we'd stay

Arico is more of a day trip destination than a base for a holiday as there's an almost complete dearth of life in the villages, but for a true 'far from the madding crowd' experience, book into one of Arico Nuevo's *casas rurales*.

Best time to visit

The default setting for the east coast tends to be sunny, so it's good all year. However, coastal settlements have far more life in summer months with Canarios from Tenerife and other Canary Islands moving into their summer homes in the small villages found along the coast.

THE ABANDONED LEPER VILLAGE

For a long time we thought it was a developer's folly; a never-completed resort beside a quiet bay on Tenerife's breezy east coast. From a distance the buildings look like bare breeze block. It's only when you spot the naked structure of a church – not a normal resort ingredient – that you suspect all is not what it seems. When you get closer to the curious town and notice the breeze blocks are *jable* you realise this ghost town has stood empty for a lot longer than it might at first seem. This is a jilted bride waiting for a groom that is never coming.

The town with no name exudes a slightly disturbing air; probably thanks to an imagination fed by films about abandoned towns where no good lurks, or video games where you know at any moment some mutant creature is going to leap from a shadowy doorway and go for your throat. The other strange thing about the ghost town is that it sits like a shadow beside what actually is a newish development at Abades on Arico's coast. If anything, with its church, the ghost town looks more like a real town than the small settlement below it, which has the appearance of an out-of-place housing scheme. Despite the presence of the nearby development combined with sandy coves that are about as inviting as any you'll find on Tenerife, few people walk these empty streets. Possibly that's got something to do with the ghost town's past. To call it an abandoned town is not technically correct as it was never actually populated. Maybe it retains a stigma as potent as that which affected the people who were meant to live there. This is a leper colony that never was.

The idea was conceived toward the end of the Spanish Civil War. This part of Tenerife's arid, windswept east coast was considered ideal as a location for housing Spain's lepers at a time when the disease was rampant; there were 200 cases on Tenerife alone. Nobody lived here. The big centres of population lay to the north, so it was conveniently out of the way. The plan was that a village colony be constructed, to be managed by Franco's military. Everything was almost in place ... just as scientists discovered Dapsone, a drug that revolutionised treatment and changed the world for those people suffering from leprosy. The leper colony was no longer needed.

Now it sits impassively above Abades; a Mary Celeste of a town with houses, barracks and buildings that look as though they were designed to house shops. There are broken beds in box rooms, exposed wires and bad graffiti everywhere. Exploring its empty streets and maze of interlinking corridors really does feel like you've stumbled across a 'The Walking Dead' scenario. What it's like after dark I can't say. And what's more I don't have any plans to find out, even though it gets used for raves; so not all spooky. Step into the church and the urge to rapidly exit the ghost town is ramped up. The town may be devoid of residents, but from the painted symbols adorning the walls of the church there is no question that somebody still worships in this place. Who, or what, they worship there is another matter.

CANDELARIA

Where is it and what's it like?

Lying on the east coast 18 km south east of Santa Cruz in a long, thin strip, Tenerife's spiritual capital of Candelaria is a Mecca for Canarios, and nothing more than a brief coach excursion stop for those visitors who even know it exists. Despite its importance as a religious place of pilgrimage, its impressive basilica, its selection of tapas bars and souvenir shops and its default setting of year-round sunshine, Candelaria remains primarily a day visitor destination for those on a round-island tour.

Thousands of pilgrims annually travel to Plaza de la Patrona where the Virgin of Candelaria, Patron Saint of the Canary Islands, is housed in a grand basilica. Beside the basilica is the wide Plaza de la Patrona where nine bronze, life-sized statues of the former Guanche *menceys* who ruled the island before the Spanish conquest, stand guard over the virgin's home.

In the narrow streets around the plaza, shops cater for both pilgrim and visitor, from food and drink to souvenirs and curious religious icons.

From the old quarter around the basilica, a pleasant promenade follows the 3km coastline past a harbour, marina and beaches to the most northerly section of the town at Las Caletillas where Candelaria's hotels are located and where you'll find supermarkets, a handful of good restaurants, dangerously fabulous cake shops and one or two cool bars.

On Wednesdays there's a small but lively farmers' market on Avenida de la Constitución which sells fresh fruit, vegetables and local produce.

What's the story?

The history of Candelaria is inextricably bound up with the discovery of the Black Madonna, or the Goddess Chaxiraxi to give her her Guanche name, on the beach at Chimisay by Guanche shepherds in 1392. The Madonna and child were allegedly discovered by two shepherds who were driving their goats along the shore. Finding their way barred by the woman who made no attempt to move out of the way, and forbidden by law to speak to a female on her own, one of the shepherds picked up a stone to throw at the woman and as he did so, his arm apparently locked. Shocked, the other one armed himself with his knife and accidentally almost severed his own finger.

Terrified, the two ran back to the ruling Mencey Acaymo who declared the whole affair a miracle, took the Madonna and child to a nearby cave for safekeeping and put the word of the discovery out. The statue's appointed keepers were effectively Candelaria's first inhabitants and from that day forward, Guanche travelled from across the archipelago to worship her, as pilgrims still do today.

178

In 1599 the Virgin of Candelaria, as she had become known, was declared the Patron Saint of the Canary Islands but tragically, the statue was washed out to sea in a storm in 1826 so a new statue was commissioned the following year, sculpted by the Master craftsman Fernando Estévez. Naturally, convents, churches and homes began to spring up around the site of the cave and the settlement of Candelaria began to grow. In 1947 work began on a safer and more appropriate home for the virgin and in 1959 the Basilica of Our Lady of Candelaria was completed.

Who'd want to stay here?

Candelaria would suit people who want a hybrid travel experience – mostly traditional but with some of the trappings of a resort. It's also a very sunny part of the island, so good for mixing beach time with cultural exploration.

The food scene

We say that Puerto de la Cruz is the only big town which successfully fuses the traditional with the characteristics of a tourist resort, but in a way Candelaria is similar, albeit on a smaller scale. The restaurant scene reflects this. In the area around the basilica, restaurants are mostly traditional with an emphasis on fish and seafood. At the other end of town in Las Caletillas the scene feels more geared towards visitors, resulting in a more diverse choice than is generally found in traditional towns. As well as Spanish restaurants there are ones with a Belgian/French influence, Latin American, and even Indian. The greatest concentration of restaurants are to be found around Cabezo de la Barca.

Where we'd eat

Tapas - There are plenty of traditional Canarian restaurants and tapas bars in Candelaria but not many are a fun and funky as **CerViTapas** which serves attractive looking tapas which are far more creative than the average Tenerife restaurant – think rabbit meatballs or mozzarella tempura. *Rambla Los Menceyes 27; +34 922 197 365; open midday to midnight daily, closed Monday; average cost of a tapa €5.*

Traditional - The restaurants around the basilica in Candelaria are in an envious position, and they know it. You're more likely to find locals eating traditional food at places like **La Casona del Vino** on the other side of the TF1 motorway. The speciality is rice dishes, but there's an extensive menu of traditional dishes, and also vegetarian options. *Carretera General Sur 44; +34 922 500 095; open 13:00-16:00 and 20:00-23:00 Tuesday to Saturday, 13:00-16:00 Sunday, closed Monday; average cost of main course €13.*

Why visit

Plaza de la Patrona with its bronze statues is where most visitors head, enjoying browsing at the religious and souvenir shops that line the route from the car parking.

The basilica is worth visiting to see the murals, paintings and of course, the Black Madonna herself. Beyond the basilica is the Cueva de Achbinico, also known as the Ermita de San Blas, the location of the first place of worship dedicated to the virgin. Another nearby cave was used as a stable for the camels which were used to transport wares, so all very Biblical.

Climb the steps behind the basilica, cross C/La Palma and the cream building above the red tiled roof straight in front of you is Centro Alfarero Casa las Miquelas (*open Tues-Sat 08:00-15:30; +34 922 505 216; C/Isla de La Gomera, 17; www.candelaria.es*), a small pottery museum where they still throw pottery by hand. Traditionally the craft of women, the workshop shows the rudimentary tools and methods used to produce the red pots which are typical of the area. Visitors can watch the pottery being made, buy a genuine piece of Tenerife's history and help to keep this once vital craft alive.

On the beach

An uninviting pebbly shoreline hems the town around the Plaza de la Patrona but further along the promenade towards Las Caletillas, finer sand, beach volleyball courts, exercise areas and kiddies playgrounds provide popular leisure space for the residents of the apartment blocks that line the coast between the two ends of the town.

After dark

It's hardly bouncing after dark, but the Las Caletillas side of town does have some decent modern bars serving a good range of beers as well as wines, so not the 'sitting in a draughty bar with four old blokes wearing fedoras and playing dominoes' experience you get in some traditional towns on Tenerife. There are also occasional music festivals in Candelaria.

Where we'd stay

Accommodation isn't exactly inspirational in Candelaria, mostly perfectly decent apartments, but nothing to get excited about. There's only one hotel which is the **Catalonia Punta del Rey** (*Avda. Generalísimo, 165; +34 922 501 899; www.hoteles-catalonia.com*). Located at the Playa de las Caletillas end of town and recently refurbished, the Punta Del Rey is as popular with locals as visitors which means it can get lively at weekends. Rooms are clean and comfortable, but upgrade to a superior for best views and quiet. Short on outside space so expect elbow to elbow sun loungers. Its biggest plus point is it's the only hotel in town, and it's within easy reach of Santa Cruz.

Best time to visit
The biggest religious fiesta in Tenerife's calendar is the Virgen de Candelaria which takes place on the 15th August to commemorate the discovery of the Black Madonna and child by two Guanche shepherds. On the eve of the fiesta, tens of thousands of pilgrims who have travelled by foot from all over the island arrive in Candelaria, some of them ending their journey on hands and knees as they approach the basilica where a re-enactment of the 'miracle' of the Virgen's discovery is acted out in the Plaza de la Patrona. It is crazy busy and quite an experience, but not for everyone.

GÜÍMAR

Where is it and what's it like?
Once known as the 'Gateway to the South', Güímar is a town of two halves. The main commercial centre and old quarter sits at 300 metres above Tenerife's east coast on the road which was formerly the only link between the north and south of the island. On the other side of the TF1 motorway which changed all that in the 1970s, is Puertito, Güímar's delightful little coastal settlement.

Hogging the coastline beside Puertito de Güímar is volcanic *malpaís*, or badlands, with a desert-like landscape of grasses and cacti and plentiful indigenous plants, lizards and butterflies. Criss-crossed by trails that gently undulate along the coast, it's an easy and tranquil walker's delight.

Home to the late Norwegian adventurer Thor Heyerdahl, of Kon Tiki fame, Güímar is the site of his brainchild and Tenerife's most enigmatic theme park, the Pirámides de Güímar.

What's the story?
The proliferation of Guanche archaeological sites around the caves and ravines of Güímar are testament to the importance of the area before the Spanish conquest of the island. Two kingdoms were the most important on Tenerife, Taoro in the La Orotava Valley which represented the *menceys* of the North, and Güímar which represented those of the South and which was led by Acaymo, succeeded by his son Añaterve. Like the rest of the island, land in the Güímar Valley was given over to livestock rearing – goats, sheep, pigs – with animals being moved between the high summer grazing grounds and the winter coastal areas. Abundant in water springs, barley was also produced here.

Prior to the Spanish conquest, a process of self-Evangelization had already begun amongst the Guanche population around Güímar following the discovery of the Black Madonna and Child on the Chimisay beach in 1392 (see Candelaria

What's the Story). It's thought that this existing move towards Catholicism, coupled with ongoing conflict between the southern and the northern *menceys*, led the Güímar *mencey* to join forces with his southern neighbours in signing a peace pact with the Castilian army and agreeing, not only to not try to prevent the invasion but actually to assist the conquistadors under the leadership of Alonso de Lugo. As a result, with friendly relations already established, Güímar was one of the first areas to be settled by the Spanish and is one of Tenerife's oldest towns. The pact did not however prevent the Guanche of the south being taken into slavery by the conquerors, many being taken to the Peninsula to work in the estates of Andalusian gentry while others were forced to work for the new 'owners' of Tenerife. After the spoils had been divided up, very few indigenous people owned any part of their ancestral lands.

Güímar's rich supply of water was ingeniously tapped by farm workers through aqueducts, galleries and wells, ensuring a constant flow to the sugar plantations that were created in the first months and years of colonisation. Sugar mills and plantations were worked by Guanche and Berber slaves and by Portuguese workers specializing in sugar production. Along with the sugar, cereals and vines were cultivated, and livestock-rearing and honey production continued. As the estates of the rich expanded, orchards of fruit trees were planted, along with tomatoes, potatoes and avocados, making Güímar the principle supplier of produce to the south of the island. As in the case of other parts of the island, it was around this time that a deal of damage was done to the environment with massive deforestation of the upper reaches in order to provide pine resin to make and export pitch and tar for Spain's shipbuilding industry.

The bottom fell out of the sugar market in the second half of the 16th century when cheaper produce came to market from the Antilles and Brazil. Displacing sugar cane, more vineyards began to be planted and wine production kept the economy steady. Inevitably, divisions arose between the vast estates of the wealthy, many of whom were absentee landlords, and the poor who struggled to survive on the meagre plots of land they rented without also having to work for the rich estates to supplement their livelihood. By the 18th century, the wealthiest of the poor had begun to form a middle class who, taking advantage of the absentee nature of the big landowners, began to take up political offices and increasing their own lands. Control of water became a source of permanent conflict, frequently giving rise to litigation and sometimes, as in 1810, to riots.

At the end of the 18th century, when the wine trade collapsed, it was a local boy, Isidro Quintero Acosta who introduced cochineal production to the island and ensured its economic survival for the next seventy years. With synthetic dyes displacing the ugly, bug-covered prickly pear leaves that had blighted the landscape, vines were once again planted, supplemented by the domestic produce of potatoes and cereals.

Top: Arico Nuevo, bottom left: church at leper village, bottom right: Pyramids of Güímar

182

By the late 19th- and early 20th century, the balance of land ownership in Güímar had begun to shift from the absentee aristocracy to the local bourgeoisie, still leaving a sizeable population of those at the bottom of the agrarian ladder who emigrated to Cuba and Venezuela in their droves.

Today, tomatoes continue to be the mainstay of the economy with Güímar being the largest producer on Tenerife while its main export product is avocado.

Who'd want to stay here?

Tenerife's east coast tends to get overlooked by most visitors, and yet there is much of interest. Güímar and its surrounding valley deserves more attention than it gets. It's one of the most historic towns on the southern side of the island and has a tad more sophistication than most other hill towns. Its history is fascinating and it's in a good position for accessing Teide National Park via roads that few travel. And it's got good restaurants as well as a choice of hotels with character. It's ripe for exploration by those who want to experience an underrated area of Tenerife.

The food scene

In traditional terms you get the best of both worlds in Güímar; hearty, meaty fare in the main town, and fish & seafood at the coast. But there's also a splash of culinary sophistication to be found in Güímar, mostly from the kitchens of the area's small, colonial hotels.

Where we'd eat

Contemporary Canarian - Probably the best restaurant which isn't in a hotel in Güímar, **Rincón de Tara** is one of the new breed of traditional restaurants serving Canarian dishes which have been modernised for a more sophisticated palate. So you may get the likes of cod coated with crunchy Parmesan on a bed of avocado sauce, and *puchero* croquettes with a cheesy *mojo*. *Calle Imeldo Seris 2; +34 922 514 227; open 13:00-16:30 and 20:00-23:00 Tuesday to Saturday, 13:00-16:30 Sunday, closed Monday; average cost of a main €12.*

Head to El Puertito de Güímar for fish and seafood, however it's not easy to recommend a particular restaurant there as we've enjoyed good experiences in restaurants and also indifferent service in the same places. From other reviews we've read this isn't uncommon. **La Charcada** at the harbour serves good, basic fish and seafood beside the sea (*open 08:00-midnight daily*).

Why visit

The Pirámides de Güímar (*+34 922 514 511; www.piramidesdeguimar. es*) park is based around the discovery of the remains of what Thor Heyerdahl believed were stepped, solar-aligned pyramids like the ones in Mexico and Peru. The tranquil, enigmatic park is a showcase for Heyerdahl's evidence to support the theory that ancient peoples could have sailed the Atlantic in reed boats long before Columbus laid claim to being the first to do so. A museum, film show and replicas of Heyerdahl's reed ships all add interest to the pyramids themselves and make up one of Tenerife's most enduring mysteries. You can also enjoy an Easter Island exhibition, a poisonous garden and a sustainable garden (all with an additional entrance fee). Some people are disappointed the pyramids don't look like Egypt's, but we think it's a fascinating, thought-provoking place.

The *malpaís* might be volcanic badlands, but they're badlands full of interesting curios including former bunkers turned into fishermen's (underground) huts, salt pans, and a cave which was used to dump dead donkeys. Maybe the last isn't so much of an attraction.

On the beach

Small, black sand, pebbly coves dot the coastline around Puertito de Güímar and its little marina but there are no facilities or lifeguard and to be honest, not much beach either. Better by far are the decking and the long pier that border the harbour providing attractive sunbathing areas beside clear, turquoise waters.

After dark

Although very much a local scene, there are a few decent bars in Güímar. The summer months, like much of the more traditional coastal areas, are far more lively than the rest of the year. Near the harbour at El Puertito is one of Tenerife's popular wild camping spots, with a convoy of RVs filling any rough parking areas throughout summer. It's also a good place for music festivals during summer.

Where we'd stay

Surprisingly, given the choice in similar areas, there are some great places to stay in and around Güímar. It has more than its fare share of small, atmospheric hotels in colonial buildings, as well as some eclectic accommodation. At the time of writing there was even a honeymoon van. Yes, it is what it sounds like – a bed in an old van.

Enticing though the van sounds we'd opt for **Hotel Rural Finca Salamanca** (*+34 922 514 530; C/ Güímar; www.hotel-fincasalamanca.com*). A former sugar cane and coffee plantation now hosting splendid botanical gardens, surround a converted manor house and provide the setting for a genteel, de-stress getaway. Guests are on the mature side and the whole place has a delightful air of bygone times about it. It's not far from the seafood restaurants of El Puertito and the

Pirámides de Güímar, but a car is essential.

Hotel Rural La Casona De Santo Domingo (*+34 922 510 229; C/Santo Domingo, 32; www.casonasantodomingo.es*) has oak floors polished to a blinding shine, low doorways to crack your skull on, beamed ceilings and antique beds; all the joys of a beautifully restored 16th century house in the heart of town.

Best time to visit

Bajada de El Socorro - When two Guanche shepherds encountered a woman and her child on the beach at Socorro it changed their lives and the history of the archipelago. Every 7th September, thousands of devotees carry the statue of their Patron Saint back to where they found her and re-enact that historic day.

One of the barmiest celebrations on Tenerife taking place during carnival is Las Burros de Güímar, an event straight out of a Stephen King novel that involves 'naked' witches fighting angels on the streets of the old town. Because it's linked to carnival, the date changes every year but this bizarre good vs evil battle always takes place on a Friday.

THE MYSTERIOUS TENERIFE PYRAMIDS

"Borders? I have never seen one, but I heard they exist in the minds of most people." Thor Heyerdahl

Güímar's most celebrated resident, the anthropologist and explorer Thor Heyerdahl lived in the town for the last eight years of his life, brought to Tenerife by the discovery of what appeared to be step pyramids on the island in 1990. Believing the pyramids to be the same type of construction as those found in Peru, Mexico and Egypt, Heyerdahl partnered up with shipping magnate Fred Olsen to construct an ethnographic park around the site as a showcase for his theories on the migratory patterns of ancient civilisation. But local opposition to the plan was fierce. The land on which the pyramids stood was earmarked for development, promising a nice payout to the landowner and locals who insisted the pyramids were nothing more than stones cleared from the land by farmers.

Awakenings

Heyerdahl first started to question the established view of how civilisation spread when he was a young student living in Polynesia and studying the origins of the Polynesian Islands' animal life. Whenever he went fishing with his friends, they constantly had to battle the prevailing easterly winds and currents, and yet, according to popular scientific belief, the Polynesian Islands were first settled by

Stone Age immigrants from South East Asia, more than 16,000 kilometres on the wrong side of the wind and currents.

Heyerdahl theorised that the first settlers could have come instead from the east; from Peru and Easter Island, carried on balsa rafts by the same wind and currents that brought the flora and fauna to the Canary Islands. But he faced a wall of opposition to his theories and so, in 1947 he set out to prove that such a voyage could have been made. Using balsa logs from Ecuador, he constructed a craft based on a pre-historic South American vessel and on 28th April, he and his crew of five set sail from Callao in Peru bound for the Polynesian Islands. The small crew suffered a harrowing voyage of storms, dead calm and constant circling sharks but they also breakfasted on flying fish that landed on deck and were occasionally escorted by playful whales. After 101 days at sea and 6880 kilometres, the craft sailed into the French Polynesian island of Raroia and the names of Thor Heyerdahl and Kon Tiki sailed into history. Heyerdahl told the story of the voyage in a documentary which won an Oscar in 1951 and in a book, Kon-Tiki, which has since been translated into more than 66 languages. In 2014 the Norwegian movie that chronicles the journey of the Kon Tiki expedition was nominated for an Academy Award in the category of Best Foreign Film.

Step Pyramids and Sun Gods

One of the things that Thor Heyerdahl saw as evidence of the movement of early settlers was the existence of step pyramids in Mexico, Peru and Ancient Mesopotamia. These were not the flat sided, sloped pyramids of school text books; these were a series of stepped platforms leading to a flat summit; a temple for sun worshippers, with a stairway built into the westerly side, perfectly aligned according to sunset on the summer and winter solstice and they were what first brought Thor Heyerdahl to Tenerife.

Newspaper reports of the discovery of pyramids on the island in 1990 were met with the same scorn and derision as Heyerdahl's original westerly migratory theories. Seeing the photographs, Heyerdahl came to Tenerife and confirmed that the extensive pyramid site in Güímar was in fact the same type of construction as those in Peru, Mexico and Egypt. Investigation of materials on the site by the University of La Laguna in 1991 dated the construction of the site to the mid-nineteenth century which tied in with documentary evidence from the deeds of sale of the land which made no mention of the structures in 1854 whereas the same deeds in 1872 do refer to them. Although the pyramids were not constructed by ancient civilisations, Heyerdahl argued that they were nevertheless, part of the cultural heritage of the island. Having won his case with the authorities, Heyerdahl set about developing the grounds around the pyramids and creating a museum crammed with artifacts and information supporting his theory that early migrating people could have sailed the currents of the world's oceans in reed crafts long before Columbus 'sailed the ocean blue'. Included within the park are replicas of the reed ships Kon Tiki, Tigris, Ra, Ra ll (named after the Egyptian god who every day sailed his ship, the sun, across the sky) in which Thor Heyerdahl and his crew of six sailed from Safi in Morocco to Barbados, thus blowing out of the water the established belief that Mediterranean vessels built prior to Columbus could not have crossed the Atlantic. The replicas were constructed by members of the same Aymara tribe from Bolivia who helped Heyerdahl construct the original vessel in 1969. The original Kon-Tiki raft now sits in the museum of the same name in Oslo, Norway.

The museum and auditorium at Pirámides de Güímar pose questions about the possibility that the first navigators of the world's oceans were sun worshippers who built their temples across three continents; all the Norwegian voyager, Thor Heyerdahl, asked of today's sun worshippers, is that they keep an open mind to the possibilities placed before them; a mind without borders.

Pirámides de Güímar *(+34) 922 514 510; www.piramidesdeguimar.es/en; Open every day from 09.30-18.00 except Christmas Day and New Year's Day; entrance from €12.50 for adults, €6 for children (aged 9-12 years) depending on how much of the site you plan to visit.*
Most tour groups tend to visit on Thursdays so best to avoid that day.

LA ESPERANZA, EL ROSARIO

What's it like?
Sitting on the spine of the island, La Esperanza is the last town before the road from La Laguna wends its way into the dense pine forest in the direction of Mount Teide. Those passing through are often on their way to Teide National Park. Subsequently, it tends to be overlooked by most visitors to the island. And yet, it's an area with an interesting history and more quirks than many other traditional Tenerife towns.
La Esperanza is located in the municipality of El Rosario which sweeps from the *cumbre* (island's spine) down to the 'new' towns of Tabaiba and Radazul on the coast; places which have little in common with their hill top administrative centre. The countryside around La Esperanza is a mix of fertile farmlands and lush forests, both of which have added their own contribution to an agricultural heritage which stretches back to the first settlers. Statues in town pay tribute to the people who have worked the lands over the years; *las lecheras* – the women who used to carry pots of milk on their heads to the markets in La Laguna before the arrival of the '*Guagua de Las Lecheras*' (the milk bus). Then there's *los pinocheros*, the people who collected pine needles from the forest floor. These

were used as animal bedding, for fertilizer, and as padding in crates of fruit. The removal of pine needles also helped reduce the spread of forest fires, so somewhat of a symbiotic relationship between humans and nature.

El Rosario is one of those towns which feels like it's stuck in a time warp.

What's the story?

Although the name of the municipality, El Rosario, only dates back to 1813 when it was established and took its name from a hermitage in the hamlet of Machado, on the route pilgrims followed from La Laguna to Candelaria, the town's name stretches back to the conquest. Fleeing the battle of Acentejo in the area now known as La Matanza, Alonso Fernández de Lugo and his decimated troops reached the island's spine and saw their camp on the coast below at Añaza (now Santa Cruz). For the first time since escaping the massacre they were given hope they'd survive. Grateful to be alive, de Lugo vowed to build a hermitage on the spot in honour of la Virgen de la Esperanza – the virgin of hope.

Tenerife's most famous pirate, Amaro Pargo, chose El Rosario for his home, the ruins of his house (declared a site of cultural interest) lie near Machado, just off the Camino de Candelaria, the pilgrims' route leading to Candelaria. Pargo was considered the Spanish equivalent of Sir Frances Drake. In the 18th century he terrorised ships belonging to enemies of Spain he encountered on sailing routes between Cadiz and the Caribbean. When Amaro Pargo died it was believed he'd stashed some of his ill-gotten gains in his house or in the Tenerife hills, leading to treasure hunters ransacking his house. For centuries people have searched for Pargo's treasure without success. One story tells that the belief there is treasure was fuelled by Amaro Pargo often commenting he could see his treasure from his house. Some think this was just a piece of mischief on the pirate's part; the treasure he was referring to being the sea. His body is buried in a tomb in the Convento de Santo Domingo in La Laguna. It isn't difficult to spot, the skull and crossbones give it away.

In more recent years, the picnic zone at nearby Las Raíces was where army officers loyal to General Franco met to plot to overthrow the Spanish government. A concrete obelisk marked the spot, until it was torn down in 2015.

Who'd want to stay here?

La Esperanza would suit people who enjoy the great outdoors and a traditional setting, but also like being relatively close to bustling urban centres. Many walking routes criss-cross the nearby forests, it's in a good position for getting to Teide National Park, and Anaga with even more hiking options is on the opposite side of the Aguere Valley.

The food scene

This is meat, meat, and more meat country. Restaurants in La Esperanza are big (to cater for the folk from the metropolis who flock here at weekends) and so are the portions they serve. There's nothing fancy, and it's culinary hell for vegetarians, but for anyone who likes mountains of perfectly cooked grilled meat in an authentic, no frills Canarian setting, this is the place.

Where we'd eat

Traditional - Bodegón Campestre doesn't look particularly appealing from the outside (many traditional restaurants don't) but inside is a rustic sanctuary with chunky wooden tables, and walls decorated with traditional farming implements. Huge steaks and chops are popular, but best of all is the selection of various sausages which arrive at the table on a thick board with flames still engulfing them. Weekends and fiesta days can be mad busy.

(+34) 922 548 057; Calle Bethencourt, 2; average cost of a main course €14; open midday-17:00 Tuesday, Wednesday, Thursday & Sunday, midday-midnight Friday & Saturday, closed Monday.

Why visit

La Esperanza is the sort of place where there are curios rather than attractions, like the statues of the milkmaids and pine needle collectors. The town's plaza leads into the Bosque del Adelantado, a small *laurisilva* forest. Between steps leading into the forest is a statue of *La Manta Esperancera*, a coarse cloak traditionally worn by livestock farmers. Anyone who's been at agricultural fiestas in the hills during winter months should have spotted shepherds wearing this traditional, warm and waterproof beige woollen cloak supposedly based on a similar garment worn by the Guanche. The cloak originated in La Esperanza, where conditions in winter can be cold and humid. Although uniquely Canarian in design, the material used to make these cloaks came from blankets imported from Britain.

Located deep in the pine forest at Las Lagunetas is the Las Raíces *zona recreativa*, a sprawling picnic zone with tables, barbecues, free camping, and toilet facilities. It's packed at the weekends, as is the surrounding forest as residents of La Laguna and Santa Cruz head into the hills to walk and cycle the network of hiking trails which pass through this area.

Not far beyond Las Raíces on the TF-24 road is the Mirador de Montaña Grande which has views north across El Rosario's farmlands to Anaga, and south across the Güímar Valley all the way to El Médano.

Further along the TF-24 is the Forestal Park, an adventure playground of zip lines, Tarzan swings and treetop walkways with courses designed for all members of the family (*(+34) 630 385 742; entrance is €22 for non-resident adults, and €17 for non-resident children (5-12 years); open 10:00-16:00 daily).*

Finally, beside the Los Toques bar is a shrine which illustrates how strong the relationship between Tenerife and Venezuela is. On display is a statue of a moustached man who looks a bit like Charlie Chaplin; it's Doctor José Gregorio, a Venezuelan medic from the early 20th century who dedicated his life to helping the poor. He achieved saint-like status among the poor of Caracas after Venezuelans claimed miracle cures when they invoked his name during their prayers. In 2017, the Catholic Church attributed a miracle to Dr Gregorio in relation to an incident when he saved the life of a young girl who had been shot in the head during a robbery. In June 2020, Pope Francis approved his beatification.

On the beach

Although La Esperanza is most definitely a hill town, the municipality does stretch to the coast where there are a handful of decent beaches, the most popular being La Nea which is backed by gardens and has all the usual town beach facilities. A marina in Radazul attracts Canarios who enjoy water sports such as sailing, water skiing, and diving. Radazul is considered one of the top freediving spots in Europe.

Where we'd stay

For anyone seeking a rural base, where you can both have wild countryside and yet also be not too far from the likes of La Laguna and Santa Cruz, La Esperanza offers a few interesting choices. There are a couple of small hotels/ hostels in, or not far from, the centre of the town; a good choice of rustic cottages, and a campsite (Quimpi) which has chalets of various sizes for those wanting a more back-to-basics experience.

Best time to visit

Canarios flock to the woods at weekends throughout the year, but we think spring, followed by early autumn are the best times to enjoy this area. Being located at 900m above sea level means it can be quite nippy during the cooler months, hence the need for a blanket cloak.

SAN ANDRÉS

Where is it and what's it like?

The white houses of the little fishing village of San Andrés tumble down the Anaga Mountains to the edge of the sea on the north east tip of Tenerife. Just around the headland is the frenetic capital city, but it might as well be a hundred kilometres away for all the impact it has on San Andrés.

191

Top: Playa de las Teresitas, bottom left: fish market, Santa Cruz, bottom right: Noria district, Santa Cruz

Characterised by its precipitous setting and the 'Broken Tower' of Torre de San Andrés which lies in pieces at its feet, the village has had more titles than the Queen's Honours list. Throughout the 16th and 17th centuries it was known as 'the pirate port' because it was subject to constant incursions from corsairs. Water rich from its position at the confluence of two *barrancos*, the village produced so much fruit and vegetables for Santa Cruz that it was known as 'the city's larder'. Today it's known as 'the gateway to the Anagas'.

But wander its streets any time after 1pm and the all-pervading aroma of fresh fish grilling on open coals will tell you that it's also known for its fish restaurants and is a lunchtime favourite with *santacruceros*.

What's the story?

The fishing and farming heritage of San Andrés changed little from its Guanche days right up until the beginning of the 18th century.

Following the conquest when Anaga was taken from the Guanche under the command of Beneharo and given instead to the conquering army, it was a Castilian named Don Lope de Salazar to whom the lands were ceded. Fishing boats came ashore at the old beach of Los Melones and produce from the *barrancos* was taken to Santa Cruz by footpath, the only means of access to the village until the road was built by the military in the 1940s.

Against continual harassment by pirates, the San Andrés castle, known as Torre de San Andrés, was constructed in 1706 and became a symbol of protection for that part of the coast. By 1724 more than 100 soldiers were stationed there and eight cannon decorated its turrets. Throughout the 18th century the presence of militia here helped to dispel the title of 'pirate port' from the village.

In 1797, the tower played an important role in defending the attack on Santa Cruz by Nelson. Ordered by General Gutiérrez to fire on the British fleet, a salvo of cannon fire from the tower destroyed part of the masts and equipment of the ships Theseus and Emerald. When the ship Rayo approached shore and began firing on the Valley of San Andrés, the reply from the tower to her broadside almost capsized her and sent her into retreat. The site of the tower at the confluence of two ravines proved to be its literal downfall; heavy storms in 1878 and 1898 damaged it beyond repair.

At some point in the 20th century (the exact date is unknown) an incredibly well-preserved mummy was discovered in a ravine alongside San Andrés. Thought to be the body of a *mencey* due to the care that had been lavished on its preservation, it is known as the San Andrés Mummy and is now on display in the Museum of Nature & Archaeology in Santa Cruz. In 1973 four million bags of sand were brought from the Spanish Sahara and laid at the door of San Andrés, creating the golden expanse of Las Teresitas for the residents of the capital – the *santacruceros* - to enjoy.

193

Who'd want to stay here?

San Andrés would suit people who have a wide range of likes. Quiet traditional Canarian town – tick. Good local food – tick. Superb beach – tick. Mainly sunny weather – tick. Close to a city for a change of scene – tick. Easy access to rural areas for pursuing outdoor activities – tick.

The food scene

Where many of the former fishing villages of the south have largely been taken over by upmarket restaurants, San Andrés resolutely remains a fishing community boasting some of the best fish and seafood restaurants on Tenerife. The smell of fried fish as you walk through its streets is enough to drive a person crazy. We once visited with a friend who doesn't eat fish. It was embarrassing to ask at every restaurant 'do you have steak' to which the reply was invariably a perplexed 'no, this is San Andrés.' This is decidedly fish and seafood territory.

Where we'd eat

Contemporary fish & seafood - Chef Carlos Villar is highly regarded on the island and **La Posada del Pez** isn't your average fish restaurant. His fishy creations are as good looking as they are tasty. It's the sort of fish restaurant where the menu includes ceviche, tuna tartar, and sardines that arrive carefully arranged in a neat tower rather than lined up like dead soldiers on your plate. Make sure to leave room for their equally creative and delicious desserts. *Carretera Taganana 2; +34 922 591 948; open 13:00-16:30 and 20:00-23:00 Tuesday to Thursday, 13:00-23:00 Friday and Saturday, 13:00-17:00 Sunday, closed Monday; average cost of main course €15.*

Fish & seafood - You'll know what's on the menu at the same time as the owner of **Rincón de Pescadores**; it's whatever is in the fisherman's basket when he knocks on the side door mid morning. Fresh fish and seafood at its simplistic best. *Corner of C/ Chana Cabrera; +34 609 231 891; open midday to 16:30 and 20:00-23:00 Monday to Saturday, midday to 18:00 Sunday; average cost of main course €10.*

Why visit

As well as having the best-looking beach on the island, and some of the best seafood, San Andrés is simply a pretty little fishing town which remains unspoilt. Its one attraction is the broken tower, the Torre de San Andrés and which takes all of a minute to visit.

On the beach

The tropical paradise of Las Teresitas may have been constructed for the citizens of Santa Cruz but it's on San Andrés doorstep (quite literally, as the near constant east coast breeze carries the fine sand), lending villagers a picture-postcard vista from their front terraces.

Framed by the stunning backdrop of the Anaga Mountains and backed by rows of lush palms swaying in the breeze, the gold sand beach is one of the most attractive on the island and is invariably used in press photos whenever Tenerife's beaches are mentioned, regardless of where the feature is actually about. Clear, turquoise waters are tamed by a man-made breakwater and provide a haven for tropical fish and a free-form swimming pool for the beach, which at 1.5 kilometres in length, can swallow half the city without even looking busy. There are kiosks, toilets, showers and changing rooms along the back of the beach and loads of parking spaces. The facilities have been given an upgrade in recent years with swish modern beach bars replacing the old rough 'n' ready kiosks. There's no arguing the new bars have given the beach a more upmarket look ... but they've stripped it of some of its local charm.

After dark

At times of the year it can be surprisingly lively after dark, thanks to the presence of the beach. Mostly though this is a place which bounces during daylight hours only.

Where we'd stay

There have been plans for years to build a hotel behind Las Teresitas but, thankfully as it would turn this beach built for the *santacruceros* into just another resort beach, they remain plans. For the moment only rural houses and apartments offer a place to lay your head.

Best time to visit

Summer can be very busy, but outside of Spanish summer holiday periods (June to September) you still get the warm sunshine most of the year, but not the crowds on those golden sands.

SANTA CRUZ

Where is it and what's it like?

"Probably many people have shared my feeling of disappointment on landing at Santa Cruz.

...but even so, the utter hideousness of the capital of Teneriffe was a shock to me." – Florence Du Kane, "The Canary Islands" published 1911

Not the most auspicious of introductions to the island's capital city it has to be said, and one which until recently, it was difficult to argue with. But with the 21st century has come a vast, and vastly overdue, facelift for Santa Cruz, shared capital of the Canary Islands along with Las Palmas de Gran Canaria.

Today, the millions of people who annually arrive at the port in the world's ocean liners are greeted by the white iconic tsunami of Calatrava's Auditorium, César Manrique's Parque Marítimo, and Plaza España's strikingly eclectic blend of Franco symbolism and urban modernism. This is a small, compact city, which means it's easy to explore on foot ... when you know the best places to wander.

Although the sprawling ugliness of the CEPSA oil refinery remains a blot on the south side of the city, a great deal has been done in the last couple of decades to bring Santa Cruz into focus as a potential tourist destination. Not least, the addition of a sleek and sexy tram system and the development of the Noria District with its contemporary bars and chic restaurants. Add that to its impressive shopping; myriad parks and plazas; magnificent, out-of-town beach; galleries and museums; one of the most flamboyant festivals in Europe, and a default weather setting of sunshine, and what you've got is a vibrant European capital and the perfect winter sun, city weekend break destination.

What's the story?

Spreading south from the foot of the dramatic Anaga Mountains on the north east coast of Tenerife, the settlement now known as Santa Cruz was part of the Guanche kingdom of Anaga, ruled by Mencey Beneharo. Allying himself to the southern menceys who made a pact with the Castilian conquerors, on 1st May 1494, Beneharo allowed the invaders, under the command of Alonso Fernández de Lugo, to land at the coast in his kingdom and to set up camp. To celebrate his safe landing, de Lugo placed a cross in the ground around which a mass was held and the place became known as Santa Cruz, or Holy Cross. Using it as his base, De Lugo took another two years and a sound thrashing from the rebel Guanches before finally securing Tenerife for the Crown of Castile in February 1496.

With its deep waters and relatively easy accessibility, the port of Santa Cruz became the nucleus of a burgeoning settlement of mud houses and landing piers which enabled the import and export of trade and the provision of supplies for vessels bound for the New World. The surviving Guanche, mostly women, were integrated into a society comprised of soldiers, sailors and merchants while the surviving Guanche males were taken into slavery. The population largely settled around the Castillo de San Cristóbal which was on the site of today's Plaza España, the creation of which heralded the destruction of the castle. In the latter part of the 16th century the first plaza was created, Plaza de Pila, on the site of what is now Plaza de Candelaria. New defensive structures were installed along the coast to protect the population from the ever-present threat of attack from English and Barbary corsairs and pirates, most notably by the British Navy under the command of Horatio Nelson on July 25th 1797 (see Admiral Nelson and the Battle of Santa Cruz 1797). The piracy attacks that the islands suffered forced the archipelago to become more militarized and the towns and villages to be located hidden from view from the coast.

Santa Cruz continued to expand and soon reached the edge of the Santos *barranco* which stagnated its growth until several bridges were constructed. After that, the population gradually settled on both sides of the *barranco* and an urban network of housing, streets and paths began to take shape. In 1706 when the port of Garachico was destroyed by a volcanic eruption, Santa Cruz took up the mantel of the island's premier port and a booming trade at the crossroads to the New World brought further expansion. The middle of this century saw the Commander General leave La Laguna and set up home in the Castillo de San Cristóbal, effectively transferring the status of capital to the new settlement. A growing bourgeoisie took control of exports and began to demand better trade and leisure facilities, spawning the creation of the Alameda del Duque, the Plaza del Príncipe, the Plaza de Weyler and the La Recova market.

From 1833 there was a new impulse in the city as a consequence of the fact that Santa Cruz de Tenerife was granted the capital of the province of the Canary Islands and was granted status as a free port with its own tax scheme and the ability to offer trade incentives which placed it at the heart of trade between Europe and the emergent markets of Africa and the Americas. The 20th century saw one Francisco Franco, then Captain General of the Canary Islands, rise up from Santa Cruz to overcome the Spanish Republican government and start the Spanish Civil War.

Who'd want to stay here?

Santa Cruz is ideal for people who enjoy city breaks, not just because it's a perfect size for discovering on foot over the course of a few days, or because the weather is conducive to pavement pounding, but because you get two cities for the price of one as La Laguna is only a short tram ride away.

The food scene

As with any city, there's an overwhelming choice of restaurants to be found in Santa Cruz. These range from Michelin Star to bustling and basic. And, also like any city, there are the good and the mediocre. Apart from areas like the Noria district, and a couple of other pockets, there isn't a restaurant district as such, so there can be significant distances between one choice restaurant and the next.

Where we'd eat

A mixed plate - Instead of one restaurant, here's a mini restaurant district to

197

get your teeth into. The Noria district between Plaza España and the Museum of Nature and Archaeology is café society central with lots of deliciously attractive restaurants to choose from. We found it a nightmare to pick one the very first time we walked its colourful streets. In all honesty, we're no better now. It's always a toss up between **El Bulan, Baobab, El Porrón, Mirador de Noria, Mojos y Mojitos** and **Los Reunidos** – all on Calle Antonio Dominguez Alfonso. Restaurants here can be a bit pricier than in other parts of the city but there are good value *menu del día* options at lunchtime.

Creative cuisine - It might seem strange that the top restaurant in Santa Cruz is Japanese rather than Canarian, but Japanese cuisine is very popular in traditional areas of Tenerife and **Kazan** is one of the island's Michelin star restaurants. The smorgasbord of flavours in the food here explains why. Sublime dining and not overly expensive for a restaurant with a Michelin star. *Milicias de Garachico 1; +34 922 245 598; open 13:30-15:30 and 20:30-23:00 Tuesday to Saturday, 14:00-16:00 Monday, closed Sunday; tasting menu around €75, average cost of main course €14.*

Traditional - For more locally-inspired food in a traditional setting, try bustling **La Hierbita**, a restaurant in an old town house. There are two entrances leading to different dining areas, either in a dimly lit bar, or cosy rooms. La Hierbita can get very busy and hectic and this style of Canarian dining can frustrate those who aren't familiar with it, but this is authentic Canarian. If it's busy you might have to be assertive to get a waiter's attention. *Calle Clavel 19; +34 922 244 617; open midday-17:30 and 18:30-23:30 Monday to Saturday, midday-17:00 and 19:00-23:30 Sunday; average cost of main course €10.*

Fish and seafood plus – we love food markets, but they're thin on the ground on Tenerife. However below ground, amid the fish stalls at **Nuestra Señora de Africa Mercado La Recova,** are a handful of tiny tapas bars serving traditional dishes and contemporary creations featuring ingredients straight from the stalls around them. Despite cruise passengers strolling the aisles of the above-ground market, few make it down to what, for us, is the best bit. Opening hours reflect the market, so this is a lunch venue.

Contemporary international – One of the most unique spots for lunch is overlooking the Black Castle from beneath the snow-white hood of Tenerife's Auditorium. The food at **MAG Café Bistro** matches the modernity of its surroundings and, given the menu is overseen by one of Tenerife's top chefs, the *menú del día* is excellent value at around €12.50. And if the service seems slow, so what? This is a place to chill out and enjoy the scenery. If anyone gets bored they can always amble over to the sea wall to see how many 'stars' they can spot painted onto the sea defences below. *Open midday-21:00 Thursday & Friday, 10:00-21:00 Saturday & Sunday, closed Monday to Wednesday.*

Why visit

As well as museums, theatres, and parks, Santa Cruz is a pocket-sized city with lots of curios and quaint corners.

Slip on the comfy shoes and follow the city's sculpture trail, walking the length of La Rambla to discover a cornucopia of eclectic sculptures, most of them the legacy of an exhibition in 1974, by such luminaries as Joan Miró and Henry Moore. The route will take you into the city's oasis of Parque García Sanabria to see the voluptuous 'Fertility' in her fountain and then back to port side for the 'Angel of Victory' and more. Pick up a guide at the tourist office in Plaza España or go on one of their tours.

Parque García Sanabria (*Accessible from Calles Numancia, Mendez Nunez, Dr. Jose Naveiras y Rambla de Santa Cruz*) is the green heart and lungs of the city where you'll find a blend of street sculptures and magnificent landscaped gardens including the lovely Italianate garden; the flower clock; the bamboo tunnel and the water lily ponds. *Santacruceros* use this park for lunch time relaxation, to meet with friends and to stroll post-work.

TEA (*Tenerife Espacio de Las Artes; Ave de San Sebastián 10; +34 922 849 057; www.teatenerife.es; open Tues-Sun 10:00-20:00; entrance €7*) is a modern art museum with permanent and temporary exhibitions, state of the art design and a good restaurant. A full programme of events includes screening of art-house movies in their original language.

The iconic, tsunami-shaped Auditorio de Adá Martín (*Ave de Constitución 1; http://auditoriodetenerife.com*) fronts the port and was designed by celebrated architect Santiago Calatrava. Events range from the Tenerife Symphony Orchestra and international rock artists to Spanish pop idols.

Las Teresitas, the city's beach, is set 8km outside the centre (jump on the 910 bus which runs every 10mins from the *intercambiador* outside the bus station) and is a golden paradise fronted by a calm bay and backed by palm trees, and kiosks selling sandwiches and beers.

Housed in the splendid 19th century, Neoclassical former hospital for the homeless, the Museum of Nature and Archaeology (*+34 922 209 320; Calle Fuente Morales; www.museosdetenerife.org*) has three floors of exhibitions taking you from the explosive birth of the Canary Islands through their climate and biodiversity to the mummified remains of their first known inhabitants, the Guanche.

Located beside the 17th century Castillo de San Juan Bautista – known as the Black Castle – and the Parque Marítimo César Manrique swimming pool complex is the Palmetum, a former rubbish dump which has been transformed into quite beautiful botanical gardens covering 12 hectares and specialising, as the name suggests, on palms. Strolling these lush gardens it's mind-boggling to think years and years of rubbish lie below your feet. (*Open 10:00-18:00; entrance €6 for adults*).

On the beach

Playa de las Teresitas, the golden beach built for the '*chicharreros*' (the nickname for residents of Santa Cruz) actually lies eight kilometres outside the city. Being a port city, Santa Cruz doesn't have a beach as such. There are a few places along the coast where residents get prone, but anyone who wants their Canarian city to come with a convenient beach should head across the water to Las Palmas de Gran Canaria. However, there is the César Manrique-designed swimming pool complex of Parque Marítimo (*open 10:00-18:00 daily*) squeezed between the Auditorium and the Palmetum for anyone who wants to soak up some city sunshine in pleasant surroundings.

After dark

Head into the Noria District which runs from the foot of the landmark grey stone tower of the Iglesia de La Concepción to find many of the city's newest and coolest bars where live bands feature on summer weekends and you can drink until the early hours. After that, in summer months, head over to the area around Parque Marítimo near the auditorium for the clubs. The seafront facing Avenida Francisco la Roche is also traditionally a stretch which is popular for late night drinking. Personally, we prefer some of the more intimate scenes found in back streets and alleys where small clusters of bars are hidden away. If you're in the city in June, don't miss the excellent Santa Blues festival which features top US Blues artists beneath the flamboyance trees in Plaza Concepción.

Where we'd stay

There's a good range of hotels in Santa Cruz, from the luxury to clean and comfortable budget places.

One of our favourite hotels on Tenerife, the **Hotel Iberostar Heritage Grand Mencey** (*+34 922 609 900; C/ Dr Jose Naveiras, 38; www.sheraton.com/ mencey*) is the sort of 5 star hotel where you might rub shoulders with the rich and famous, at least, the rich and famous who come to Tenerife. Given a head to toe Iberostar makeover in 2011, this iconic, old dame of a hotel is beautifully located alongside the Ramblas, opposite Parque García Sanabria, and offers contemporary city style combined with colonial splendour. Beautiful gardens, state of the art spa and gym facilities and excellent à la carte dining – there are regular themed gourmet events featuring some of Spain's best chefs. Breakfast can be underwhelming but the gin & tonics mixed in the bar are legendary, if pricey.

At the opposite side of the city, the **NH Hotel** (*C/ Candelaria 3; +34 916 008 146; www.nh-hoteles.es*) is a good value for money option with a bit more of a business hotel feel. Décor is contemporary in chocolate, charcoal and grey with a splash of crimson supplied by the bed coverlets. Inward facing rooms are a tad dark and floor space is what you'd expect for a city centre hotel but beds are comfy and water is piping hot. On the edge of the Noria district, it's in a great location.

Best time to visit
Being a city, it's good any time of the year. But THE time to experience Santa Cruz is during carnival – There really ought to be loud music and ticker-tape at the very mention of the word. One of Europe's largest, Santa Cruz Carnival is the highlight of the year. Originating from the Catholic practice of using up all the meat and dairy produce before entered the abstinence of Lent, it's now an excuse for one almighty blow-out in which party stamina and endurance are tested beyond the limits.

Characterised by parades at the beginning and end of the main week in which hundreds of costumed revellers, scantly clad dancers and flamboyantly decorated floats thread their way through the heart of the city, the real spirit of carnival is in the nightly street parties held in and around Plaza España and attended by hundreds of thousands of people.

Whereas the event which is most popular with tourists is the closing parade (although officially the closing parade, carnival continues for another few days afterwards) which takes place on Shrove Tuesday, it's the street parties which get the *santacruceros* the most excited. To really go native you need to get into fancy dress for the nightly parties (many people have a different costume for every night) and don't bother arriving much before midnight.

SOUTH TENERIFE

The first views of Tenerife experienced by the millions of people who fly into Reina Sofia Airport in the south will cause scenery lovers' hearts to plummet. A hot, dry, lifeless, pumice terrain where rain is an infrequent visitor, accompanies coaches along the TF1 autopista on their journey from the airport to the southern resorts.

But once you get away from the construction site landscape of the motorway there's beauty to be found. Beaches are lapped by turquoise waters, wind erosion has created surreal rock formations; the Adeje mountains add drama to the skyline, and the countryside between the coast and hills is pockmarked by volcanic cones.

Much of the coast is characterised by purpose-built modern resorts with immaculate man-made beaches. The biggest, Playa de Las Américas and Costa Adeje cater for people who want sunshine and amenities more than culture and tradition, whilst others like Los Cristianos and El Médano retain their fishing village roots and still, to some extent, feel Canarian.

A popular criticism of the south of Tenerife is that it has been over-developed and therefore spoiled. It's a romantic, but ill-informed view. Prior to the advent of mass tourism, there were only a few tiny fishing communities along the south coast. Most of the area was *malpaís* which was of little or no use to neither man nor beast. Its transformation into a year-round, sun kissed playground for northern Europeans provided a much needed boost to the island's economy.

Ultimately, anyone seeking the authentic southern Tenerife can still find it where it always existed, in the original centres of population in the hills; in towns like Granadilla de Abona and Vilaflor where tradition and culture remain strong and life at the edge of the pine forest continues much as it always has done.

COSTA ADEJE

Where is it and what's it like?
Located just west of Tenerife's southern tip, Costa Adeje has been the cause of a renaissance in terms of how the south of Tenerife is viewed as a tourist destination. The construction of a spate of luxury hotels at the beginning of the 21st century transformed the coastline at the western end of the resort and now the area is invariably referred to as the 'upmarket' resort of Costa Adeje.
The name has become an umbrella term for Playa del Duque, Fañabe,

Left: Las Rocas,
Costa Adeje

Torviscas, Puerto Colón and San Eugenio. Whether all are worthy of the
'upmarket' tag is a matter of opinion. Some of these areas were previously
known as being in Playa de las Américas, so the change confused the hell out
of some people who'd been holidaying for years in what they thought was
las Américas. It was understandable, as both the las Américas Casino and las
Américas bus station actually turned out to be in Costa Adeje. Whereas it had
been convenient to tag resort areas in Adeje onto the tourist magnet of las
Américas, once the brand Costa Adeje became known in its own right, especially
with the 'upmarket' tag attached, the municipality of Adeje reclaimed and
renamed the parts that didn't fall within neighbouring Arona's borders. The term
Costa Adeje should really be applied to all coastal resorts which lie within Adeje,
but it tends to be used just for the block running west from the border with Playa
de las Américas to La Caleta.

This Costa Adeje boasts all the trappings that anyone seeking a beach
resort could want. There are beaches galore; ultra-modern shopping centres;
fashionable bars and stylish restaurants; a golf course with colonial styled
clubhouse (*www.golfcostaadeje.com*) and a marina at Puerto Colón where
visitors can charter yachts, go whale watching and even explore Adeje's undersea
vistas from the safety of a BOB (*an undersea scooter - www.bob-diving.com*).
What it lacks is the soul that you find in the Tenerife towns that weren't purpose-
built for pleasure.

For a bit of authentic local colour, travel a short distance inland to Adeje
town nestling below the mountain range of the same name. The town, a favourite
haunt of Sir Francis Drake who had dubious business dealings in the vicinity,
lies at the opposite end of the spectrum from its coastal cousin. Cobblers and tile
makers toil away inside dim doorways on tree-lined streets leading to the 16th
century *Iglesia de Santa Úrsula*. It's a location which should appeal to anyone
wanting to experience authentic Canarian living within a stone's throw of the
sort of facilities that attract millions of visitors annually.

On Costa Adeje's western perimeter, the fishing village of La Caleta has
almost been engulfed by the plush developments threatening to devour it but, for
the moment, still retains the air of a sleepy fishing community.

What's the story?

The name Adeje is believed to originate from the Guanche – Tenerife's first
inhabitants – and to mean 'mountainous massif'. Records suggest that Tenerife
was originally ruled by a single king, Tinerfe, who resided in Adeje. Tinerfe
died at the end of the 14th century and the kingdom passed to his nine sons who
then divided the land into nine distinct kingdoms. With the division, came power
struggles and the northern kingdom of Taoro emerged as the strongest, led by
Bencomo. The Adeje kingdom was ruled over by Pelinor who made a pact with

his southern brothers to sign a peace treaty with the armies of Alonso Fernández de Lugo. When the Spanish invaded in 1495, while his brother Bencomo fought and died for the protection of their ancestral lands, Pelinor was baptised into the Christian faith, received the new name of Don Diego de Adeje, and was given lands. He was the only Guanche mencey to remain living on Tenerife and the only Guanche to be allocated land after the conquest.

Following the conquest, the first settler families were allocated land around the Adeje river, amongst them was Pedro de Ponte who, in 1555 was granted permission to build a manor house fortress as a means of defence against pirate attacks which were common on this coast. The construction was named Casa Fuerte and on its completion in 1558, Pedro requested jurisdiction for the domain of Adeje but was denied due to strong opposition from his neighbours and from the island government. A century later, when the land was awarded the title of Villa, Pedro's descendant, Don Juan Bautista de Ponte y Pagés was granted the title of Lord of the Villa. As Lord, Don Juan Bautista was empowered to appoint a mayor, councillors, juries, scribes, bailiffs, guards and the ministers of justice. In addition, he controlled the military which he used effectively in defence of the southern coast against attacks by corsairs and pirates. Consisting of more than 7000sq meters incorporating a castle and keep, warehouses, granaries, a sugar mill, a blacksmith's, stables, bakery and ovens, servants' quarters, archives room and the main palace itself, Casa Fuerte became the political, economic and social centre of the region, a role it maintained for three centuries. In the 19th century, the old feudal regime was swept away in favour of democratic elections and Casa Fuerte lost its pivotal role in the life of Adeje.

Having its own water sources, Adeje did not suffer the same socioeconomic deprivation of the 19th century as much of the rest of Tenerife following the collapse of first sugar, then the wine market. Planting cochineal, and then replacing it with tomatoes and bananas destined for the European markets, kept Adeje`s economy buoyant and placed it at the centre of Tenerife's agricultural recovery. With its continued growth came the building of ports and roads which improved accessibility with the rest of the island. All this was to pale in comparison to the development Adeje experienced in the 20th century when tourism arrived on Tenerife. Sun-seekers began to arrive in their numbers, heading to the south west coast and prompting exponential growth in the development of Playa de las Américas. From 1996, the area became known as Costa Adeje and developed into one of Europe's largest tourist destinations. Today, the municipality has the highest rate of immigration on the island and, with 50,000 inhabitants, is one of the most densely populated.

Who'd want to stay here?
With areas catering for the luxurious end to ones aiming for a more budget

market, Costa Adeje would suit families, couples (younger and older), groups of friends - any combination of holidaymakers seeking a dependable sunshine destination but not necessarily authenticity.

The food scene

Costa Adeje was partly responsible for elevating gastronomy on Tenerife, making it the culinary capital of the Canary Islands, and yet it's also the place we've had the most mediocre meals, usually paying a lot more for the privilege than we would in traditional areas.

The reason for these extremes is whilst the growth of 5 star hotels brought top chefs to hotel kitchens, what's generally on offer outside of those hotels doesn't come close to reaching the same level. Subsequently, there are some excellent restaurants in Costa Adeje, but the ones we know tend to be inside the luxury hotels which characterise the western end of the resort. At the time of writing, the restaurant considered number one in Costa Adeje by Tripadvisor reviewers was an Indian restaurant. In fact out of the top ten, six were Indian/Asian, two were cafes, and one was Irish. There was one restaurant serving contemporary Spanish cuisine ... inside a luxury hotel. It speaks volumes. Outside of its hotels, Costa Adeje's restaurants exist to provide the wide range of choice you expect from a sun and sand destination. They're not going to give any insight into the Canarian food scene. For that you need to head inland.

Where we'd eat

Traditional Canarian - There is one place we'll go out of our way to visit. Adeje is known for *pollo al ajillo* (garlic chicken) which is lip-licking good and once tried bound to become a favourite. The best speciality restaurants are in Adeje town behind the resort area. **Otelo** dishes up some tasty specimens. It's unpretentious fare and excellent value. Simply tell them for how many people and they'll bring you a mountain of crispy, garlicky chicken bits. Garlic chicken fans tend to argue over which is the better restaurant – Otelo or Oasis on Calle Grande in the centre of Adeje Town. *C/ Los Molinos beside the Barranco del Infierno; +34 922 780 374; open 13:00-21:00, closed Tuesday; average cost of a plate of chicken €5/6.*

International - Jutting out over the ocean gives the terrace of **Las Rocas** a secluded air making it one of the most romantic spots for dinner on the south coast. Opt for a seafood dish when the setting sun bathes the terrace in a golden glow and you're asking for an aphrodisiac overdose; although the ardour might be doused when the bill arrives. *C/Gran Bretaña; +34 922 746 000; open 13:00-15:30 and 18:00-22:00; average cost of main course €20.*

International - If stylish dining overlooking the beach is your thing, then **La Terraza del Mare** is one of the better looking restaurants in Costa Adeje. The menu is a mix of Spanish influenced dishes and ones with a more international appeal (pizzas and pastas). The food looks good and tastes better than the fare you'll find at many restaurants in Costa Adeje. Plus it's a great spot for sunset cocktails. *CC Salytien, Ave. Rafael Puig Lluvina; +34 922 716 617; open midday-02:00; average cost of main course €15.*

Why visit

Sun and fun is the main reason. Costa Adeje offers all of the sort of attractions found in just about any sun-kissed, purpose-built resort; its whole raison d'être is to give people a good time during their precious breaks from work.

The biggest 'WOW' attraction in town is the Thai-themed Siam Park (*www. siampark.net*). A beautifully landscaped water park with imaginative white knuckle rides (the Tower of Power is only for the bravest, or foolhardy) set amidst rich tropical gardens. Built by the owners of Loro Parque, it's a little bit of Thailand in Tenerife.

Aqualand (*www.aqualand.es*) is another water park located next door to Siam Park which has managed to keep its head above water thanks to the fact that it has something Siam Park doesn't; a dolphin show. Interestingly, and despite it not having the same level of facilities, it doesn't come in for quite the same amount of negative publicity as Loro Parque on the other side of the island.

One of the most popular walks in Tenerife is Barranco del Infierno at the edge of Adeje town. A one and a half hour trek each way through a ravine ends at a small waterfall over 200m high. It's a bit manicured for experienced hikers, but its proximity to resorts keep it busy. There's a daily limit to the number of people who can walk the *barranco* so booking ahead is essential and there's a €8 charge for the privilege of walking it. If you show up in flip flops you'll be refused entry; ensure you have proper footwear, sunscreen, a hat and at least a litre of water per person. *Open daily 08:00-18:00 (last entrance 16:30); entrance €8; book online at www.barrancodelinfierno.es*

On the beach

Costa Adeje boasts a number of attractive, man-made beaches; all spotlessly clean, with lifeguards, sunbeds and toilet facilities. They're protected by breakwaters, making swimming a leisurely and more current-free experience.

Playa del Duque is the most exclusive, probably because it fronts swish hotels, and views to the main tourist developments in the south are blocked by a volcanic outcrop. Turquoise seas, thatched umbrellas and striped huts give the beach a Caribbean meets St Tropez appearance.

The sweeping beaches of Playa Fañabe and Playa Torviscas merge into one another; there's an inflatable green iceberg in the centre of Playa la Pinta at Puerto Colón for water babies of all ages to practice their penguin impersonations.

Choose Playa del Bobo in San Eugenio for windsurfing and sailing lessons. Next door are Playas de Troya I and II which have a whole range of activities from parasailing and jet skis to diving.

It's still possible to get away from the crowds without having to travel too far. Trek across the headland at La Caleta and you'll be rewarded with some secluded coves inhabited by only the occasional hippy or two.

After dark

The main hub of bars and clubs are located in the San Eugenio area; these are aimed at people who want familiar environments and on-tap entertainment when they go abroad; any number of interchangeable Irish, Scottish, English, karaoke and sports bars are the order of the day. There are lots of decent live music bars like Harley's featuring talented bands.

Costa Adeje's renaissance has seen a few international-style chill-out bars creep onto the scene but they're scattered about the resort. Some of these are located around the more select del Duque area whilst others are dotted along the promenade, a bit of a trek from each other. Some of these types of bars attract more of a young Spanish crowd than visitors, especially at the weekend and in summer months. If seeking lively nightlife, it's worth researching as there are areas of Costa Adeje that can be very quiet after dark.

Where we'd stay

Nearly all of the best resort hotels are to be found in Costa Adeje. If you want luxurious surroundings and high end dining, then Costa Adeje's 5 stars are where you'll find it. But reflecting the contrasting personality of the resort, there are plenty of good mid-range and budget options as well.

Iberostar Anthelia Hotel (*Calle Londres, 15; (+34) 922 71 33 35; www. iberostar.com/hoteles/tenerife/iberostar-anthelia*) is a gourmet, all-inclusive, Italian-styled hotel in the heart of Costa Adeje with extensive grounds and swimming pools backing directly onto the promenade. The bedrooms are nice, although nothing special unless you upgrade to the Salomé Suites, and the grounds are delightful, but it's the food that really sets this hotel apart. Foodies will love it.

Iberostar Grand Hotel El Mirador (*Avenida Bruselas; (+34) 922 716 868; www.thegrandcollection.com*) is a romantic, adults-only hotel adjoining the Bahía del Duque in Costa Adeje. Arabian Nights turrets and jasmine-scented walkways; billowing white drapes on four poster beds; a profusion of Bali beds scattered around the pool; and extensive grounds with quiet, private alcoves, this is a fairytale of an environment.

The **Hotel Jardín Tropical** (*+34 902 250 251; C/Gran Bretaña; www.jardin-tropical.com*) is a good mid-range choice that punches above its weight. Located within easy access of both the main areas of Costa Adeje and Playa de Las Américas, it has an attractive Moorish design and the lush subtropical gardens are popular with guests looking for quiet corners to lose themselves in a good book. Ask for a room with sea view.

Royal Garden Villas (*Calle Alcojora s/n; (+34) 922 78 84 82; www.royalgardenvillas.com*) consists of Asian-chic-styled villas set within perfumed gardens alongside Costa Adeje golf course on the western edge of the main Costa Adeje resorts. Opulent furnishings, beyond generous floor space and a private pool are just some of the attractions of the gorgeous villas. Immaculately maintained, if a tad twee, gardens and grounds; a lovely spa and an excellent restaurant.

Best time to visit

Winter is the obvious answer as Tenerife's resorts are perfect for winter sun. But as every night is Saturday night in resorts and the weather is good all year, there's little difference in character from one month to another.

Adeje town comes over all 'luvvy' on Good Friday, when many of the townspeople take a role in a full blown re-enactment of the Passion of Christ that would rival Mel Gibson's version; it's surprisingly evocative. Another increasingly popular fiesta is the Romería de San Sebastián in January that sees 35,000 onlookers crowd Playa de la Enramada to watch horses being ridden into the sea as part of the festivities.

COSTA DEL SILENCIO

Where is it and what's it like?

Marking the 'join' with Las Galletas and the resort of Costa del Silencio are the concrete boxes and militarily ordered sunbeds of the Alborada Ocean Club (formerly Ten-Bel).

Built in the 1960s with Belgian money, Ten-Bel was the island's first purpose-built holiday complex. It's had a revamp and a change of identity, but still feels like it belongs to Tenerife tourism days from the past. It does have a great swimming pool area on the ocean's edge which is its best feature. The area which grew up around it, and which generally lacks charm, is known as Costa del

Silencio. The name pre-dates the existence of the nearby Tenerife South Airport and is now more of an ironic statement than a description.

Row upon row of near-identical holiday, residential and retirement apartments sit in complexes alongside commercial centres filled with estate agents, souvenir shops, supermarkets, and restaurants offering familiar menus to mainly Brits, Germans and Belgians.

For us, Costa del Silencio has just two redeeming features, the wonderfully quirky fountain of bathers outside the Chaparral Commercial Centre, and Montaña Amarilla, a splendid volcanic mountain layered in shades of yellow from deep ochre to mustard. Climb Amarilla's height for excellent views across to El Médano; join the locals on the rocks at its base for a unique sunbathing spot or follow the coastal path to Golf del Sur.

Who'd want to stay here?

Every time we visit the resort we ask ourselves the same question. A friend who lives there says it's a nice place to live, with a multi-national personality. But we just don't see the attraction.

The food scene

Pub grub and standard British menus are the order of the day or night in the bars and restaurants that fill the resort.

Where we'd eat

It might seem harsh, but we wouldn't. By all accounts there are places in the resort serving decent food, but the setting (often in *locales*) just doesn't appeal.

Why visit

Apart from Montaña Amarilla literally standing out from the rest of the resort, the seas around this part of the coast have some of Tenerife's best dive sites. It's also convenient for the golf courses of Golf del Sur, and a taste of a more traditional side of the south in Las Galletas.

On the beach

Other than at Las Galletas, the coast around this part of Tenerife is sheer, rocky and for the most part devoid of beaches. A coastal path leads from Las Galletas to the Alborada Ocean Club where there's a pleasant but small, black sand beach favoured by locals. As the rocky coast continues, the occasional crumbling steps down to churning rock pools are handy for those who like their daily dip to have that frisson of danger attached.

After dark
Endless bars showing sports and nightly karaoke or cabaret. Most are to be found in and around the Coral Mar centre.

Where we'd stay
In a nutshell, we wouldn't stay in Costa del Silencio.

Best time to visit
Any time of the year is good ... or not, depending on how you view Costa del Silencio.

EL MÉDANO

Where is it and what's it like?
In everything but the weather, El Médano is possibly Tenerife's coolest resort. Seldom absent easterly winds attract local and international kite-boarders and wind surfers who spend their days in hand to sail combat with the elements, skimming the ocean alongside three kilometres of natural pale gold sands. The same winds keep the serious suntan seekers of the more popular southern resorts at bay, leaving El Médano to a laid-back, Bohemian clientele who take their sunshine with a healthy helping of local culture.

Grown from a small fishing village, El Médano has retained its Canarian population and swelled their numbers with sports-minded incomers who have opened surf schools, bars and shops along the wooden *'paseo'* that lines the seafront. Plaza de Asturias, which is the focal point of the village, is busy with its pavement cafes, doubling as the venue for a weekend market where neo-hippies lay out their clothing, jewellery and craft stalls, and as the open air stage for world music concerts and the occasional theatre production.

The landmark red volcanic cone of Montaña Roja lies to the west of the resort, acting as a stunning backdrop to the gold sand and petrol waters of this vibrant, photogenic part of Tenerife's southern coast.

Provided you suit the 'windswept and interesting' look and can ignore the constant daily aircraft as you're right under the flight path, El Médano represents the perfect blend of a coastal resort with long, golden sand beaches, near-guaranteed year-round sunshine and some genuine *tinerfeñan* culture; there aren't many places on the island that can boast the same.

Who'd want to stay here?
People who enjoy board sports. But it's also a good base for anyone who likes a chilled-out, beach scene with a local vibe and who doesn't mind the constant stiff breeze.

The food scene

El Médano's culinary offerings are as diverse as its visitors and you'll find Canarian, Mexican and even a Japanese sushi bar amongst its eclectic collection. As you'd expect for such a Bohemian venue, there are plenty of veggie offers on menus.

Where we'd eat

Snacks, international, Spanish - Just the fact that it's in a prime position on Plaza El Médano makes **Veinte 04** worth a stop but the food is varied and interesting too with something to keep you satisfied whether it's breakfast, lunch or dinner. Plus it doubles as a centre of culture, so you get great live music occasionally as a bonus. *Plaza El Medano; +34 922 176 079; open 09:30-22:30 Sunday to Wednesday, 09:30-23:00 Thursday, 09:30-midnight Friday & Saturday; average cost of main course €9.*

Tapas & traditional - We particularly like **Bar Playa Chica** because of its seafront position overlooking the tiny beach it shares a name with. Grab a table on the small terraces or on the rooftop terrace, order tapas or fresh fish dishes, and soak up the view and that sea air. El Timón next door offers a similar experience. *Paseo Marcial Garcia, 32; +34 922 178 938; open 11:00-23:00 Tuesday to Sunday, closed Monday; a selection of tapas for €10.*

Why visit

This is the wind surfing and kiteboarding capital of Tenerife; if it's got anything to do with riding waves, you can hire it, learn it, wear it and buy it here. With up to 290 days of wind a year and sea temperatures that hover around 20C, you can surf your way through the calendar. Equipment hire is around €35 per day and lessons start from around €30 a session including equipment.

There are also decent coastal walks around El Médano, the best being across the sands to the top of Montaña Roja and then to a cave where the Canary Islands' only saint, Hermano Pedro, once lived.

On the beach

If beaches were currency, El Médano would be the Jeff Bezos of Tenerife. No less than seven sandy sites grace the resort from Playa de la Pelada in the east to Playa la Tejita in the west. Many of the natural golden sand beaches are given over to El Médano's first two loves; surfing and naturism.

Surfers have the whole of the beautiful Playa Machado to themselves and its fine sand is constantly littered with their boards and sails. At the headland on the east of the village is Playa el Cabezo which hosts international windsurfing competitions, and further along to the east is Playa la Jaquita which also fills the

Top: El Médano, bottom left: banana plantation worker, bottom right, Costa Adeje

horizon with sails.

Those who prefer to have no 'white bits' head out to Playa la Pelada and scramble down the rocks to the resort's main nudist spot where the sheltered coves keep out the wind and the 'sightseers'. Around the base of Bocinegro to the west is the small beach of La Playita which is popular with male naturists and the cove at the foot of Montaña Roja on Playa la Tejita is also given over to nude sunbathing.

If neither surfing nor nudism ring your bell, the town beach of Playa El Médano has fine sand and a gently shelving shoreline and is very popular with families. Backed by bars, restaurants, ice cream parlours and kiosks, you'll want for nothing all day.

For endless sandy space, walk for 20 minutes towards Montaña Roja, past the sand dunes and through the *malpaís* until you arrive at the white sand beach of Playa la Tejita which could absorb coach loads of visitors should they choose to arrive but luckily, they don't. Wander the turquoise shore leaving virgin footprints in the sand and try not to trip over the semi circular walls that protect nude sunbathers from having their sensitive bits sandblasted. The vibe could change once/if plans to build a hotel on Playa la Tejita go ahead.

After dark

After a hard day on the boards, the order of the night is laid back and mellow. Indulge in an early beer with the surf dudes at Flashpoint, on the boardwalk behind Playa Machado, before heading over the other side of town to Plaza Roja where you can kick back at Manfred's Soul Café and enjoy the sunset chill-out or join in the jam sessions.

Where we'd stay

Apart from a handful of hotels, there are a proliferation of apartments in and around the town, from cheap bedsits to swish apartments overlooking Playa Machado.

Hotel El Médano (*Picacho, 2; +34 922 177 000; www.hotelmedano.com*) is the town's iconic hotel and in a superb position but more comfortable, is the **Hotel Arenas del Mar** behind Playa la Jaquita (*Avda Europa, 2; +34 922 179 830; Avda Europa,2; www.hotelarenasdelmar.com*) where you can leave the hippy surfer look to the locals and indulge in spa style and chic comfort.

Best time to visit

If music and a lively local atmosphere is your thing, then July/August is ideal. The Sansofé Festival brings events most days including music concerts, tapas tastings, traditional dances, and open-air cinema.

GOLF DEL SUR

Where is it and what's it like?
Move further east along the coast and some of the concrete of the Alborada
Ocean Club and Costa del Silencio is replaced by green, or rather greens, as the
eponymous courses of Golf del Sur undulate in the heat haze. Overwhelmingly
British in both its population and its visitors, Golf del Sur's hotels, shopping
arcades, restaurants and bars are predominantly geared towards satisfying their
needs. Rows of blackboards announce sports TV coverage, cabaret, karaoke and
burger and chips.
A shiny marina, San Miguel, is filled with yachts and cruisers even though,
save for the greens that sweep down the headland and a small kiosk, there's
nothing else there. There's been a move to re-brand Golf del Sur as Costa San
Miguel, and the resort is now sometimes referred to as San Miguel de Abona,
which is the name of the traditional town located inland and in the hills. Getting
them confused isn't going to end well for either golfers or those seeking a more
authentic Canarian experience.

Who'd want to stay here?
Golfers are the obvious target, but also holidaymakers seeking a quiet resort
with a British feel to it. With accommodation being limited at neighbouring Los
Abrigos, it might also suit people who want to be close to a traditional fishing
village.

The food scene
Restaurants in Golf del Sur are aimed squarely at the mainly British visitors
and ex-pats who frequent the resort. It's not the place for authentic Canarian
dining. But you'll get a decent curry there and you won't struggle to find a
restaurant dishing up a Sunday roast.

Where we'd eat
Contemporary international - The food at **Old Fashioned 1986** is nicely
presented and interesting enough to tempt us through its doors. *San Blas
Commercial Centre, 73; +34 922 059 036; open 18:00-23:00 Monday to
Saturday, closed Sunday; average cost of main course €10.*

Why visit
Golf is the main attraction – The Golf del Sur course (*www.golfdelsur.net*) (27
holes, par 72) and the Amarilla Golf course (*www.amarillagolf.es*) (18 holes, par
72) have greens sweeping down to the sea and an easterly breeze to notch up the
difficulty factor.

The marina also means easy access for some sea-going trips, such as hiring yachts or taking an undersea voyage on the Submarine Safari. This popular trip takes you into the awesome underworld of Las Galletas without the aid of an oxygen tank and flippers. Packed with 'wow' moments, you'll have a memory stick full of eels, wrecks and rays and if you're old enough, 'Yellow Submarine' going round your head for days afterwards. (*922 73 66 29; www. submarinesafaris.com; €48 adults, €28 children*).

There are a couple of good, short walks around Golf del Sur. One heads south west along the coast to Costa del Silencio and Montaña Amarilla. The other is a cracker of a route through the San Blas Barranco which has a few surprises along the way. The downside to this one is, unless you're staying at the Barceló Hotel, there's a fee to enter the ravine and you need to book (organised via the hotel).

On the beach

There's not really a beach at Golf de Sur, or at least there wasn't. There have been attempts to convert pebbly stretches of coast into something more comfortable, especially outside the Barceló Hotel.

After dark

Nightlife in Golf del Sur is most definitely aimed at British holidaymakers seeking a flavour of home.

Where we'd stay

There are a handful of hotels in and around Golf del Sur, some aimed at golfing visitors, others not. We're not golfers so ...

Nature is the VIP guest at the **Barceló Tenerife**, formerly Sandos San Blas, (*San Blas Reserva Ambiental, Los Abrigos; +34 971 78 33 02; www.sandos. com*), a stylish, five star, all-inclusive set alongside a nature reserve on the south east coast, a stroll away from golf courses and great seafood restaurants. Eight pools, a small lake with kayaking and canoeing and fabulously stylish rooms, all at four star prices.

Best time to visit

There's nothing really to separate one month from the next so, apart from it being hotter in summer months, any time of year is good.

GRANADILLA DE ABONA

Where is it and what's it like?

Granadilla de Abona nestles into Tenerife's southern flank at around the 600 metre mark, where the buff *jable* (pumice) landscape meets the edge of the pine forest.

There's a pleasantly nostalgic feel to Granadilla's streets. Some shops are reminiscent of the kind of independent affairs found in British towns in the 1960s, with shoe and shirt boxes piled high behind wooden counters and shelves full of all sorts of household goods. The butcher, fishmonger and greengrocer are all located in the same courtyard with a bar and takeaway tapas bar (fast food – Granadilla style) thrown in for good measure. It's close enough to the tourist resorts to be convenient for commuting but has more in common with the other agricultural communities dotted along the old Carretera General del Sur.

Some pavements on the main street are ridiculously narrow, forcing pedestrians onto the road and into the path of oncoming 4x4s. Better to stick to the mainly traffic free and more picturesque streets around the Convento Franciscano San Luis (once a military headquarters complete with dungeon, now the town's library and tranquil courtyard) and the 17th century Iglesia de San Antonio de Padua whose midget gem-shaped tower has a Russian Orthodox quality to it.

In 2015 the municipality's coast was re-branded as Costa Magallanes, a tenuous link to the famous Portuguese explorer (Magallanes is Spanish for Magellan) who briefly hid his ships behind Montaña Roja, but it's a tag that's yet to catch on.

What's the story?

Before the conquest of Tenerife, Granadilla was part of the *menceyato* (Guanche kingdom) of Abona, under the rule of Adjona. Ironically, although Adjona had been one of the so-called *menceys* of Peace, those who signed a pact with the Castilian army in support of the conquest of the island, it was Abona which saw the fiercest and longest-held Guanche resistance following the ceding of the island to the Crown of Castile. After the last of the rebels were defeated, the settlers arrived, predominantly from Portugal, and made their homes in the valleys where there were springs to provide water and Guanche paths connecting settlements. On October 1st 1519, the coast briefly hosted the fleet of Ferdinand Magellan on the first circumnavigation of the globe.

The first church, dedicated to San Antonio Abad, was awarded the rank of parish church in 1617 but was subsequently destroyed by fire. The church that was constructed atop its ruins in 1885, is still in use today. Becoming a municipality in the 19th century, the region remained isolated with no access by land except over the mountains on foot with mules or horses, and the only way to reach other municipalities being by sea. It wasn't until the 1930s that the first road was built by the military, finally connecting Abona, re-named Granadilla de Abona in the 16th century, to the rest of the island.

Who'd want to stay here?

As well as those wanting to experience life in a traditional Canarian town not too far from the coast, the location of Granadilla de Abona makes it suitable for visitors interested in outdoor pursuits such as walking, rock climbing and mountain biking.

The food scene

Granadilla de Abona isn't blessed with a great choice of restaurants. There are a few very run-of-the-mill traditional affairs, but dining options are definitely limited here.

Where we'd eat

Contemporary Canarian - El Secreto de Chimiche (formerly named Casa Fito) is in Chimiche, a 15 minute drive from Granadilla, but it's worth making the effort as it is considered one of the best Canarian restaurants on Tenerife (it has a Michelin Bib Gourmand rating). The restaurant is set in a former tomato packing warehouse (much nicer looking than it might sound) and although the menu sounds very traditional, what arrives at the table is presented in a more sophisticated manner than is usual. A good place to try the Tenerife speciality of *cochino negro* (black pig). *Carretera General del Sur 4, Chimiche; +34 922 777 279; open 13:00-17:30 Monday to Thursday, 13:00-22:30 Friday & Saturday, closed Monday, and also 19:00-23:00 on Friday and Saturday; average cost of main course €20.*

Why visit

The town's History Museum (*C/Arquitecto Marrero; 11*) is tiny, but beautifully designed with interesting exhibits about rural living in the south of Tenerife pre-tourism (information in Spanish only). One darkened room reveals a couple of grotesque-looking mummified Guanche and scattered human bones. It's delightfully macabre.

There are quite a few walking routes around Granadilla – an old trading route links the town with neighbour San Miguel de Abona, whilst a pilgrim trail from Vilaflor leading to the coast passes through the town.

After dark

Basically, it's very quiet when the sun drops below the horizon.

Where we'd stay

There are a few rural houses for rent in and around Granadilla, but whenever there's a good rural hotel we'll opt for that every time.

Hotel Rural Senderos de Abona (*C/Peatonal Iglesia; +34 922 770 200; www.senderosdeabona.es*) is the former village post office now converted into a rural hotel. It's an enchanting, rustic 19th century house with courtyards, polished wooden floors and low doorways. Lots of character in its period furniture and assorted ornaments and a great library of information about walking routes.

Best time to visit

As a base for walking and outdoor activities, winter months are best. But for anyone wanting warmth in a rural setting, summer and autumn are best.

LAS GALLETAS

Where is it and what's it like?

Las Galletas is the least commercialised centre along the whole of the south coast of Tenerife from Costa Adeje to Golf del Sur. Its history as a fishing village pre-dates the Spanish conquest and it has managed, against all odds, to fend off the armies of mass tourism and retain a large Canarian population and commensurate culture.

The focus of the town is the marina whose offices, cafés and tower are painted as if they were destined for Blackpool pier. White-hulled, elegant-masted yachts bob lazily alongside bright blue fishing boats and every morning the daily catch is sold from stalls at the top of the beach and then served up for lunch in the restaurants that line the promenade.

Southwards from the marina the sandy bay follows the coast around to the Malpaís de Rasca. Literally meaning 'badlands', eight kilometres of arid desert is populated by an abundance of Tenerife's endemic flora and the occasional 'bender' constructed of straw and old surf boards where the heat-hardiest of hippies hangs out. A hike across the *malpaís* takes you to the Faro de Rasca lighthouse, a lonely spot on a deserted headland which can be seen from all along the east coast.

Life in Las Galletas has a mellow pace, which is closely guarded by the locals who have no desire to mirror their neighbours to the east, or to the west of the island, evidenced by the shortage of hotels and holiday apartments in the town.

What's the story?

There are two schools of thought as to why the name Las Galletas was given to this area. One theory is that the name has its roots in Guanche heritage where it refers to a ceramic dish with a twisted spout, several of which were discovered here. Alternatively, it's thought the name could be a derivation of the Portuguese word '*calheta*' referring to a cove, the Portuguese 'lh' being pronounced the

219

same as the Spanish 'll'.

Whatever the origins of its nomenclature, Las Galletas' roots as a fishing village date back to its Guanche heritage when it was a favoured fishing ground for the indigenous people of the island; on Holy Days, pilgrimages were made to Las Galletas and bonfires were lit on the rocks. Until the end of the nineteenth century little changed in the small fishing village; poor soil, a lack of rainfall and susceptibility to attack from pirates ensured little development of this stretch of coast.

Who'd want to stay here?

Anyone looking for local flavour in a coastal setting. There aren't many places on the south coast where a Canarian personality dominates. Subsequently, Las Galletas isn't a place which suits everyone.

The food scene

As you'd expect for a town with a fishing harbour, fish and seafood figure highly on menus in Las Galletas. There is also a bit of a Belgian connection and as a result it's the place to try *moules et frites*.

Where we'd eat

Spanish & international - We like **El Pantalan's** position, jutting out over the harbour. You simply won't find many restaurants like this on Tenerife. It's a great location for enjoying *gambas al ajillo* (garlic prawns), *gueldes* (small fried fish) and mussels in green Thai sauce. *Rambla Dionisio González, local 1; +34 691 674 556; open 10:00-16:00 Monday to Friday, and midday-22:00 Saturday 6 Sunday; average price of tapas €5.*

Contemporary Belgian - We haven't eaten at **Le Grand Bleu** yet, but friends with palates we trust highly recommend it for its imaginative, fun and exquisitely presented food combined with sea views, Le Grand Bleu should probably be first port of call for visiting foodies. Plus they have *moules et frites Paseo Marítimo, Rambla Dionisio González; +34 655 708 547; open 09:30-15:00 and 19:00-22:00 Tuesday to Saturday, 09:30-15:00 Sunday, closed Monday; average cost of main course €18.*

Why visit

The seas around Las Galletas are deep, calm and clear, offering the perfect diving conditions for exploring rusting wrecks and volcanic rock formations teeming with life. There are dive clubs aplenty, amongst them Dive Tenerife (*+34 922 785 910; www.divetenerife.com*) and Tenerife Scuba (*+34 922 785 584; www.tenerifescuba.com*)

On the beach

Las Galletas has a pleasant, sheltered, sand and pebble beach where the lack of sun loungers for hire ensures it's never too busy. There are no facilities or lifeguard but you're only a stroll away from the promenade's restaurants and ice cream parlours. At the other end of the promenade is a second, smaller beach favoured by locals where you can snooze away your post-lunch drowsiness undisturbed by the sound of traffic.

After dark

There are some decent local bars around the harbour, along the promenade and in the back streets.

Where we'd stay

Although there are a handful of apartments for rent, there's still a lack of accommodation in Las Galletas itself. Costa del Silencio is joined on to the town and so offers a wider range of options, starting with the **Alborada Ocean Club** (formerly Ten-Bel) which is right on the border between the two. However, we'd base ourselves somewhere else and visit during the day, or to eat.

Best time to visit

Like other traditional coastal settlements, summer is liveliest. However, any time of year is good for a visit.

LOS ABRIGOS

Where is it and what's it like?

Los Abrigos means overcoat in Spanish, and mariners have been taking advantage of the natural, protected harbour at Los Abrigos since the days when Ferdinand Magellan sailed these waters.

Although the small town behind the harbour front is typical of many modern Canarian towns – not particularly attractive – the harbour area itself is one of the most picturesque on Tenerife, especially when the moon sends a silver trail across the water after dark.

A small fishing fleet still brings their catch to the restaurants lining the curved promenade ascending from the harbour and it's not uncommon for local men to be seen sitting mending their nets in the shade provided by the harbour wall.

There's a nice little, relaxed scene in Los Abrigos. The village plays host to small scale fiestas and festivals such as the Tapas y Cañas Festival each August. There's also a weekly night market each Tuesday between 5pm and 9pm.

Top: Barranco San Blas, bottom left: Playa las Vistas, Los Cristianos, bottom right: Las Galletas

What's the story?

Originally known as Caleta de los Abadejos, on October 1st 1519, the fleet of Ferdinand Magellan berthed at the beach of La Tejita in El Médano, just along the coast, and hid in an inlet behind Montaña Roja as they had heard that a Portuguese squadron was looking to arrest them.

Although the port was one of the busiest in the south during the 16th century, it wasn't until the 19th century when it became the port of call for San Miguel de Abona, that a nucleus of population settled. In 1922 the road connecting San Miguel to the port of Los Abrigos was completed, enabling the transport of bananas, potatoes and tomatoes for export. In the 1940s the Canal del Sur brought water to the area and greenhouse plantations were established for the cultivation of tomatoes. With the arrival of mass tourism, Los Abrigos became commuter territory for many of the workers from the tourism industry and it almost doubled its population from 395 to 777 between 1981 and 1991. Today it still retains a small fishing fleet and is known for its seafood restaurants surrounding the harbour.

Who'd want to stay here?

Los Abrigos would suit anyone who wants a tranquil base in the south that's on the coast and has a traditional feel to it. It's not a place for beach lovers though.

The food scene

The main reason people visit Los Abrigos is because of its reputation for fish restaurants. These days there are as many contemporary restaurants as there are traditional fish ones, which has resulted in some ex-pats heading further along the east coast in search of a 'more authentic' fish and seafood scene. However, Los Abrigos remains a romantic setting for dinner which is worlds away from that in the purpose-built resorts.

Where we'd eat

Fish & seafood - There are lots of good restaurants along the promenade, but for a decidedly local fish and seafood experience try **Restaurant Los Abrigos** right on the harbour. The fish is fresh daily; they have their own fishing boat so Squid, octopus, moray eel, mussels, limpets, oysters, prawns and lobster are constant regulars. *Calle Marina 3; +34 922 170 264; open midday-23:00, closed Wednesday & Thursday; average price of main course €10.*

Why visit

It's on the coast, the weather is good, it's small but with a great choice of fish and seafood restaurants.

On the beach
The closest beach is Playa de San Blas which links Los Abrigos with neighbouring Golf del Sur. It's a cobble beach but the former San Blas Nature Reserve Hotel (now the Barceló Tenerife Hotel) constructed a sandy strip with straw umbrellas.

After dark
There aren't many places on Tenerife where you can sit around a picturesque harbour drinking local *vino* after dark. Los Abrigos is one of them. It's not exactly Greek standards, but it's still a romantic setting.

Where we'd stay
Although it is possible to rent an apartment in Los Abrigos, for hotel accommodation it has to be Golf del Sur which is only a short walk away. Closest is the **Barceló Tenerife** (formerly Sandos San Blas Resort).

Best time to visit
Any time of year is good.

LOS CRISTIANOS

Where is it and what's it like?
Gateway to the Western Canary Islands of La Gomera, La Palma and El Hierro, Los Cristianos near Tenerife's southern tip is characterised by its bustling, colourful port; golden beaches; and hotels, apartment blocks and sundry developments built to cater to its mass tourism industry. Despite its breakneck expansion, the resort still has fishing and the sea at its heart and retains some semblance of a Canarian character which separates it from its purpose-built neighbours.

Narrow streets lined with shops, bars, restaurants, ice cream parlours and souvenir outlets criss-cross their way back from a wide, wheelchair-friendly promenade. On the hills behind the centre, complex after complex of holiday and residential apartments climb towards the motorway, and construction cranes are an ever-present feature of the horizon. The further away from the harbour-side centre, the less traditional it feels.

Home to a large British expat population and preferred destination of retired Brit 'swallows' who over-winter on its sunny beaches, Los Cristianos is considerably quieter than its neighbour, Playa de las Américas, whose boundaries have extended so far south that it's now impossible to see the join between the two resorts.

What's the story?

Located between two mountains – Guaza and Chayofita – and with no natural water sources in its arid, volcanic landscape, there is little evidence of this stretch of coast being populated by the Guanche who preferred to live in the upper reaches of the kingdom of Arona. The same lack of water meant that little attention was paid to the area post-conquest, the first Tenerife lands to be settled being those that could support the cultivation of sugar cane. Save for a handful of fishermen's huts, the constant threat of incursions by pirates kept settlers away and as there was no sizeable population, no defences were built. It wasn't until 1860 that the first permanent settlement of Los Cristianos took place and consisted of three one-storey houses, a two-storey house and a shack. By the time it was officially recognised in government deeds in 1888, its dwellings had swelled to 29 houses and a cave.

In 1909 the first quay (now known as El Puerto Viejo) was built, taking advantage of the natural harbour and, with the threat of pirate attacks now a distant memory, Los Cristianos' importance as an export point for fish, salt and pine resin for tar, began to grow. Agriculture began to feature in the landscape from 1914 thanks to the efforts of one man, Teofilo Bello Rodriguez who ran a pipe from his land in Vilaflor, down to his father's land in Los Cristianos. The introduction of irrigation fuelled economic expansion with the planting of tomatoes and bananas attracting new labour. In 1934 a much larger port was constructed which could accommodate larger fishing vessels and commercial shipping. Fearing a possible invasion by the British, at the outbreak of WWII a number of defensive bunkers were constructed along the Los Cristianos coastline, some of which remain intact today.

But by far the greatest influence in the development of Los Cristianos and subsequently of the whole of the south of Tenerife was sparked by two significant events. In 1957, a Swedish vet suffering from Multiple Sclerosis arrived in Los Cristianos and changed the course of its history. The Swede, Bengt Rylander, known to the locals as El Bonito (the handsome one), immediately found the dry air and the warm sunshine improved his condition beyond anything he had found on his travels. Being a writer and a TV presenter, Rylander broadcast the news of Los Cristianos' climate to his home country. Before long, a group of Swedes, all suffering from related disabilities, settled in the village and bought a house which they adapted into ten wide rooms for wheelchair access, naming it Casa Sueca (Swedish House). Some of the village men went to Sweden to study medicine and returned to work in Los Cristianos and so the mutual benefit derived from the arrivals set the pattern for the future. The Vintersol rehabilitation centre was constructed in 1968 with funding from the Swedish National Health Service, attracting ever increasing numbers of rehabilitating invalids and their families to the village. As friends made trips to visit them, so the local population grew to cater to their needs.

The second most important event was the inauguration of the Reina Sofia Airport in 1978 fuelling mass tourism and a huge influx of British ex-pats retiring to the sun or relocating and opening bars and restaurants catering to the tastes of the tourists. Tourism displaced all other economic activity; the last banana crop was harvested in the early 1990s and commercial shipping has been replaced by pleasure cruises and the daily ferry services to La Gomera, El Hierro and La Palma. A small fishing fleet still operates from the harbour.

Who'd want to stay here?

Los Cristianos suits visitors who want a quiet resort with excellent weather where English is largely spoken and there's just a hint of local flavour. It's also a good base for exploring other islands.

The food scene

At first glance it might seem as though there's a glut of Italian restaurants and blackboards offering all day English breakfasts in Los Cristianos. Once you know where to look, you'll discover the gastronomic scene is more varied and there are plenty of traditional restaurants mixed in with the international crowd-pleasers. The harbour area is best for going local whereas restaurants along Avenida San Francisco are most definitely aimed at those looking for familiarity abroad. One of the best areas for dining is at CC San Telmo.

Where we'd eat

Fish & seafood - Despite being right at the entrance to the port **El Cine** is easy to miss as it's hidden away at the end of a narrow passage behind the chemist. The seating is simple as are the fish and seafood dishes on the menu. People queue to get in, but we think although it's raved about in the south of Tenerife, this local institution is fairly run-of-the-mill compared to similar restaurants outside of resort areas. But it is cheap and the food is good. *Paseo Juan Bariajo 8; +34 609 107 758; open 11:00-23:00 daily, closed Monday; average price of main course €9.*

Lebanese - The San Telmo Commercial Centre is a good hunting ground for establishments which are better than the average resort restaurant. The **Water Melon** and **Sal Negra** are both good, but our pick is **Habibi**. Lebanese restaurants are popular all over Tenerife, even in the bigger tradition towns, and Habibi is one of the best on the island. We're meze fans and Habibi's are excellent, as are mains of various meats in ginger, mango and light curry sauces. Here you get the flavours of the Middle East overlooking Las Vistas beach. *CC San Telmo 11B; +34 922 750 951; open 13:00-midnight, closed Monday;*

average price of main course €12.

Mixed bag - If, like us, you enjoy munching your way around food markets, it's worth a visit to **La Pepa Food Market** on the roof of Pasarela Oasis. Stalls serve food with flavours from across the globe, including Spanish, Mexican and Asian. There are also cocktails, wine stalls and local beers. In truth, it doesn't compare to food markets in other destinations such as Santa Cruz but food markets are thin on the ground on Tenerife which makes La Pepa a welcome addition. *CC Passerella ; +34 922 794 885; open 09:00-01:00, closed Monday & Tuesday.*

Why visit

Take advantage of the ferry portal to visit any of the other Western Canary Islands of La Palma, La Gomera, and El Hierro to discover locations under two hours sailing but which feel half a century away from Los Cristianos.

Take to the warm seas that surround the resort to see whales and dolphins in their natural environment. Choose any trip that flies the yellow 'Barco Azul' (it would have been so much more sensible to make the flag blue) to ensure ethical practices and then prepare to be wowed.

Seeing animals in captivity isn't anything like as thrilling as watching them at play in their natural habitat, but there are two establishments near Los Cristianos which are popular with visitors. At Monkey Park (*www.monkeypark.com*) the assorted primates show no respect for personal space, eat the food offered, and your hair, then steal anything they can get their little hands on. Kids love it.

Las Águilas Jungle Park (*www.aguilasjunglepark.com*) is for those who want to act out Indiana Jones fantasies over narrow suspension bridges in thick jungle with the cries of leopards and jaguars in the still air. The big attraction is the bird of prey show, when eagles, vultures and falcons fly centimetres above your head. Not a good place for wig wearers.

On the beach

In the centre of town, overlooking the port and its constant activity, is the golden sand beach of Playa de Los Cristianos. Rows of umbrellas and sunbeds occupy the shoreline while at the back of the sand, beach volleyball courts are in near-constant use.

Through the tunnel towards Las Américas is the vast expanse of Playa de Las Vistas, arguably the south's most popular beach. Fine white sand has been imported, cleaned and pressed and lies in its Sunday best clothes in the shimmering heat haze while regimented rows of sun loungers crowd the water's edge. The western edge of the beach strays into Playa de Las Américas, but it's all the same municipality.

In deference to its origins, Los Cristianos is Tenerife's most disability friendly resort with beach terraces set aside for those with mobility problems and wheelchair users. Amphibian chairs and Red Cross staff are on hand to ensure that everyone can enjoy the seaside experience of a 'barrier-free paradise'.

Beyond the crazy golf and petanque courts, small, sandy coves dot their way from the centre of the resort to its southern end. The further you walk, the fewer people occupy them, until you reach Playa Callao where the sand is less disciplined, the vegetation has a mind of its own and you can find quiet corners and rocky platforms on which to be alone. Perfect for anyone who prefers their beaches a little less manicured and their tan a little more 'all over'.

After dark

Nightlife south of the Las Vistas tunnel is aimed at the resort's visitors with a multitude of cabaret bars with tribute acts which close at or around midnight, sending the more mature Brits home to bed with the strains of 'Simply the Best' still ringing in their ears. However, the eclectic style bars of San Telmo will just be warming up about then, attracting a more local clientele, and you can be anything but mature there until the early hours.

Where we'd stay

There's no problem with finding accommodation in Los Cristianos, there are plenty of hotel and apartment options. The luxury end of the market is more limited, but there are some good mid-range hotels.

Sensimar Arona Gran Hotel (*Avda Juan Carlos, 1; +34 922 750 678; www.aronahotel.com*) is a large and perennially popular hotel at the southern extreme of the resort. In 2016 the Arona Gran was refurbished, re-branded and relaunched as a couples-only hotel under the name Sensimar. The gardens and swimming pools offer a relaxed space in which to soak up the sun while the spa promises couples treatments and a state of the art gymnasium. It's a 20min walk along the sea front to the centre of town.

Best time to visit

The fist Sunday in September sees the municipality's largest fiesta when the Virgen Del Carmen is taken from her home in the white church of Nuestra Señora del Carmen in the little plaza and carried by fishermen to the harbour. There, amidst a colourful regatta of fishing boats, she's taken for a trip around the bay and returned amidst a barrage of fireworks and much merrymaking.

PALM-MAR

Where is it and what's it like?
What is the purpose of Palm-Mar? It's a question we ask ourselves every time we visit. It's not a town, neither is it a resort. Yet it's more than a housing development. In Spanish it's called an *urbanización*. Basically it's still a bit of a work in progress – a place with aspirations of becoming a fully-fledged resort.

The dry, sunny area tucked into the eastern side of Montaña Guaza was identified as having the potential to be an exclusive tourist resort and development started in the 1990s. The construction work sort of fizzled out during the crisis years leaving an *urbanización* that looks unfinished and which remains more residential than a place for visitors to stay. It's a curious place with a small, fort-like construction which is actually for housing utilities. It's also a non-busy area to park for anyone who wants to explore the protected volcanic badlands of Malpaís de Rasca. In recent years Palm-Mar has had a boost, with part of its stony beach being developed and a handful of stylish bar restaurants opening. However, for the time being it remains neither one thing nor the other.

Who'd want to stay here?
You don't have to be Sherlock Holmes to have gathered Palm-Mar is not our cup of *té*. However, if sunshine and tranquillity are the main goals, then it ticks both those boxes.

The food scene
To be fair, there's not a bad little food scene in Palm-Mar, with choices ranging from tapas and Italian to Belgian and British. There's even a *guachinche*, or at least a restaurant with the *guachinche* tag; although anyone who thinks they'll find an authentic *guachinche* in a coastal development in the south of Tenerife is going to be disappointed.

Where we'd eat
International - One of the reasons we would visit Palm-Mar would be to chill out at **Bahía Beach**. We spent a very nice Noche de San Juan there, lounging on the Bali beds watching the sun go down and fire-dancers do their thing. The food isn't cheap, but with wraps, fish, pastas, burgers, vegetarian, meat and fish dishes there's something to suit most tastes. Good music as well. *Paseo Marítimo; +34 922 103 030; open 11:00-22:00 daily; average price of main course €18.*

Why visit
If anyone can answer that question, we'd love to know. Flippancy aside, it is

handy for an explore of Malpaís de Rasca which separate Palm-Mar from Las Galletas.

On the beach

Arena in Spanish means sand, so you tend to find a few Playa de las Arenas (sandy beach) about the island. There's a tendency to add 'ita' or 'ito' to words when locals want to emphasise something is small. The beach at Palm-Mar is called Playa de la Arenita as most of it is stony and just a small section has been given a sandy makeover.

After dark

The scene at Bahía Beach after dark draws a mixed bag of nationalities.

Where we'd stay

There are no hotels in Palm-Mar but there are plenty of apartment complexes. In all honesty, we wouldn't stay there.

Best time to visit

If Palm-Mar is the sort of place which appeals, any time is good.

PLAYA DE LAS AMÉRICAS

Where is it and what's it like?

Playa de las Américas on Tenerife's sun-kissed southern coast in the municipality of Arona has long held a reputation as a hedonistic holiday destination for under 25yr-olds seeking boozy nights and lazy days on the beach, and people who were looking for 'Blackpool in the sun'. However, the times they are a-changing.

Following its development from virtually uninhabitable badlands to bustling tourist resort in the 70s, Las Américas spread outwards, joining up with Los Cristianos on one side and into the neighbouring municipality of Adeje on the other. In recent years, realising that Las Américas had become synonymous with cheap, package holidays, Adeje re-branded their part of the resort as the upmarket 'Costa Adeje'. A smart strategy; it's not uncommon to hear people who would have baulked at the idea of staying in Las Américas remark: "Stay in Las Américas? Good God no, we're staying in Costa Adeje".

Consequently the area once known as Playa de las Américas seems to be shrinking. Las Américas has responded by attempting to re-invent itself. Bars for the 'beer and burger brigade' still exist, with their 'we sell normal food here' (whatever 'normal' is) proclamations etched on blackboards, but much of the resort has undergone a revamp. Stylish restaurants, trendy bars, five star hotels

230

and shopping centres filled with designer brands have become the norm on the resort's wide, palm-lined avenues. Nowadays Las Américas is a bright, clean modern resort which is becoming increasingly popular with nationalities other than the British, especially Eastern Europeans. The new image has given it an international ambience; although one which has more in common with Las Vegas than it does with the rest of Tenerife.

Who'd want to stay here?

It's known as the resort for people seeking lively nightlife in a warm climate, but that's around Veronica's on the border with Costa Adeje. We also recommend the area around the Safari Centre at the other end of the resort to friends and family seeking sunshine, a nice beach, a good choice of restaurants, and some decent music bars, all in an upmarket setting.

The food scene

There are plenty of Italian, Indian, Chinese, Tex-Mex, Greek, Lebanese and 'international' (code for conservative cuisine) restaurants about the resort although a shortage of traditional Canarian restaurants speaks volumes about Las Américas' lack of cultural identity. In recent years, the opening of cosmopolitan eateries with food as imaginative as their décor has added a chic flavour to the choice of cuisine on offer. We prefer the choice of restaurants here to that of neighbouring Costa Adeje.

Where we'd eat

Spanish - As the name suggests, **Mesón Castellano** is more Castilian than Canarian, something that's instantly obvious once you step inside to see Serrano hams, salami and *salchichas* hanging from the rafters, and wild boar heads staring down from the walls. One of the best Spanish restaurants on Tenerife. It gets some poor reviews online because, well, it's authentically Spanish. Go figure. *Avda. Antonio Domínguez Residencial El Camisón; +34 922 796 305; open 13:00-01:00; average price of main course €18.*

Contemporary Spanish - The best meal we've had in Las Américas was at the gourmet restaurant Tiziano. But as you've got to be a guest at the Hotel Villa Cortes that's not much use. However, the hotel does have restaurants open to the public, one being the Beach Club located in what is our favourite part of the coast in that area. It's a lovely spot for lunch or a sunset cocktail. They do a very good gazpacho and a mean *barraquito. Avda. Rafael Puig S/N; +34 922 757 700; open early to late daily; average price of main course €12.*

Traditional Canarian - El Gomero is a refreshingly unpretentious traditional Canarian joint, a rarity in Playa de las Américas, with big portions and low prices. Opposite the Magma Centre's architectural masterpiece, or muddle depending on personal taste, it's a popular haunt with taxi drivers and police but hey, everybody's got to eat. *Ave. V Centenario, 1; +34 922 750 713; open 07:00-midnight; average price of main course €8.*

British - Empire describe their menu as a modern take on classic pub grub, and that's pretty much what it is. Good looking, quality pub food in pleasantly stylish surroundings. All the crowd-pleasers are there – beef Wellington, bangers and mash, steak and ale pie and, of course, fish and chips. If you're going to eat British fare on a Spanish island, it might as well be quality. *CC Safari Centre, Avenida de las Americas; +34 922 789 971; open 13:00-23:30; average price of main course €15.*

Why visit

It is so unlike much of the rest of Tenerife, that strolling its glitzy streets is like visiting a completely different destination. There isn't a better example of Las Américas' aspirations to be the Vegas of Europe than the row of bare-breasted archers atop the columns of the mock Roman-themed Pirámide de Arona, home to the lavish Carmen Mota Ballet (tickets €36). The building's so outrageously tacky that it's wonderful. The show itself is an enjoyable visual extravaganza, mixing Flamenco with opera and contemporary music. Las Américas doesn't pretend to be anything other than it is, a fun-filled playground for holidaymakers seeking sunshine.

On the beach

Despite many a travel guide waxing lyrical about the beaches of Playa de las Américas, most of the resort's coastline is rocky with a few natural and man made rock pools. The main sandy beach is Playa del Camisón. Backed by a strip of palm trees, it's a picturesque, sheltered, man-made affair of golden-ish sand with sunbeds and pedalos. Part of the long wide Playa de las Vistas which stretches almost to the centre of Los Cristianos also falls into Las Américas

A pleasant promenade running the length of the resort is accentuated by modern sculptures and benches which overlook the rocky Playa Honda and La Montañeta; an area with high waves which attracts surfers by the VW bus load. It's a surprisingly un-touristy spot for a romantic dusk stroll.

After dark

A diverse, lively nocturnal scene is one of the reasons why visitors return year after year. No other resort can match the range of sports bars, fun pubs, drag and tribute acts, karaoke bars and clubs that are dotted about the neon lit streets; it's

Top: Iglesia de San Pedro, Vilaflor, bottom left: traditional hamlet, San Miguel, bottom right: Safari Centre, Las Americas

Tenerife's cabaret capital.

Younger visitors, whose holiday aspirations are to drink as much as they can without the aid of a stomach pump and try to strike up a 'holiday romance' in the process, populate 'the strip'; an area around the notorious CC Veronica's and CC Starco. This is the Tenerife of TV's 'Tenerife Uncovered' infamy; the place to party the night away at any number of venues. It's matured somewhat these days, and is now also home to chic chill-out beach clubs.

More mature night owls who enjoy a sing-a-long should head to the 'patch', near the Hotel Parque Santiago II and the Hotel Las Palmeras or Parque de la Paz. There's a host of bars featuring comedians and live music; a place where time stands still and the likes of Billy Idol and Shirley Bassey soundalikes still haven't passed their 'sell by' date. But there are some decent musicians to be found in bars like The Bull's Head.

If the idea of cabaret holds about as much appeal as sunlight does to a vampire, there are some 'style' bars around the CC Safari end of the resort which cater for the local 'in crowd.' This is also home to the Hard Rock Cafe.

Where we'd stay

It's a purpose-built resort so there is accommodation to suit all budgets, from low end and basic to upmarket enough to keep international divas like J. Lo satisfied.

Hotel Villa Cortes (*+34 922 757 700; Avda Rafael Puig; www.europe-hotels. org*) is Mexican hacienda-themed luxury in the heart of Playa de Las Américas. We love the vibrant décor and the art work (lifts feature Frida Kahlo artwork); the hidden corners and romantic courtyards within the grounds; and the excellent beach club lunch venue and *chiringuito* beach bar. With a couple of Spain's top chefs overseeing the kitchen, the food is outstanding. You've got to love a hotel whose grounds include a Mayan pyramid with a church on top. We like it so much, we'd travel to Las Américas just to stay here.

Best time to visit

It's fun in the sun here all year round.

SAN MIGUEL DE ABONA

Where is it and what's it like?

San Miguel de Abona sits at 600 metres above the coast, capital of the municipality of the same name which includes the resorts of Golf del Sur and Amarillo Golf. It's one of the oldest towns in the south of Tenerife.

The TF28 which runs through San Miguel was built in the 1940s to connect the barren south to the populated north of the island and many of the town's old buildings were demolished to make room for it. The new centre that grew around it is work-a-day, nondescript and indicative of what all of the south would look like today had the tourism boom of the 1970s not changed much of the face of the coast beyond Tenerife recognition.

Leave the main road and wander down streets that would test the stamina of a mountaineer, into the old quarter where the austere beauty of the Iglesia de San Miguel Arcángel marks the start of a picturesque old quarter. Nicely renovated 18th and 19th century houses line narrow, cobbled streets with views over the volcanic landscape to the south coast.

San Miguel's best selling point is its semi-rural setting just a few kilometres but a million miles away from the busy coastal resorts so you still get the sunshine (albeit a degree cooler) along with characterful accommodation and great restaurants.

What's the story?

Part of the Guanche kingdom of Abona, ruled by Adjona, many archaeological sites around the surrounding area are testament to the Guanche origins of San Miguel, such as the ceremonial complex of Guargacho excavated by L. Diego Cuscoy in the 1970s in which he claims to have found a space of some 150sq metres incorporating an incineration pit, furnace and two stone slabs. Other researchers claim the site was actually a settlement of several huts of the type seen in North Africa. In 1933 the remains of 70 Guanche bodies were discovered in a necropolis in the Barranco de la Tafetena.

After the conquest, the area was populated by conquerors, settlers and those surviving Guanche who had not been taken into slavery. At this point, San Miguel was under the jurisdiction of Vilaflor and part of Chasna. The nucleus of today's San Miguel came into being in 1665 when Fernando Garcia del Castillo, a descendant of the conqueror Alonso Fernández de Lugo, built a church dedicated to San Miguel (The Archangel) and a village began to form around it. In July 1796 the church was granted the status of parish and two years later, San Miguel won independence from Vilaflor. The first road connecting San Miguel to Los Abrigos was completed in 1922 allowing the transport of goods to the coast for export but the development of agriculture did not gain any real economic importance until the construction of the Canal del Sur in the 1940s which brought water from the galleries of Fasnia and Arico to the south.

San Miguel de Abona is particularly known for its potatoes, tomatoes and wine. Despite the addition of the Canal del Sur, in order to prosper, the area has to overcome the problem of rain scarcity and so its terraces are lined with *jable* or pumice; a white, porous volcanic material which draws moisture from low cloud and traps it below the surface helping to retain precious rainfall and effectively self-irrigating crops.

Who'd want to stay here?

It's handy for the coast and the airport, and is about as traditional a town as you'll find in southern parts, making it a good base for anyone who wants to explore the authentic face of the south of Tenerife, but who also might want to be not too far from a beach or two.

The food scene

For a small southern Tenerife hill town, San Miguel de Abona punches well above its weight in relation to its gastronomic scene.

Where we'd eat

Traditional Canarian - La Bodega de San Miguel is a lovely looking restaurant in an historic Canarian building. The menu is traditional Canarian but presented with more style than is the norm and with some dishes you don't normally find on local menus, like chunky savoury pies. Also a good place to go for a drink in the evening. *Calle Jose Hernandez Alfonso 2; +34 922 700 127; open 13:00-22:00, closed Monday; average price of main course €12.*

Why visit

There's a small museum in Museo Casa de El Capitán (*www.teneriferural. org, +34 922 700 887*) at the town's El Calvario where they have displays of pottery and ceramics and lots of local history including a room dedicated to the use of camels for farming the south of the island.

A five minute drive or a pleasant hour's walk along a former Guanche trail takes you to the viewpoint of La Centinela from where you get widescreen vistas of the south airport and the resorts of Golf del Sur and El Médano set amidst arid, volcanic terrain.

If a mock medieval castle, skills of horsemanship, jousting and pulling chicken flesh from the bone with your bare hands while cheering on your Knight Errant rings your bell, the Castillo San Miguel (*www.castillosanmiguel.com*) will be right in your arena.

After dark

For a Tenerife hill town, there are a couple of nice spots to enjoy a drink, such as La Bodega de San Miguel.

Where we'd stay

There's quite a decent choice of accommodation in small, traditional hotels and rural houses.

Hotel Rural San Miguel (*+34 922 167 922; C/Las Morales, 2; www. hotelruralsanmiguel.com*) in the heart of town is an exquisitely restored 17th century mansion set around courtyards with its own thermal baths, rooftop Jacuzzi & solarium, and individually-styled bedrooms where you may find yourself sleeping in the former hen house or the goat farmyard.

Best time to visit
Hill towns can be cooler than the coast in winter, but that's relatively speaking. Spring, summer, early autumn is best for warmer weather. But if exploration is the goal, the time of year doesn't really matter.

VILAFLOR

Where is it and what's it like?
Vilaflor, lying at around 1500 metres above the south coast, is Spain's highest municipality and not the place to stay if a tan is your goal. At this height, clouds can sneak through the pines and fill the town's streets with a bone-chilling mist. Most of the time the town nestles above the clouds; its temperate climate attracting visitors since Victorian times when it was a popular spa destination. Nowadays, millions of tourists pass Vilaflor annually on their way to Mount Teide, but few venture onto its streets.

The heart of the town is a collection of historic houses, including one from the 19th century known as la Casa Inglesa (the English house), around the Plaza and Iglesia de San Pedro, named after a humble goatherd born in Vilaflor who became the Canary Island's one and only saint. It's a pretty little community with an Alpine-esque flavour thanks to the proximity of the pines and the high altitude setting, but it doesn't take more than an hour to wander around.

What's the story?
Popular legend has it that Vilaflor got its name from one of the Castilian conquerors, Captain Pedro de Bracamonte, who fell in love with a Guanche girl whose beauty was so mesmerizing that he had her captured in order to court her. Giving her the nickname Flor de Chasna (the flower of Chasna, as the area was known until the 17th century), the girl managed to escape and legend has it that the Captain went into a deep depression for three months and finally died, still ruing his loss with the words - *'vi la flor de Chasna'* (I have seen the flower of Chasna). Those of less romantic inclinations have concluded that Vilaflor is actually the name bestowed on the area in 1286 by the poet D Dinis who, passing through and noting the proliferation of flowers, called it *Vila Flor* (flower town). In 2014 the Cabildo de Tenerife approved a change of name for the municipality, restoring it to its original name of Vilaflor de Chasna. The town's residents have

always been, and still are, referred to as *chasneros*.

Pre-conquest there were no Guanche settlements at this height, instead Chasna was where the summer grazing grounds lay to which the Guanche would lead their livestock before returning to the coast for the winter. Falling within the jurisdiction of the Mencey of Abona, one of the so-called peace *menceys* who signed a pact with the Castilian conquerors, following the conquest in 1496 the highlands of Chasna became a refuge for Guanche rebels who held out for many years as the slow process of colonization began at the coast.

It wasn't until 1514 that the lands around the Chasna River were given to four conquerors. Just four years later the four ceded the land to Sancho de Vargas, senior Mayor of Tenerife whose heirs then sold the land to Juan Martín de Padilla. The town of Vilaflor finally came into being when Juan Martín's daughter, Juana de Padilla and her husband Pedro Soler built a hermitage dedicated to San Pedro Apóstol (St Peter the Apostle) in 1533. When the church was elevated to the title of Parish in 1568 it heralded the acquisition of Arona, Granadilla and Arico to the Parish of Chasna-Vilaflor.

Unfortunately, the arrival of the Solers was characterised by authoritarianism and launched a state of constant conflict between the ruling class and the local people whose lands and water were systematically seized leaving the poor with no choice but to emigrate to seek their fortunes in the New World. The conflict continued right through to 1840 when the Seventh Marquis of Soler was murdered by twelve masked men. The murderers were never apprehended and the *chasneros* never spoke a word about the incident.

Granadilla and Arico both achieved independence in the 17th century as each was awarded the status of its own Parish church. It would take until the late 18th century for Arona and Abona to establish their own parish and leave Vilaflor with the boundaries it still has today.

During the 19th century, Vilaflor increasingly played host to explorers, naturalists and scientists, including the likes of Philip Barker Webb and Sabino Berthelot, illustrious English and French botanists who penned the influential Natural History of The Canary Islands. Around this time Vilaflor also became popular as a spa town, its climate and mineral waters being considered advantageous to good health and particularly for those suffering from respiratory problems. In 1929 the development of Vilaflor took a leap forward when the road connecting it to Granadilla was completed, and again in 1947 with the completion of the road linking it to La Orotava, this latter highway being constructed by prisoners of the Spanish Civil War under jurisdiction of the military.

Hermano Pedro

In 1626 Pedro de Betencourt was born to Amador and Ana, poor farmers who lived in the village of Vilaflor. One of four children, at the age of 12yrs Pedro was indentured to one of his father's creditors in payment of debts for which the family goats had been possessed. A quiet and pious boy, he lived in a cave at the coast near El Médano from where he tended his father's herd on behalf of the creditor until the debt had been cleared. At the age of 23yrs he left Tenerife and 2 years later, arrived in Guatemala where he became seriously ill. Unable to afford medical help, he was cared for by the poorest of the city until he made a complete recovery. Wanting to become a priest but unable to pay for ecclesiastical college, he entered a Franciscan convent and began a systematic programme of visiting hospitals, prisons, poor houses, emigrant centres and orphanages, tending to the sick and needy. Setting up a Foundation, he oversaw the building of a school, an infirmary and an inn for student priests and for clergy passing through the city. He called the inn Bethlehem, in honour of the humble birthplace of Jesus.

Way ahead of his time, Pedro established social services unheard of at that time, including a convalescence hospital, and produced spiritual writing which became highly influential. His practices became known as the Order of Bethlehemites. Hermano Pedro died in Guatemala in 1667, just 41 years of age, and 350 years later, Pope Paul VI approved his beatification. He is the first, and only Saint in the Canary Islands.

Who'd want to stay here?

Set on the edge of the pine forest, it's quite a unique setting as far as Tenerife is concerned, so the experience of staying here is about as far removed from the coastal resorts as you can get. It's a superb base for outdoor activities, especially walking – a number of trails lead into the forest, and you're as close to Teide National Park as you can get without actually staying in the park.

The food scene

Vilaflor's southern approach is lined with potato terraces, so the *papas arrugadas* are particularly good, although restaurant choices are somewhat limited. This is also wine country, so it's worth keeping a lookout for some truly local wines.

Where we'd eat

Traditional Canarian - El Rincón de Roberto is a rustic little restaurant with attractive slate walls and a log fire, essential when the cloud invades the streets. Try the delicious degustación of Canarian dishes – cheeses, *chistorras* (Canarian sausages) and *morcillas* (blood sausage with almonds and raisins). As you might expect, given the town's speciality product, you get proper *papas arrugadas* here. *Avenida Hermano Pedro 27; +34 922 709 035; open midday-*

239

22:00 Wednesday to Saturday, midday-21:00 Sunday, midday-18:00 Monday, closed Tuesday; degustación of Canarian dishes €15.

Traditional Canarian - We nearly always stop at **Fuente Hermano Pedro** when passing through Vilaflor. It's in a super location right on the main plaza and its Canarian menu is cheap as chips. As well as a place to try Canarian favourites like rabbit and goat, it's also good for snacks, coffee and cake, or just a beer in the sun. *Plaza Obispo Perez Cáceres; +34 922 725 022; restaurant opening times in Vilaflor can be erratic, Fuente Hermano Pedro is one of the more reliable ones, open 09:00-21:00 daily ... mostly; average price of main course €9.*

Why visit

The town boasts some examples of traditional rural architecture; an old water mill, communal wash house and a quirky little museum at the Hotel El Sombrerito. As you would expect from a town surrounded by mountains and forests, nature provides the best bits. Just outside the town is an oversized ancient pine, El Pino Gordo. The route to some of the most unusual rock formations on the island, Paisaje Lunar, begins from the centre of Vilaflor. It's a three hour trek to reach, so those spa treatments are very welcome afterwards.

The night skies in Vilaflor are truly magical. A combination of the clarity of light, altitude and things that only an astronomer would understand make it possible to view stars that should be mathematically impossible to see from Tenerife.

After dark

There's not a lot going on once darkness descends. The cosy lounge at the Villalba is where we'd usually spend an hour or so relaxing after dinner.

Where we'd stay

There's a range of appropriately rural accommodation in Vilaflor, but we keep returning to the same hotel.

The Hotel Villalba (*Ctra San Roque; +34 922 709 931; www.hotelvillalba. com*) is one of our favourite hotels on Tenerife. Pine scented, luxurious retreat on the edge of Vilaflor with great rooms and generous en suites; a very good restaurant in La Vendimia; their own wines and *bodega*; and a cosy little basement spa which is included in the price of the room.

Best time to visit

It really doesn't matter if outdoor activities are your thing. We've stayed in

Vilaflor at various times of the year, enjoying the walking trails in all sorts of weather, including the only time on Tenerife, outside of Teide National Park, we've found our car's windows frosted in the morning.

WEST TENERIFE

The most westerly point of Tenerife is at Punta de Teno, reached via a road that cuts through the mountains and can only be accessed from the north coast, but it's the best spot to absorb one of the most spectacular views on Tenerife, the Teno Massif. Unfortunately, following an incident in which a large section of surface broke away and slipped down the cliff, the access is now controlled.

These ancient monoliths, one of the oldest parts of the island at 7 million years old, rise up from the sea providing a spectacular backdrop to the area's main resort, Los Gigantes. It's a relative newcomer to the western shores, barely a twinkle in developers' eyes until the late 1960s, unlike the remote hamlets characterised by traditional rural architecture which lie hidden in the folds of the mountains; the most famous of which is the beauty spot of Masca.

The coastal landscape, like the south, is dry and barren, enjoying the most sunshine hours and least rain on Tenerife. Until tourism transformed bad farming weather into the sun-seekers' Holy Grail, the only people who lived there were mainly fishermen in small communities at Alcalá, Playa San Juan and Puerto de Santiago.

Nowadays the area has become popular with expatriates and visitors seeking a quieter alternative to the more lively resorts thirty minutes drive to the south.

Head inland, past banana plantations and tomato crops and the scenery and the character of the west changes dramatically. At the wide plateau of Valle de Santiago, where agricultural practices have hardly changed in five centuries, two micro-climates meet head-on and you can virtually see the line where the low lying shrubs of the arid south meet the pine forests of the verdant north. The west of Tenerife provides a perfect illustration of the diversity of scenery, climate and culture which can be found in even one relatively small area of Tenerife.

ALCALÁ

Where is it and what's it like?

The south and south west coast of Tenerife are often viewed as having been developed purely for tourism. Admittedly, there aren't many coastal communities which are uniquely Canarian, but the small fishing village of Alcalá is one of them.

A mishmash of streets are clustered around a small plaza and fishermen's jetty. Life, as with most Spanish communities, centres around the plaza. The village is populated by a mix of families from La Palma, La Gomera (in clear view across the water) and returning emigrants from Venezuela, lending it a spicy Canarian/Latin American character.

Despite being the most authentic village in the area, Alcalá was overlooked by visitors for decades, possibly because its rocky coastline was devoid of any decent beaches. The opening of a luxury hotel in 2008 brought it onto visitors' radar screens and businesses noticed an increase in trade within weeks of the hotel opening. Any concerns that a village-sized hotel complex may change the nature of Alcalá were dismissed by locals like Domingo, a restaurant owner, whose uncomplicated philosophy illustrated the strength of culture that shapes the village.

"The hotel is there," he said, pointing to the banana plantations at the western edge of town. *"We are here."* - Simple as that.

What's the story?

The inhospitable coastline coupled with a lack of water meant that few Guanche settled in the coastal region of Guia de Isora and it wasn't until after the conquest that their presence became known here, the hills providing refuge for small groups of rebel Guanche. A handful of fishermen and the occasional lone goatherd would have been the sole residents of the area known as Alcalá right up until the beginning of the 19th century when the cochineal market took off. With new labour needed to cultivate and harvest the cochineal, there was an influx of workers from La Gomera who settled on or near the coast, their home island still in view.

The cochineal market collapsed with the introduction of synthetic dyes at the end of the 19th century and the ensuing economic recession, aided and abetted by plague and pestilence, sent much of the population emigrating to the New World, depleting the population until well into the 20th century.

When the returning émigrés – known as *Indianos* – used their wealth to dig galleries and lay pipelines to bring water to the coast, it heralded an upturn in the economy and prompted the cultivation of tomatoes and bananas for export. It wasn't long before this area became one of the largest exporters of agricultural produce on the island.

By the end of the 20th century, tourism had arrived and gradually began to displace agriculture as a dominant economic force.

Who'd want to stay here?

Alcalá is perfect for anyone seeking a Canarian coastal vibe in a sun-kissed setting.

The food scene

Having a luxury hotel on its doorstep has been a catalyst for Alcalá to up its gastronomic game. Once there was a handful of decent traditional restaurants, now the choice is more sophisticated and diverse. This 'new' restaurant scene is still finding its feet in Alcalá and as a result, restaurants come and go on a relatively regular basis. What were some of the best restaurants in the village a couple of years ago have changed hands/names. Check back in another couple of years and the names are likely to be unfamiliar yet again. But there are some who look as though they could be around for the long haul, and there are always going to be good places to eat.

Where we'd eat

Italian - Sauco used to be located in Playa de la Arena but it's probably better suited to Alcalá's new-found style. It's in a great position overlooking the sea and is very convenient for guests staying at the Palacio de Isora. Chef Jorge Campos specialises in pastas and pizzas as well as fish and grilled meats, so most tastes are covered. It also opens for breakfast. *Calle la Fabrica no. 5; +34 922 860 744; open 13:00-16:00 and 19:00-23:30 Monday, 09:00-16:00 and 19:00-23:30 Wednesday to Sunday, closed Tuesday; average price of main course €13.*

Why visit

There are no stand-out attractions, it's just a pleasant little Canarian village on the coast. It's also a handy base for exploring the south west coast and hills, including the old quarter in the town of Guía de Isora, as well as popping across to the north west coast.

On the beach

Some golden sand has been added to the tiny cove where the plaza meets the sea and a lifeguard has been employed to keep watch, but most locals sunbathe on the attractive boardwalk linking the plaza and the small harbour.

A walk south along the top of the village leads to Playa Mendez; a smuggler-like cove where you'll have only the lapping of the waves for company.

Showing a desire to give something back to the community, the Gran Melià Palacio de Isora developed the coastline in front of the hotel, creating a new beach and sprucing up rock pools along the promenade of La Jaquita. It has transformed what was a forgettable stretch of coastline.

After dark

It's a nice place for a sundowner, or to relax in the plaza on a hot summer evening, but mostly nightlife is low key. There's a far livelier scene for anyone staying at the hotel on the western edge of the village.

Where we'd stay

There are quite a few decent apartments and *pensións* in Alcalá. There's even a rural hotel (El Navio) not far from the village. But there's only one hotel in the village itself, and it is quite a hotel. Despite its size, it does a better job of blending into the surrounding terrain than some of its peers further along the coast.

Gran Melià Palacio de Isora (*Avenida Los Océanos s/n; +34 922 869 000; www.granmeliapalaciodeisora.com*) has fabulously stylish rooms, oodles of floor space, lively bars, glitzy surroundings, the largest saltwater pool in Europe and a good choice of on-site restaurants. Not cheap but cracking value for money. Leave value behind and upgrade to Red Level for unadulterated pampering, personalised butler service, superb contemporary style, and a plethora of amenities and in-room facilities including a Jacuzzi on the terrace. Free bar and canapés from 18:00-19:00, poolside service including sunscreens and aromatic chilled towels and gourmet breakfast by the pool.

Best time to visit

The village pulls out all the stops for the celebrations in honour of the Virgen del Carmen around the 15th August. The plaza, all decked out in its fiesta finest, is ideally sized for getting into the thick of celebrations which feel as though they're taking place in some Latin American country. Live bands (salsa of course), fiesta queens and an offshore firework display liven up Alcalá's usually sedate nocturnal scene.

CALLAO SALVAJE

Where is it and what's it like?

One of two, purpose-built resorts which lie off the TF47 coastal road on the westerly edge of Costa Adeje, Callao Salvaje is a quiet resort, predominantly occupied by residential housing and holiday apartment blocks with a decent smattering of shops and bar restaurants. The resort has a beach which raises its appeal with holidaymakers, but it still has the air of a Tenerife resort from the 1980s.

Don't book Callao Salvaje simply on its Costa Adeje label and think you're going to be anywhere near the centre of the biggest resort area on Tenerife; it's a fifteen minute drive away from the resort most people know as Costa Adeje. It's also a decent drive to reach any of the resorts to the west – Los Gigantes or Playa de la Arena. Unless you're happy to spend your holiday in your hotel or apartment block, a car is an essential as buses along this stretch of coast are infrequent.

Who'd want to stay here?

It's quiet and the weather's good. If those are the main objectives when booking a holiday, then Callao Salvaje might fit the bill.

The food scene

Callao Salvaje doesn't have the most exciting culinary scene going, but there is a quite diverse selection of restaurants given its size. There's also a French/Belgian influence in the area and this is reflected in what's on offer in some restaurants and bakeries.

Where we'd eat

Traditional Canarian - Family run **El Ancla** has been a favourite with visitors to Callao Salvaje for years. What you get is big and tasty portions of traditional fish and meat dishes. The food is classed as 'gourmet' which means prices are slightly higher than you'd pay in more traditional areas. *Calle la Lava 1; +34 922 740 468; open 18:00-22:00 Tuesday, 14:00-22:00 Wednesday to Sunday, closed Monday; average price of main course €15.*

Why visit

Is it worth a visit if you're not staying here? Not really.

On the beach

Playa de Ajabo is a very pleasant, black sand beach with a half breakwater to protect the little bay from the ravages of the Atlantic Ocean. A gently sloping shoreline and sheltered position make it a good choice for families.

After dark

There are a handful of resort type bars along Calle La Lava.

Where we'd stay

There's a decent choice of typical resort-style hotels, apartments and villas in and around Callao Salvaje. Most are comfortable but none really stand out enough to warrant a special mention.

Best time to visit

Callao Salvaje is one of those resorts where, apart from fluctuations in the weather, nothing really changes from one month to another.

LOS GIGANTES

Where is it and what's it like?

Los Gigantes lies on the sunny west coast in probably the most stunning location of all Tenerife's resorts. Its low-rise white buildings cluster at the foot of the 500 metre high, sheer face of the Acantilados de Los Gigantes (cliffs of the giants) from which the resort derives its name.

Los Gigantes is very much a British resort which many British ex-pats have chosen to make their home. Unable to spread further west due to its precipitous position, it's managed to maintain a certain village feel about it; one where aerobic workouts for thighs and calves come as standard every time you walk out of your front door.

Despite being hemmed in by the *acantilados*, apartment blocks continue to be built into the cliff face, for which there really ought to be access via a ski lift, to meet the seemingly endless demand for residential and holiday accommodation in the resort.

Life tends to revolve around the pretty marina, the small square and the main street of Avenida Marítimo de Los Gigantes where shops, bars and restaurants cater almost exclusively to a British clientele. Without the clubs and late bars of the south, it's given a wide berth by the 18-30s and is better suited to families and those for whom Veronica's holds no allure.

What's the story?

The first development of Los Gigantes began in the 1960s when the Spanish Juan Manuel Capdeville realised the area's potential to attract a new breed of tourist that was emerging in Franco's economy, one who enjoyed long sunshine hours unavailable in their home country. But it was British nationals who began to build on the barren land at the foot of a 300m high section of the cliffs at the end of the 1960s and then built the first tourist accommodation - the Hotel Los Gigantes. The hotel was officially opened in 1973 by the King and Queen of Spain, then still Prince and Princess.

Who'd want to stay here?

As a resort with a village feel to it, Los Gigantes tends to attract people who want the amenities of a small, quiet resort in a stunner of a setting, but one which has its own distinct personality. It also enjoys more sunshine hours than just about anywhere else on Tenerife's coast. An added bonus is it's a great base for accessing Masca, the Teno Massif, and the north west coast.

The food scene

Generally speaking, we've never found restaurants in Los Gigantes to be particularly inspiring; too many fit into the British food abroad category. The very first time we ate in Los Gigantes we sat ourselves down at a table outside one of the harbour restaurants and asked for tapas, to which the English owner replied "ah, you must be the people who won the radio contest." We gathered from this that folk seeking tapas must be a rarity. The food scene has moved on since then, but it still has its moments. Last time we ate in Los Gigantes, a waiter in a supposedly Canarian restaurant tried to palm us off with a Spanish bottle of wine when we asked for a Canarian one. Restaurants on the whole are decent, but many are just not what we look for in a culinary scene on a Canarian island. Saying that, Los Gigantes does boast one of the best restaurants in the Canary Islands.

Where we'd eat

Creative Canarian - In the very first edition of this book we said chef Juan Carlos of **El Rincón de Juan Carlos** produced food of Michelin star quality. We got that one spot on, he's had his Michelin star for a few years now. It's a family run restaurant serving superb, theatrical and even witty dishes. It's the best restaurant we've eaten in on the Canary Islands with food by who is officially one of the best chefs in Spain (Juan Carlos was voted runner-up best young chef in the country a few years ago). Simply a must for foodies. *Paisaje de Jacaranda 2; +34 922 868 040; open 19:00-22:00, closed Sunday & Monday; taster menu is €95.*

Tapas – TAS-K is a friendly little place on the street running parallel to the harbour. The tapas are tasty, nicely presented and dishes are a bit different from those found on standard Canarian tapas menus. *Calle los Guíos 16; +34 922 862 328; open 21:30-23:00; average price of tapas €6.*

Why visit

The cliffs which gave the resort its name are spectacular, almost mythical in certain light, especially with La Gomera in the scene as well. However, Los Gigantes has a bigger WOW experience to offer visitors.

Sheltered from the trade winds by the *acantilados*, the waters off Los Gigantes are deep, still and warm sustaining a host of microscopic marine life which attracts dolphins and whales. A large community of bottle-nosed dolphins live in these waters and many more cetaceans pass through on their migratory routes so that it's not uncommon to spot minke, Bryde's, and even killer whales. Various whale and dolphin safaris sail from the marina twice a day in boats ranging from small craft to a mock pirate ship. We don't think booze cruises and eco-friendly dolphin-watching trips mix, so stick to ships whose focus is purely on the stars of the sea.

On the beach

The only beach in Los Gigantes is the small, black sand Playa Los Guios behind the marina, but more than adequate compensation comes in the form of the César Manrique-designed complex of El Laguillo and further along the *avenida*, the garden setting of Club Oasis. Both offer swimming pools, sunbathing and poolside snacks. At the residential area of Crab Island there's a natural rock pool with a couple of conveniently flat rocks, nice for a late afternoon dip.

After dark

Along Avenida Marítimo de Los Gigantes are bars and pubs screening Eastenders, hosting karaoke and offering nightly cabaret, but don't expect to be crawling home as the lizards come out, they all close around the midnight hour.

Where we'd stay

Despite being a purpose-built resort, there's a severe shortage of hotels in Los Gigantes. Apart from a couple of aparthotels, most holiday accommodation is found in apartment complexes.

Best time to visit

Although a resort first and foremost, Los Gigantes does embrace local traditions, holding its own lively little carnival after the main ones in other parts of the island are over. As it's not linked to Lent in the same way as the traditional carnivals, the dates are impossible to predict but it does tend to be around March.

MASCA

Where is it and what's it like?

Even seasoned travellers will find it difficult not to say 'WOW' when they first set eyes on Masca. Tucked away in the folds of the seven million year old Teno Massif in the west of the island, it occupies a uniquely special location and is often referred to as Tenerife's Shangri La or Machu Picchu. The approach, a series of switchbacks twisting and turning downwards through an overwhelming landscape, may shred some nerves, but there are plenty of *miradors* (viewpoints) en route at which to break up the rollercoaster descent and marvel at the scenery.

It's not only the vistas in Masca which are magical; tales of witchcraft and shape-changers abound in these parts. Once a rural farming community, narrow terraces still line the valley's slopes. Tourism is now the main source of income. Daily, between 11:00 and 15:00, coaches and jeep safaris fill the car park above the hamlet, unloading their charges to wander its bougainvillea- and palm-lined cobbled walkways. The path between upper and lower Masca is steep and slippery and shoes with a decent tread are essential.

There's a view that the daily influx of tourists has diluted Masca's charm; we don't subscribe to that view. Tourism has brought prosperity and renewed life and the hamlet is immaculately maintained. Without tourism, Masca could have become just another abandoned rural community, much like ones found on the neighbouring island of La Gomera, perfectly framed on the horizon.

Masca is simply a 'must see' for anyone visiting Tenerife. The time to catch it at its best is early morning and late afternoon, when it's devoid of the bulk of tourists. Escape the crowds at other times by making the short journey to adjoining Lomo de Masca which is equally picturesque.

What's the story?

Due to its hidden position at the top of a deep ravine inside the Teno Massif and hemmed in by Roque Tarucho on land and by the natural breakwaters of Abache and La Fortaleza to sea, Masca Barranco was a stronghold of the Guanche. Believing that, unless bound, Roque Tarucho would fall on them, the Guanche bound the dominant monolith with rope twined from reed, a practice which continues to this day, the rope being renewed every year. Also still in evidence are the paths which seam the landscape, carved by feet and hooves as the Guanche moved their livestock between coastal and mountain grazing. Many of the rebel Guanche who refused to bend the knee to the Crown of Castile, continued to hide within its inaccessible ravines for years after the conquest of 1496 and, walking through hidden folds and rock overhangs in the Masca Barranco, you could well imagine that some may yet remain hidden here!

The houses that make up the settlement of Masca are grouped into five hamlets – Lomo de Masca, Lomo de Medio, La Piedra, El Turrón and La Vica - sitting between 650 and 800 meters above sea level and are fine examples of Tenerife's rural construction methods which, given the inaccessibility of the settlement, were driven by the availability of materials. Walls are constructed of roughly hewn basalt rocks, held fast by a mortar of clay, water and a little lime. Houses are either single storey in an L-shape with each individual room accessed from outside and no interior connections, or are two-storey set around an inner courtyard. The roofs are constructed of curved Arabic tiles lined with cane to prevent small rodents from passing through into the living space.

Accessible only on foot, across the mountains from Santiago del Teide, or by sea via a long and arduous hike up the ravine, Masca remained virtually hidden from the rest of the world until the 1970s when the road was constructed along the route of the old mountain path which now connects the hamlet from Santiago del Teide all the way to Buenavista del Norte. Today it's the second most visited destination on the island, after Teide National Park. In 2007 wild fires swept through the Masca Valley destroying lush vegetation and several traditional houses in its wake. The vegetation has largely recovered over the intervening years but the old architecture is irreplaceable.

Who'd want to stay here?

The great majority of visitors are day-trippers so if serenity in a sensational setting appeals, after around 17:00, Masca is *the* place on Tenerife to find it.

The food scene

Considering it's a mass tourist hotspot, Masca actually has a couple of decent restaurants with some interesting concoctions to try, like cactus lemonade and cactus cake.

Where we'd eat

Vegetarian – First of all, you get what is one of our favourite Masca views from **El Guanche**, the old schoolhouse. Secondly, if vegetarian you're in for a treat. Thirdly, if you're not it doesn't matter, you won't notice there's no meat. The freshest local ingredients are used to create super soups, tasty tortillas and fabulous fried cheeses. *Calle El Lomito 9; +34 922 860 074; open midday to 17:00 Thursday to Monday, closed Tuesday & Wednesday; it's worth trying the set menu at €17.*

Why visit

Masca is a marvel, which is reason enough to venture down those winding roads. A hugely popular activity is hiking the Masca Barranco, but it's not a stroll. Descend into an ancient landscape where narrow ravines close in overhead; a Jurassic trek perhaps. Sensible walkers can arrange to be picked up by boat when they reach the bay three hours down the line (tickets available from Restaurant El Fuente in the village before setting off); masochists can dip their toes in the water and make the return journey. Too many of the people who undertook the route weren't actually prepared for the challenge and subsequently there were far more accidents than on any other hiking trail on Tenerife. After one too many rescues, Masca Barranco was closed to the public in 2018 and plans were drawn up to make the route safer. At the time of going to print, there's still no sign of it opening again, although much of the work to improve the path has been completed. The improvements will come at a cost. It is expected numbers will be limited and walkers will have to pay to hike the barranco.

On the beach

Masca does have a beach, a couple of hours or so away at the end of the hike through the ravine. In truth, the beach itself is a tad disappointing, especially if you've read reports which wax lyrical about it. But the beach shouldn't be the

Top: Los Gigantes, bottom left: Playa de la Arena, bottom right: Alcalá

reason to tackle the *barranco*.

After dark
It's a tiny hamlet in the mountains. Do we have to say anything else?

Where we'd stay
Pensions and rural houses are available for rent in the hamlet for those who fancy experiencing the solitude of staying in such a remote community…and maybe seeing a local metamorphose into a pig.

Best time to visit
Any time of year will deliver a WOW experience.

PLAYA DE LA ARENA

Where is it and what's it like?
Geographically joined at the hip with Puerto de Santiago along Tenerife's western coast, it's difficult to tell where one ends and the other begins but, belonging to different municipalities, they reveal quite distinct personalities.

Playa de la Arena has benefited from investment in its infrastructure to create a clean, bright, family-friendly resort. The wide coastal promenade is lined with shops, bars and restaurants whose offerings reflect the predominantly British, and to a lesser extent German, visitors and ex-pats who choose to frequent it. Residential and holiday apartments climb up the hill behind the promenade, occupied from October to March by the 'swallows' who over-winter in this, the most benign of Tenerife's climates.

With new apartments springing up along the main road at the back of the resort, it seems clear that Playa de la Arena is set to expand. But for now, the resort's main promenade retains a village feel where life is unhurried in the near constant sunshine.

Who'd want to stay here?
Playa de la Arena is simply a quiet, pleasant little resort with oodles of sunshine hours; ideal for doing nothing except relaxing. But it's also handily placed for heading into the south west hills and beyond for anyone who fancies a change of scene.

The food scene
The restaurant scene is quite varied for a resort of this size. There's nowhere outstanding but there is a good selection of places catering for British, Spanish, and German/Austrian tastes.

Where we'd eat

Traditional Canarian - If cheap and cheerful is your dining preference, **Pancho** right on the beach is not the place to go. It's one of the more sophisticated restaurants in Playa de la Arena, with a menu which could be described as traditional with knobs on – alongside the Canarian favourite *conejo en salmorejo* you get the likes of duck in a honey and sesame sauce. Fish and seafood is probably what it does best, there's a good choice, as well as a selection of fish and seafood rice dishes for two. *Avenida Marítima, 26; +34 922 86 13 23; open 13:00-16:00 and 19:30-22:30, closed Monday; average price of main course €19.*

Why visit

Apart from the sunshine and nice little beach, there's not a lot to draw people to the resort. A coastal path links the resort with neighbour Alcalá, giving the option of a more traditional change of scene.

On the beach

The island of La Gomera is the focal point on the horizon at one of the prettiest natural beaches on the island from which the resort derives its name; the blue flag Playa de la Arena. Backed by palm trees and bordered by cafés, restaurants and residential apartments, the small, black sand beach lies in a sheltered cove below the promenade. Nicely maintained toilets and shower blocks are worth the tiny fee for using them and make the beach a firm favourite with families, plus there's free WiFi.

After dark

Nightlife is low key, made lower key by the rising popularity of all inclusive packages. Bars such as the Blarney Stone offer Irish hospitality and karaoke, but if your Saturday night simply isn't complete without a bouncing live band, head to Route 66 in neighbouring Puerto de Santiago.

Where we'd stay

This is a resort where most people stay in apartments, the prime being seafront ones with views of La Gomera. But there is one perfectly positioned hotel.

Landmar Playa La Arena (*+34 922 86 29 91; C/Lajial, 4; landmarplayalaarena.com*) is located in the centre of the village, right opposite the beach; a multi-storey 4 star looking a bit like an ocean liner in dry dock. The open plan, marble-floored reception drips with ferns and vines creating an indoor jungle.

Best time to visit

Because it's one of the sunniest spots on the island, it's particularly good for winter sunshine.

PLAYA PARAÍSO

Where is it and what's it like?

Playa Paraíso means 'paradise beach' in English. It's a name that might bring a wry smile to the lips of anyone who has booked a holiday here after being seduced by travel agents' descriptions of 'a quaint fishing village.' In many ways Playa Paraíso is exactly the sort of resort that might come to mind when the name Tenerife is mentioned; unattractive high rises, unfinished buildings, unappealing bars and tourist shops that looks as though they're stuck in the 80s. This is a purpose-built resort that has been left behind by the more stylish tourist developments at Costa Adeje just along the coast. However, things are changing in Playa Paraíso. The Hard Rock Hotel opened its doors in October 2016, bringing glamour and a much needed economic boost to this area of Tenerife. We predict an upturn in Playa Paraíso's appearance; the sooner the better.

Who'd want to stay here?

Anyone who's turned on by the idea of enjoying the facilities of top notch hotels in a quiet resort in the south of Tenerife

The food scene

Playa Paraíso is not a destination for gastronomes; there's a small selection of mediocre restaurants, many of which are aimed at undemanding British holidaymakers. With the opening of the Hard Rock Hotel the restaurant scene is likely to change for the better in the next few years; there are already signs of improvement.

Where we'd eat

Italian - This is a resort where we'd stick to eating in one of the three excellent hotels found there. Bucking the trend of mediocrity is **L'incontro**, a decent, friendly little Italian restaurant located in the nicest part of the resort above the Hard Rock's swimming pool complex. Good pizzas, pastas and more. They also own the bakery next door. *Avenida Adeje 300 ; +34 922 743 554; open midday- midnight, closed Monday; average price of pastas €12, pizzas €10.*

Why visit

Head under the waves and the resort's paradise tag becomes deserved with giant rays and turtles being amongst the marine characters who add life and colour to the area's undersea world. There are a couple of dive centres in the resort. A wander south across the headland leads to quiet, sandy coves and the coastal hamlet of El Puertito, still somewhat of a laid-back oasis on a coast where the development never seems to cease.

On the beach
Playa de las Galgas, a man-made, gold sand beach is located beside the Roca Nivaria Gran Hotel. It's not big but it's quiet and there are sunbeds for hire. Being set in a cove it's sheltered, therefore good for having a refreshing dip without being battered by waves.

After dark
This is stereotypical Tenerife resort land with the few bars offering karaoke, live football and the occasional act who may, or may not, be a notch up from the bad karaoke. Again there are hopeful signs of change.

Where we'd stay
A decade or so ago we'd have avoided Playa Paraíso like the plague, but its strong point is that it does have some very good hotels. Before the Hard Rock Hotel moved in we'd have happily stayed again at the **Bahía Principe Costa Adeje** (*Calle Idafe s/n; (+34) 922 72 31 00; www.bahia-principe.com*) or the **Roca Nivaria Gran Hotel** (*Avenida Adeje 300, Playa Paraíso; (+34) 922 74 02 02; www.adrianhoteles.com/en/roca-nivaria*). But the glitz and glamour make the Hard Rock irresistible.

Hard Rock Hotel (*Ave de Adeje 300; (+34) 971 31 42 10; www. hardrockhotels.com*) consists of two neon towers (Oasis and Nirvana), three swimming pools, 624 rooms, 259 suites, a rock spa, good restaurants, and as much old school rock glamour as you can stomach. Rock star-suitable rooms even come with a pick for your air guitar. It is not the place for anyone who doesn't want to hear a rocking sound track all day long.

Best time to visit
It doesn't change much from one month to the next.

PLAYA SAN JUAN

Where is it and what's it like?
One of a series of former fishing villages that dot the sunny south west coast of the island, Playa San Juan is an up and coming resort where, increasingly, British voices can be heard.

Sheltered from the trade winds and facing the island of La Gomera, this stretch of coast enjoys the best of Tenerife's benign climate with little rainfall and abundant sunshine.

Retaining only slightly less of a traditional feel than its nearest neighbour Alcalá, the tone of Playa San Juan's development is being set by its picturesque marina and the deluxe 5 star Abama Hotel which sits on the headland above the village. A palm tree-lined boardwalk runs the length of the promenade, many restaurants are stylishly glass and chrome, and apartments with sunset views over La Gomera sell for premium prices.

What's the story?

The coastal area of Playa San Juan existed only as a fishing centre and, up until the 1950s, a tuna factory, a lime kiln and fishermen's cottages were all that lined the natural harbour and coves of the village. Hardship and poverty forced much of the population to emigrate to South America in search of work and it was wealth brought back by those same families that financed the construction of water galleries and wells, bringing irrigation to the area and so initiating its economic development. The water enabled cultivation of bananas and tomatoes which are still the mainstay of the municipality's economy.

As cultivation grew in importance, so the fishing industry declined and the tuna canning factory closed but happily there's still a sizeable fishing fleet working out of the pretty harbour, ensuring a plentiful supply of fresh fish for the restaurants.

Who'd want to stay here?

Playa San Juan is perfect for people who want a more traditional setting accompanying sunshine and sea, and hypnotic sunsets. The nearby road link connecting the coast with the extension to the TF1 motorway means it's easier than ever to get into the hills where there are some interesting historical hamlets to explore, including Chirche which holds a Day of Traditions on the last Sunday in July.

The food scene

Playa San Juan is another south west town which has undergone a transformation in gastronomic terms in the last few years. The result is, although places may chop and change, there is usually a diverse selection of good to excellent restaurants to choose from, including the two Michelin star restaurants in the Abama Hotel.

Where we'd eat

Obviously, if feeling flush, first choice would have to be the Michelin stars

258

of **M.B.** and **Kabuki** at the Ritz-Carlton Abama. But it's more fun and less of an assault on the finances to eat some simple but good cuisine in the town.

Tapas - A bustling tapas restaurant on the promenade, **El Aljibe** is popular with locals and visitors alike. The amount of tapas on offer is huge and includes uniquely Canarian tapas such as *ropa vieja* (the translation is old clothes, but it's basically a mishmash of leftover ingredients) and the usual tapas suspects (croquettes, *pimientos de Padrón, ensalada rusa*). *Avenida Del Emigrante 8; +34 922 138 675; open 06:30-midnight, closed Wednesday; average price of tapa €6.*

Why visit
The promenade, harbour and beach area is one of the best looking of any town along the south and west coast of Tenerife. It has a completely different vibe from anywhere else in the south of Tenerife.

On the beach
Two beaches grace the sea front either side of the pier. The first is black sand and is popular with local families, the second was imported golden sand stretching all the way round the headland to the restored lime kiln. But it has a tendency to revert back to its natural colour after lively waves have assaulted it. Backed by changing rooms, watched over by a lifeguard and just a step from boardwalk cafés, it's a pleasantly serene place to enjoy the endless sunshine hours.

The best beach in the area is Playa Abama located in a cove below the hotel of the same name. It can feel as though it belongs to the hotel, and it *is* the hotel which looks after it, but all beaches in Spain are public.

After dark
Although not a town with a bouncing nocturnal scene, there are enough good bars to make if feel lively enough. Basically, there's a nice buzz to the place, especially in summer.

Where we'd stay
Despite its growing popularity, there's still not a great amount of accommodation options in Playa San Juan, save for the usual apartment scene. For luxury it has to be the hotel on the headland.

With a North African design, which looks a tad out of place on a Spanish island, the **Ritz-Carlton Abama Golf & Spa Resort** (*C/General; +34 922 126 000; www.ritzcarlton.com*) offers a championship golf course and Michelin starred dining on a cliff top overlooking La Gomera. When we first watched the Abama being constructed we were horrified at its sheer size, but clever design and extensive sub-tropical gardens completely mask its scale once you're actually inside its embrace. It's a five minute taxi ride or 20 minute cliff top walk away from the resort.

Best time to visit

Like the other towns and resorts in this part of the south west, it's ideally located for winter warmth and sunshine.

PUERTO DE SANTIAGO

Where is it and what's it like?

As the road continues west from Playa de la Arena into Puerto de Santiago you begin to notice slight differences, there are more amusement arcades, buildings need a new coat of paint and 'Se Aquiler' (for rent) and 'Se Vende' (for sale) signs decorate windows. Puerto de Santiago may not look as shiny, but at its heart it has more Canarian character than its immediate neighbours.

Beyond a narrow, pedestrian-unfriendly turn in the road, steps fall steeply to the heart of this fishing village, a small harbour where fishing boats and a tiny *ermita* sit alongside the quay. Early morning, the contents of the nets make their way to the restaurants whose dining terraces overlook the harbour.

At its westerly edge the resort drops down to a headland where the Barceló Santiago hotel has spawned a small centre brimming with bars, restaurants, supermarkets and souvenir shops.

There's a pretty coastal walkway which runs from the harbour to the most westerly headland on one side and through manicured gardens below the plaza and along the coast to Playa de la Arena on the other.

What's the story?

An important fishing port since the 16th century due to its natural harbour which is protected from the Atlantic by submerged solidified lava, in the 18th century Puerto Santiago was the hub of trade and communication between Tenerife and La Gomera, particularly in the import of Gomeran honey (*miel de palma*). Family ties between the two islands are still strongly evident in this area today. In 1812 the port settlement was included into the Valley of Santiago municipality which, almost a century later, became known as Santiago del Teide in an attempt to stop the town's mail from being habitually sent to Chile.

Who'd want to stay here?

It has much the same appeal as its neighbours – a quiet resort with great weather and views. It is more of a resort of two halves, with the part around the Barceló Santiago aimed at British visitors whilst the area from the harbour to the south is more Canarian. Being in the centre of three small resorts, means it's relatively easy to wander into both Los Gigantes and Playa de la Arena.

The food scene

Around the harbour area, the somewhat tatty exteriors of restaurants conceal terraces overlooking the harbour and the island of La Gomera where you'll find fresh and tasty, unfussy fish and seafood dishes at budget prices. Around the Barceló Santiago a clutch of bars, restaurants and cafés cater to mainly British clientele with few gastronomic exceptions to write home about.

Where we'd eat

Spanish/International - Occupying a peach of a position overlooking the sea and with views to La Gomera, **La Pergola** stands out in Puerto de Santiago for a number of reasons. It's probably the most sophisticated restaurant in the resort, the menu reflecting Spanish, Canarian and international influences. It's also one of the most expensive. However, it's hard to beat for a romantic sunset dinner. *Calle La Hondura; +34 922 860 347; open midday to midnight, closed Sunday; average price of main course €18.*

Why visit

Easy to miss as you keep your eyes on the narrow 'S' bend that centres Puerto de Santiago, is the sea blue wall of the Museo del Pescador where Bernard Romain's amazing 3D canvas has fishermen unloading their catch onto the quayside and the tails and heads of swordfish and sharks disappearing into and emerging from the wall. Inside, art exhibitions and fishing history await.

On the beach

There's a small, black sand and pebble beach bordering the harbour below the plaza. Further westwards below the walkway, low tide reveals beautiful rock pools, perfect for snorkeling and swimming.

After dark

The bars around Barceló Santiago offer live music and tribute acts most nights of the week with Route 66 taking the prize for the best with original music from good musicians.

Where we'd stay

The accommodation on offer is much the same as its neighbours.

Top: Playa San Juan, bottom left:
Santiago del Teide, bottom right: Puerto
Santiago

Whenever we stay in the area we tend to opt for the **Barceló Santiago** (*La Hondura, 8; +34 922 860 912; www.barcelosantiago.com*) as it offers stylish accommodation in a fabulous location, with views over La Gomera and the cliffs of Los Gigantes. There are infinity swimming pools, a good bar opposite with excellent live music, and shops and restaurants close by. Push the boat out for a superior room or junior suite, it's worth it for the space, balcony and views.

Best time to visit
Again, like the neighbours, winter is the time when the climate at Puerto de Santiago is most appreciated.

SANTIAGO DEL TEIDE

Where is it and what's it like?
Santiago del Teide (not to be confused with the municipality of the same name, for which it is the capital, and which includes the coastal resorts of Los Gigantes and Puerto de Santiago) sits 1000 metres above sea level in the centre of the Santiago Valley. It's where the 'white knuckle ride' drive to Masca begins. The town spans two micro-climates; one side is semi-arid, save for almond trees which fill the valley with delicate pink blossom in late January and early February. On the other, pine trees line the hillsides.

The town's main street dissects whitewashed cottages with colour-wash emerald windows and door frames. It has the feel of a Mexican *pueblo*; cactus plants lining flat roofs, and women wearing wide brimmed straw hats only serve to enhance this notion. It's a one horse town except Santiago's horse, which stands outside a *bodega* on the main road, isn't real.

Plots surrounding the town are filled with rows of gnarled vines and potato plants, all still cultivated by hand. In spring, nature goes all Van Gogh and the valley is covered in a sea of scarlet poppies, lavender and crimson *tabaiba*.

What's the story?
Part of the ancient *menceyate* (kingdom) of Adeje, Santiago del Teide has a strong Guanche heritage. After the Spanish conquest, when land was being distributed to financiers of the war, the land in Valle de Santiago, as it was known right up until the 1950s, was of little importance, being unsuitable for the production of sugar cane, and so it was given to Don Diego de Adeje, the former Guanche Mencey Pelinor who had collaborated with the Castilians. The only *mencey* to be allocated land post-conquest – the rest were shipped to the Spanish mainland and presented to the royal court – Don Diego married a Guanche girl, María de Lugo and from there the bloodline continued, vestiges still present in today's population who enjoy a deserved reputation for being notably attractive.

Diego died in 1505 and three years later the land was granted to Juan Cabeza, a supporter of the conquest. At this time, Santiago del Teide was moved to the jurisdiction of the Daute municipality.

Operating under a feudal system, in 1663 Santiago del Teide came into the hands of Fernando del Hoyo y Solórzano who built the Casa del Patio (now part of the Casona del Patio hotel) from where he ruled the Santiago Valley. As Lord of the Manor, his jurisdiction included the right to '*incarcerate, hang, spike the heads of, garrotte, whip with a cat-o-nine tails, cut off extremities or set free any or all miscreants and lawbreakers*". When he wasn't busy doing that, he oversaw the construction of a new church, dedicated to San Fernando.

Throughout the 18th and much of the 19th century, the residents of Santiago del Teide suffered great hardship and lived in abject poverty. It wasn't until the 20th century when water arrived in the form of pipes and galleries which enabled cultivation of the valley, and in its wake, the road finally arrived connecting the valley to the rest of the island, that fortunes revived and the population began to grow. But the early years weren't without their challenges. In 1909 Mount Chinyero blew its top (the last eruption on Tenerife) and streams of lava reached the front doors of the valley's villages. A disaster was averted only, so folklore has it, by divine intervention. Images of Santa Ana, Christ and the Virgin Mary were carried to the edge of the lava flow where, miraculously it seems, it stopped.

Who'd want to stay here?

Santiago del Teide is one of the best bases on Tenerife for hikers. It would also suit anyone seeking a tranquil, scenic setting in Tenerife's hinterland.

The food scene

As with all farming country, hearty peasant stews and broths figure highly on restaurant menus in Santiago del Teide. As the town has become more popular with visitors stopping on their way to Masca, there's a greater choice of places to eat. The area's known for growing figs and almonds, you can pick up locally produced almond cakes in most cafes or bars around the town.

Where we'd eat

Traditional Canarian & South American - As well as being in a eucalyptus-scented, tranquil spot (apart from weekends when locals pack the adjacent picnic zone), the **Kiosco el Parque** opposite the church in Santiago del Teide has the best *arepas* (fried and filled Venezuelan pancakes) we've eaten on Tenerife. You might have to go inside to prompt service, but that can just be their way in the hills. They're friendly once you get their attention. *Zona recreativa; +34 922 839 312; open 10:00-18:00 Wednesday to Friday, 09:00-19:00*

Saturday & Sunday, closed Monday; average price of main course €8, arepas €2.

Traditional Canarian - Although not actually in Santiago del Teide (it's in neighbouring El Tanque), **Bar Fleytus** is close enough to be worth a mention. It is a meeting spot for hikers and bikers and is especially appreciated when low cloud descends and you've been enjoying the walking trails in the area. The Canarian cuisine is of a decent enough standard but it's worth trying out some truly local specialities, *almendrados* (almond cakes). *Ctra General Erjos, 53; +34 922 830 110; open 09:00-20:00, closed Wednesday; average price of main course €7.*

Why visit

Santiago del Teide is one of those rare places on Tenerife where you can step from the front door of your accommodation and then head out on any number of walking trails. Goat trails, a legacy from Guanche times, criss-cross the valley traversing neat terraces, volcanic landscapes and pine forests. From here you can reach Masca, the Chinyero Volcano, the Erjos pools, or even walk down to Los Gigantes.

The lovely old buildings of El Señorio del Valle Visitors' Centre, opposite the fragranced picnic zone, wouldn't look out of place in a field in Tuscany. A small museum, a tasca and a riding stables share the bucolic idyll.

The valley's been a centre for pottery making since pre-conquest. Pick up Guanche inspired earthenware at Cha Domitila (*10.00-13.00 & 16.00-19.00, closed Monday*), a charming little pottery workshop museum in nearby Arguayo.

After dark

Having spent a Saturday night in summer in a bar in Santiago, where the entertainment was provided by a quartet of domino-playing locals, we can say categorically it's not for night owls.

Where we'd stay

Accommodation is severely limited in town. But there is one quite unique place we like, whatever its name (it has changed hands a few times after being restored).

Hotel La Casona del Patio (*Avenida de la Iglesia 68; (+34) 922 839 293; http://lacasonadelpatio.com*) is sited alongside the restored, 17th century, former home of the Lord of Santiago, this contemporary boutique hotel looks remarkably suited to the space. Style, comfort, good service, good food and horse riding – it's exactly the sort of hotel Santiago del Teide needed.

Best time to visit

Late January/early February is when the almond flowers are in full bloom, attracting hordes of Canarios at weekends to follow the '*almendros en flor*' walking trail. However, it can get very, very busy. Our favourite time in Santiago del Teide is spring, when the valley's flowers explode into colour.

ESSENTIAL TRAVEL INFORMATION

Emergency Telephone Numbers

There's one number to rule them all. Call 112 for any emergency; ambulance, police and fire services or sea and mountain rescue. It makes life very easy, especially as operators speak English and German as well as Spanish.

Crime

Tenerife is still a relatively crime-free island, although like anywhere there are instances of petty theft, especially in the main southern tourist areas where people are more relaxed and a little less vigilant than when at home. Areas with high Canarian populations generally experience fewer problems.

The best approach to avoid becoming a victim is to apply common sense. Don't leave valuables on display in cars, or handbags unattended in bars, or on the beach. One of the nice qualities about Tenerife is that it's generally a safe place for women travelling on their own. Across most of the island, young girls walk home alone on dark streets or on country roads in the early hours without any fear of harassment. However, once again this doesn't necessarily apply in areas which have a predominantly transient population.

Driving

Tinerfeños are not the best drivers in the world; they suffer from a lack of concentration combined with an apparent lack of understanding of the rules of the road, so minor bumps are commonplace. In fact they're almost expected. When we took our car in for its first service, the mechanic was sceptical that we ever took it on the road because it didn't have a dent in it.

Being armed with the knowledge that drivers around you are likely to do the unexpected is half the battle won, particularly if you're doing what many of your fellow drivers aren't ... concentrating. Despite the unpredictability of some *tinerfeño* road users, confident drivers shouldn't experience any problems and on the whole should find Tenerife's country roads a pleasure to drive on.

Some visitors are surprised to return to where they parked their car to find that it's been towed away; usually because it was parked illegally. There's a simple solution to avoid this, don't behave any differently than you would in your own country. It might look as though the locals get away with double parking, parking on pedestrian crossings, and any number of minor traffic offences ... they don't. Car pounds are full of vehicles with cars belonging to *tinerfeños*.

Speed traps have become commonplace in Tenerife, so drive within the limits, not always easy as these can fluctuate wildly over short distances, otherwise you could be hit with a hefty fine. Local wags claim that Guardia Civil presence on the roads increases when a fiesta is due and they need to boost their fiesta funds.

Health

As a semi-autonomous province of Spain, Tenerife has a very good public health service which is free for anyone who pays Spanish national insurance contributions, or has a European Health Insurance Card (EHIC). The main public hospitals on Tenerife are HUC (*Ctra. Ofra s/n, La Cuesta, La Laguna; 922 67 80 00*) and La Candelaria (*Ctra. Gral Del Rosario, Santa Cruz; 922 602 000*). There is a third just outside Los Cristianos, Hospital del Sur (*Ctra. de Arona; 922 174 744*) which, although it will be a fully functioning hospital in time, has been operating on a limited service since it opened in 2015. There are also private hospitals in both north and south of the island, and most towns have public medical centres. If you can't speak Spanish, some centres won't deal with you unless you're accompanied by a translator.

Using the public health service can involve long waiting periods, whereas having private medical insurance will mean any health issues are dealt with quickly, professionally and efficiently; private hospitals on Tenerife are excellent and staff speak English and German as well as Spanish. There are private hospitals (www.hospiten.com) in Santa Cruz, Puerto de la Cruz and Playa de Las Américas.

Whilst, if you're an EU citizen, the EHIC entitles you to free health care, it doesn't cover the cost of repatriation. In the case of a serious health issue, private insurance is essential to cover the cost of transport back to your home country. Anyone who finds themselves with a minor ailment should forget queuing at a medical centre and head to the nearest *farmacia*. Pharmacies are great places for seeking advice relating to minor ailments and can prevent unnecessary visits to the GP.

Appendix 1 - A Quick Guide to Resorts/Towns

In our opinion, these are the best Tenerife resorts/towns for:-

Families

Most of Tenerife's main resorts have plenty to offer families. Particularly good are Torviscas and Fañabe in Costa Adeje which offer the choice of a number of beaches, water sports, boat trips from Puerto Colón and aren't far from attractions like Siam Park, Aqualand and Aguilas Jungle Park. There are plenty of budget, family-friendly eating options too.

Party Animals

Playa de las Américas is still the place to party on Tenerife but knowing where to stay is crucial. The infamous C.C. Veronica's actually lies on the border with Costa Adeje. Staying in San Eugenio and Torviscas in Costa Adeje can put you closer to the action than some accommodation in Las Américas.

Tradition

Puerto de la Cruz is a traditional Canarian town first and foremost, something that sets it apart from the resorts in the south where even the more traditional ones grew from tiny fishing village roots. The partying in Puerto de la Cruz comes in the form of traditional fiestas of which there are a lot. Entertainment is aimed at the local population and the numerous restaurants are mainly traditional Canarian or Spanish.

Extreme Sports

El Médano is the place for windsurfers and kite-boarders. Long sandy beaches and a surf scene vibe gives the small resort near the airport a bohemian atmosphere.

Tranquility

The three resorts of Los Gigantes, Puerto Santiago and Playa de la Arena in the south west of Tenerife have a gentle charm and although there are plenty of bars and restaurants, the nocturnal scene is low key (most places wind down around midnight).

Luxury

The Del Duque end of Costa Adeje is the place for a bit of pampered luxury. There is a lavishness of luxury hotels in the area (we don't know if luxury hotels have a collective noun, but that's the one we're giving them). For some get-away-from-it-all luxury, the Gran Melia Palacio de Isora in Alcalá and the Abama near Playa San Juan take some beating.

Boutique Hotels

Garachico is the centre for gorgeous boutique hotels, with two of our favourite hotels on Tenerife. Both the San Roque and La Quinta Roja are small, exquisitely designed and located in historic buildings.

269

City Break

Tenerife's capital city of Santa Cruz has history, art, shopping, parks and some of the island's best restaurants, bars and clubs. This is the cultural centre of Tenerife with the sort of urban buzz you'll never find in a beach resort. It's small enough to explore the best parts on foot easily.

Rural Beauty

There's not a lot of choice of places to stay, but Santiago del Teide is perfect for stepping from the one rural hotel in town and onto a number of trails that lead to quite diverse countryside.

Unique Experience

The Parador de Cañadas del Teide in Teide National Park is a unique place to stay. Once the crowds have departed the park, step outside into that incredible landscape and wallow in the extra special surroundings.

History

It's a toss-up between La Laguna and La Orotava. But La Orotava wins by a margin thanks to having more charming, historic hotels and because of its location in the valley of the same name.

Hiking

Puerto de la Cruz is the best base for accessing many of the top hiking routes on Tenerife. We've always maintained this and the Tenerife Government would seem to agree as they chose to base the Tenerife Walking Festival in the town.

APPENDIX II - TENERIFE ZONAS RECREATIVAS (PICNIC ZONES)

Eating al fresco on Tenerife is a national weekend pastime and the interior and north of the island is peppered with *zonas recreativas*, or picnic areas. Invariably set within the shade of the pine forests, main zones have wooden tables and benches with seating capacity for anything up to 300 people; barbecues, water stand pipes, toilets and recycling bins. But head into any rural area, or even parks within towns, and you're almost guaranteed to stumble across a picnic table or two in the dappled shade, just crying out to have butties unwrapped on it.

For the *tinerfeños*, weekends are all about packing up a banquet of food and wine, cramming all the family, close relations and the dog into a convoy of 4X4s and driving into the hills for a picnic which can last from around 13:00 until late afternoon. If you'd prefer to avoid the impromptu concerts, barbecuing of entire animals and noisy joie de vivre, head up to a zone mid-week where you'll most likely have the place all to yourself. Unfortunately, you may find that the toilets are locked outside of the weekend so be prepared to extend the al fresco experience. These are our favourite picnic zones:

Las Raíces, La Esperanza (TF24 from La Laguna) - not only do you get to see one of the nicest island drives with views down both coasts, but you arrive in a wonderland of fragrant tranquillity where the pine needles provide a velvet carpet to 58 tables hidden amidst the dappled silence.

Las Lajas, (TF21 between Vilaflor and Teide National Park) – a vast woodland site with 50 tables set in scented pine forest and red earth . If you fancy the setting but can't be bothered with preparing a picnic, there's a great little restaurant on site that does a mean steak and a succulent rabbit in red wine.

Chio (TF38 above Los Gigantes and Guia de Isora) – set within Teide National Park alongside Chio, is one of the largest picnic zone areas on the island with 63 tables set beneath the trees in acres of hot pine forest with crater views.

La Caldera, (TF21 above Puerto de la Cruz and La Orotava) 48 tables are set within a crown of laurel and eucalyptus trees surrounding a volcanic crater in the pine forest above La Orotava. There's a log cabin with a sunny, garden terrace alongside and it's the setting-off point for myriad trails, some of the best walking on Tenerife.

You'll find the full list of Tenerife's *zonas recreativas* on the Cabildo website (www.tenerife.es - go to 'themes' and then to 'Environment & Landscapes')

APPENDIX III - TOP 10 THINGS TO DO ON TENERIFE

These are the top things that, in our opinion, really define the very best of what Tenerife has to offer away from its beaches and theme parks.

1. Take the cable car to the summit of Mount Teide

It's worth standing in line to take the seven minute cable car ride to stand on top of the world, just below the summit of Europe's highest volcano and Spain's highest mountain. Once at the top, walk to the old crater wall in one direction and to the perfect volcanic crater of the old peak in the other. On a clear day, most of the other Canary Islands are visible. It's a never-to-be-forgotten experience and one which every visitor to Tenerife should undertake at least once.

The cable car runs from 09:00-16:00 and the last car down leaves at 17:00. Prices are €26 adults (residents €12.50) and €13 children (up to 14 years). In strong winds, ice or snow, the operation of the cable car can be suspended, ask your hotel reception to check that it's running before making the journey to Teide National Park.

2. Watch Dolphins and Whales in the Wild.

The warm waters of the Atlantic that surround the island provide unique opportunities to get close to some of nature's most exciting sights.

No less than 28 species of whales and dolphins visit the rich feeding grounds of microscopic marine life that lie in the deep, warm waters off the west coast on their migratory routes, and it's possible to spot minke, sperm and even killer whales if you're lucky. With a community of bottlenose dolphins and one of pilot whales living in the waters too, you're almost guaranteed sightings on every trip.

Several boats operate dolphin watching trips twice a day from Los Gigantes, Puerto Colon and Los Cristianos harbours at a cost of €20 – €30 per person for a two hour trip.

3. Visit the Anaga Mountains

Head to the north eastern tip of Tenerife and you'll find an island a million miles away from the south and west coasts, where ancient forests coat rugged mountains and white cottages cling to steep ravines. This is the Tenerife that existed before tourism came to call and life here continues in much the same way it has for centuries, even down to the occasional community still living in cave houses. The best way to explore this unspoilt paradise is on foot along any of its myriad walking trails but non-walkers can explore its beauty by car, stopping to take in jaw-dropping views along the way. You'll find the best walking routes in the Anaga Mountains in Walk This Way Tenerife and a recommended driving route in Tenerife Island Drives (both available on Amazon).

4. Go to a Fiesta

Partying is quite possibly the thing the *tinerfeños* do best and rarely a week passes, particularly through the spring and summer months, when there isn't a fiesta happening somewhere on the island. Whether you join the full-on, hedonistic mayhem of the nightly street parties at carnival or simply sit on the harbour wall to watch the goats being dipped into the sea on midsummer's morn, seeing a fiesta will give you an insight into the real spirit of Tenerife.

The calendar of fiestas (page 46) gives you the what, where and when of the island's major festivals.

5. Swim in the Rock Pools of Garachico

When a volcanic eruption filled the harbour with lava and destroyed much of the town, Garachico could have given up and become a ghost town. But it didn't. Rising from the volcanic ashes of disaster, the town has retained much of its beauty and all of its resolute character and has turned some of its frozen lava into natural swimming pools. Teeming with rainbow coloured tropical fish, the pools are a joy to explore on foot and even better to cool off in on a hot day.

6. Have a Picnic in the Woods

Not so much a pastime as a national obsession, the *tinerfeños* are big on picnics and take to the pine forests most weekends in summer. You'll find picnic zones (*zona recreativa*) dotted all around the north and centre of the island, high in the pine forests and down near the coast, where there are tables, benches and usually barbecues.

7. Taste the Wine

In its heyday, Canarian wine was widely accepted to be the best in the world and today, it's enjoying something of a renaissance. In most restaurants across the island you can expect to see at least one locally produced white and one red on the wine menu while top restaurants in hotels and outside the resorts will offer a more comprehensive selection. Visiting a *bodega* is a great way to try some of Tenerife's award winning wines and learn about the grape varieties grown on the island (see Tenerife Wine (P81) for a list of bodegas)

The Wine Museum in El Sauzal is a good place to learn about Tenerife's wines and to sample and buy a range of the best annual yields. *Open Wed - Sat 09:00-21:00, Tues 10:30-18:30, Sunday 11:00-18:00; (+34) 922 57 25 35; www. casadelvinotenerife.com.*

8. Dive

Tenerife is one of the most popular diving destinations in Europe. Lava structures the size of underwater cathedrals; shipwrecks and even a DC3 plane wreck all provide a surreal underwater stage on which stingrays, striped barracudas, moray eels and more, perform their daily underwater drama. The best diving is from Las Galletas, Puerto de la Cruz, Costa Adeje and Los Gigantes and there are numerous dive sites offering everything from trial dives to full PADI courses. A boat dive incl. equipment hire costs around €40.

9. Check Out the Gardens (see Gardens of Tenerife, P25)

Blessed with a perfect climate where it's never too hot and never too cold, with long sunshine hours and adequate winter rainfall, the north west of Tenerife is a natural hothouse for tropical vegetation. And nowhere cultivates it better than Puerto de la Cruz. The La Orotava Botanical Gardens are the second oldest of their kind in existence and for more than 200 years, gardeners have travelled from across the globe to wander their chaotic paths. Other gardens in the town are the flamboyant Taoro Gardens that front the former Hotel Taoro; Sitio Litre gardens which include some fine orchids, and Risco Bello water gardens alongside the old Hotel Taoro.

Botanical Gardens, Calle Retama; *(+34) 922 92 29 81; open daily 09:00-17:30; entrance €3.*

Sitio Litre, Camino Sitio Litre; *(+34) 922 38 24 17; www.jardindeorquideas. com; open daily 09:30–17:00; entrance €4.75.*

Risco Bello, Parque Taoro; *open daily 09:30–18:00; entrance to tea garden free, to water gardens €4.50.*

10. Stargaze

One of the three best places on the planet for clear skies (along with Chile and Hawaii) and a recognised Starlight Tourism Destination, Tenerife is a must for stargazers. Even if you don't know your Orion from your Plough, it's still an amazing experience to see a night sky so filled with stars that it's easier to spot the spaces than the twinkles. The higher you get, the clearer the skies so the place to be is Teide National Park. Choose a moonless night and spend it at the Parador (see p169) for a truly special experience and if you stay on a Friday night you get a free stargazing session. Less expensive but no less spectacular as a base for enjoying the night skies is Vilaflor (see p237). And for a really romantic treat, take a champagne sunset trip up Mount Teide to watch the sunset followed by a stargazing session with Volcano Life Experience (*www.volcanolife.com; (+34) 922 67 86 76; from €51 including pick up from the south or Puerto de la Cruz, cable car for champagne sunset and Canarian dinner*).

APPENDIX IV - TEN TIPS FOR SAVING MONEY ON TENERIFE

1. Book your holiday in low season.

If you're not tied to school holidays, choose one of the island's so-called 'shoulder' seasons to book. These are the seasons that fall in between high seasons i.e. spring and autumn. As Tenerife has no off-season, most places are open year-round and with a beautiful, year-round climate, you don't have to worry too much about falling foul of the weather either (see Climate p17). Booking in low season means you'll find better hotel and flight deals and less crowded beaches and restaurants. The best months to grab a bargain are May, June, September (after kids have gone back to school), early October and early December. Avoid February and November for your best chance at not seeing rain.

2. Get around by bus and invest in a Tenmas travel card.

From September 2018 the Tenmas travel card replaced the green Bono. It can be purchased at bus stations, various kiosks, and vending machines at some bus and tram stops. It costs €2 and can be topped up with amounts between €5 and €100. Register your card with tenmas.es to ensure all discounts are applied.

3. Go on a blanket tour.

Blanket tours are the nickname given to Miller Travel tours because you have to visit a blanket sales outlet and endure a 90 minute presentation as part of the deal. The blanket sell is not like time share, there's no hard sell and no obligation to do anything other than sit through the presentation and then spend a further 30 minutes browsing the products. After that, it's just a straightforward coach tour which includes lunch with wine. Tours take you all across the island including hard-to-get-to locations like the Anaga Mountains and Masca and all for the princely sum of €12. You'll find Miller Tour brochures on walls and benches all over the main resorts. Just turn up at the pick-up point and pay on the bus. But please don't complain that the wine is low quality, bear in mind the pittance you paid for the whole day and keep expectations real.

4. Opt for menu of the day.

Most restaurants have a *menu del día* which offers a three course meal including bread and a soft drink, beer or wine and it's usually for under €10. You sometimes have a choice of two or three starters, mains and desserts from which to choose or you may not have a choice at all. The *menu del día* is a great way to get a wholesome, cheap meal for the family and then just pick up something from a fast food outlet to eat while you're strolling or maybe some tapas in the evening. Watch for blackboard menus and take your pick. Lunch times only.

5. Take a picnic.

If you're going out exploring, save money on lunch by stocking up on bread, cold meats and cheese at the supermarket and have a picnic. If you're not in self catering, you'll find cheap packs of disposable cutlery and cups in the hardware section of most decent-sized supermarkets. There are lots of picnic zones (*zonas recreativas*) dotted around the interior and the north of the island where you'll find tables and chairs, or just use the plaza benches or a nice wall on which to perch and enjoy an alfresco lunch.

6. Avoid branded goods.

Whether you're stocking up your self catering accommodation or just want a Hobnob to go with your morning cuppa, avoid buying the brands you know and love, you'll pay a big premium. Just like at home, many supermarket-own brands are just as tasty and a fraction of the cost. The same is however not true for spirits or cigarettes where the locally produced stuff will feel as if it's tearing the lining out of your throat. Opt for your favourite brands, you'll find them much cheaper anyway as Tenerife is a VAT-free island.

7. Ditch the sun lounger.

One way to really notch up the holiday cost is to hire beach sun loungers every day. The price of hiring sun loungers on Tenerife's beaches varies but averages around €7 a day and can cost as much as €10 per sunbed. For two people on a week's holiday that's a budget busting €84 to €120 just to lie in the sun. Instead, pick up a beach mat at one of the shops lining the back of the beach or at the supermarket for around €3 and lie on the sand. Nearer the water's edge will get you cooler sand and less distance to walk for a dip plus the added bonus or being away from those regimented rows of sunbeds.

8. Make Sunday sightseeing day.

All the island's government-owned museums are free to get into on Sundays so head off to Santa Cruz to the *Museo de la Naturaleza y Arqueología* for interactive exhibits and grizzly mummies or the Military Museum to see exactly how the British Navy were defeated at Santa Cruz and how Nelson lost his arm, or jump on the tram from to La Laguna for family science fun at the Museum of Science & the Cosmos. Don't forget to use your travel card (see tip number 2) on the trams as well as the buses.

9. Check pump prices.

If you're hiring a car, be careful where you stop to fill up before returning the vehicle, petrol pump prices on Tenerife vary enormously. Generally speaking, PCAN, TGAS and DISA are the cheapest and BP, Shell and Cepsa are the most expensive but prices can vary by 12 cents or more per litre according to the location of an individual station. Handily, the petrol station at Tenerife south airport is actually not bad. It's not the cheapest, but not the most expensive either so it's worth waiting until you're actually at the airport to fill up even though it will mean doing a circuit to get back to the car hire car park and departures.

10. Buy cigarettes, gifts and booze before you get to the airport.

When it's time to go home don't wait until you get to the airport to stock up on cigarettes, booze, and gifts like wine and honey to take home. Prices are much lower in shops and supermarkets in your resort area. As there is no VAT payable on Tenerife, the duty-free shops at the airport don't offer a price advantage. Remember, Tenerife and the Canary Islands fall outside EU regulations for duty free purposes so check HM Revenue & Customs website for full allowance details. Current duty free allowances from Tenerife are 1 litre of spirits and 200 cigarettes per adult traveller.

Appendix V - Tenerife Off The Beaten Track

It's hard to imagine that an island as popular as Tenerife could possibly have 'off the beaten track' places waiting to be discovered but the vast majority of visitors who annually descend to the island, some of them year on year, head straight for their favourite coastal resort to soak up the sun.

We've often heard people say: "I've seen all there is to see on Tenerife" simply because they've been to all the theme parks and taken the tour to Teide National Park, Masca, Garachico, La Orotava and possibly even La Laguna (but not many people get that far). In reality, the vast majority of Tenerife's surface area is very rarely seen by most of its visitors unless they're willing to move away from their sun loungers and explore.

These are some of our favourite places for losing the tour buses and discovering a different side to Tenerife:

Arico Nuevo (P105)

Narrow cobbled streets lined by higgledy piggledy white houses with green windows and door frames and white walls draped with crimson bougainvillea

radiate off a pleasant plaza with a pretty, 17th century church.
Candelaria (P178)
The spiritual heart of Tenerife, it seems odd to describe Candelaria as off the beaten track but the majority of people who visit this side of the island are Canarios and mainland Spanish.
El Sauzal (P107)
Perched on the north west coast with the best view of Mount Teide to be seen on Tenerife, El Sauzal's visitor quotient comes primarily from cruise passengers who travel to the little town to visit the home of its most famous daughter, Sister María de Jesús de León y Delgado, whose body has never decayed, despite being dead for almost three centuries.
Güímar (P181)
Just getting to Güímar along the old TF28 road that winds its way over numerous bridges straddling yawning ravines, you pass through a side of Tenerife a thousand miles away from the coastal resorts. Once there, the enduring mystery of Tenerife's pyramids lies on the outskirts of the town with its historic old quarter that was once the gateway to the south.
San Miguel de Abona (P234)
Head to the hills above the greens of Golf Del Sur to find the town of San Miguel de Abona whose old quarter, hidden behind its workaday main street, oozes with historic charm.
Santiago del Teide (P236)
Best known as the place where you turn off to drive the road to Masca, Santiago del Teide is a lovely little town in its own right.
Tacoronte (P160)
A busy commuter town for many people working in La Laguna and Santa Cruz, Tacoronte rarely sees visitors which is a shame because, behind its bustling and somewhat dreary frontage lies an historic heart.
Tegueste (P163)
Although entirely landlocked, this interesting little town is best known for its galleons ... on wheels, and its defence of the capital from pirate attack. It's a long story involving a plague, a saint and a local army squadron but the resulting annual *romería* (see p55) is one of the liveliest on the island.
Vilaflor (P237)
Always the bridesmaid, never the bride, hundreds of thousands of people pass through Vilaflor en route to Teide National Park, looking at its alpine-esque beauty from their coach and car windows and occasionally stopping at a café for a toilet break.

APPENDIX VI - OUR TOP TENERIFE HOTELS

Having stayed in countless Tenerife hotels over the years, there are those we'd happily return to again and again. This is our favourite top 10.

Hotel Europe Villa Cortes
Mexican hacienda-themed luxury in the heart of Playa de las Américas.

Gran Melia Palacio de Isora, Red Level
Fabulously stylish rooms, lively bars, and the largest saltwater pool in Europe. Unadulterated pampering in Alcalá.

Melia Hacienda del Conde
Colonial splendour and first class service in this adults-only, boutique, spa hotel set on a remote headland overlooking Buenavista del Norte golf course.

Iberostar Grand Hotel El Mirador
Romantic, adults-only hotel adjoining the Bahía del Duque in Costa Adeje.

Hotel Botánico
Old fashioned luxury and top notch service in one of the north's finest hotels.

Iberostar Grand Hotel Mencey
Located alongside the Ramblas and offering contemporary city style combined with colonial splendour.

Hotel Villalba
Pine scented, luxurious retreat on the edge of Vilaflor.

La Quinta Roja
Pure colonial elegance set around a patio garden on the lovely plaza in Garachico.

Hotel San Roque
The most stylish and luxurious boutique hotel on the island and probably our favourite place to stay. The fact it's in Garachico is a bonus.

Parador de Las Cañadas
Quite possibly the most unique location you will ever stay in, set at the foot of Alta Montaña in Teide National Park.

MORE IN THE REAL TENERIFE SERIES OF GUIDES

Real Tenerife Island Drives

Island Drives is a combined trail finder and guide book describing six road journeys that take you off the standard tourist trail and into the real Tenerife to experience its dramatic scenery, its historic towns and prettiest hamlets. Check out therealtenerife.com for more information.

Walk this Way Tenerife

More than just a collection of the best walking routes for the island, Walk This Way Tenerife is a complete guide to self-guided walking on Tenerife. (Available on Amazon.com) Check out our Walking Tenerife website walkingtenerife.co.uk for more information.

Real Tenerife Island Walks

Discover verdant valleys, plunging ravines, sweeping forests, remote corners, tiny hamlets and vistas galore with our series of detailed Tenerife walking routes in PDF format. Check out our Walking Tenerife website walkingtenerife.co.uk for more information.

Real Tenerife Town & City Guides

Covering Santa Cruz, La Laguna, Puerto de la Cruz, & La Orotava, our detailed urban routes include the most popular attractions, parks, plazas, museums, art galleries, restaurants, bars, shopping areas and even toilet stops. Real Tenerife Town & City Guides are available to buy online at our Walking Tenerife and Real Tenerife webistes.

And from our Buzztrips: Hiking and Dining on & off the Beaten Track stable comes a more personal travelogue ...

Camel Spit & Cork Trees; A Year of Slow Travel Through Portugal

Camel Spit & Cork Trees is a travelogue which is partly about learning to live as a foreigner in Portugal and partly about delving under the skin of areas that aren't so well known outside of the country. It's about the land, the people, the food, the weather, the wildlife… and the insects.

MOST TITLES ARE AVAILABLE TO BUY ONLINE AT AMAZON

COMING SOON - THE BANANA ROAD
Memoirs of our time in Tenerife

INDEX

285

Made in United States
North Haven, CT
04 April 2022

17880101R00163